Steve Blake and Scott Lloyd have devoted years of research to the subjects of Arthur and ancient Britain. They are founders of the Centre for Arthurian Studies at the North East Wales Institute, and have advised and promoted one of the world's leading collections of Arthurian collections of Arthurian material, housed at Flintshire Library headquarters in Mold. They have also worked with the Welsh Academic Press on a series dedicated to Welsh Arthurian source materials.

THE LOST LEGEND OF
ARTHUR

THE UNTOLD STORY
OF BRITAIN'S
GREATEST WARRIOR

STEVE BLAKE and
SCOTT LLOYD

RIDER

LONDON · SYDNEY · AUCKLAND · JOHANNESBURG

3 5 7 9 10 8 6 4

Copyright © Steve Blake and Scott Lloyd 2002

First published as *Pendragon* in 2002 by Rider

The paperback edition first published in 2004 by Rider,
an imprint of Ebury Press, Random House,
20 Vauxhall Bridge Road, London SW1V 2SA

Penguin Random House is committed to a sustainable future for
our business, our readers and our planet. This book is made from
Forest Stewardship Council® certified paper.

MIX
Paper from
responsible sources
FSC® C018179

Printed and bound in Great Britain by Clays Ltd, St Ives plc

The Random House Group Limited Reg. No. 954009

A CIP catalogue record for this book
is available from the British Library

ISBN 978 1 84 413222 5

To my son Adam Cynan, that he may grow to know the stories of his people and the land of his birth. He is a gift beyond all measure; may he find his holy grail.

Steve Blake

To my sister Fay: may your future be full of smiles.

Scott Lloyd

CONTENTS

Acknowledgements   viii

List of Illustrations   ix

Introduction   1

1 The Quest for Arthur   5

2 The Birth of a Legend   31

3 The Keepers of Tradition   47

4 The Genealogy of Arthur   79

5 Some Geographical Problems   111

6 Arthur's Battles   140

7 Arthur the Warlord   167

8 The Lost Saga of Camlan and the Death of Arthur   181

Epilogue: *The Untold Story of Arthur*   205

Appendix 1: *The Warriors of Arthur and Other Characters
       Associated with him in the Earliest Welsh Sources*   211

Appendix 2: *The Heartland of Arthur's Warriors*   225

Appendix 3: *The Source Materials*   256

Notes   273

Bibliography   293

Useful Addresses   299

Index   301

ACKNOWLEDGEMENTS

Firstly our heartfelt thanks to Sue Lascelles and to all at Rider / Ebury Press. Special thanks to Gillian and the staff at the Flintshire Library HQ custodians of the Arthurian Collection, who continue to be of immense help in our quest for understanding. Thanks also go to Professor Michael Scott and the Staff at the North East Wales Institute for their support and for giving a home to the Centre for Arthurian Studies.

Personal acknowledgements for Steve Blake:
There are many people who have shared the road since *Keys to Avalon*, but especial thanks are due to Hugh, a consummate professional whom I am now proud to count among my friends, and to his partner Sue for her patience. To Andy Wilson, for our shared dream and many wonderful days together (whatever it takes) and to his wonderful family for their hospitality. To I and A for their faith and commitment, to the Great Bear, John and Terry – keep looking for the stars. To my spiritual brothers and sisters, Ken and Karen, Jean and John, Simon, Gemma and Abby, Big Mark and especially Skeet and Sam, for always being there; Andy and Sue, for their love and reality checks; Bob and Gina Flett, for listening to my inane ramblings and for good company.

To all my family and friends who have helped and supported us along the way; to Liz, Mick and the lads; to Tish, Brook and the boys, William the poet and Elsie. To all my extended family and in particularly to Bobby, for showing what real courage is and to 'Grandad' John for everything. Finally especially to the two ladies in my life, my wife and soul mate Dee, whose love, support, friendship and patience are beyond compare, and to my mother, whose love and example gave me the belief and foundations to reach for the stars.

Personal acknowledgements for Scott Lloyd:
I would like to thank the following: John Eirwyn Williams, without whose generosity, friendship and spare room this book would not have been written. My parents for their support. John Appleby, Arnold Bantzer, James Crane, Richard Holland, Matthew Jones, Mark Olly, Murti Schofield, Stephen Whitaker, Jane Wolfe and the late Paul Davies, for the conversation, inspiration and time they have given me. Natasha, Thomas and Hazel, who have taught me more than any book, and most importantly Anne Robinson, whose love, support and companionship have helped me more than she will ever know. I would also like to thank everybody who has been kind enough to stop and give me a lift when I have been hitching in order to save money and buy yet more books!

LIST OF ILLUSTRATIONS

Black-and-White Plates

1 Church dedicated to St Marchell, cousin of Arthur, at Whitchurch near Denbigh. (Anne Robinson)
2 Church dedicated to Dehifyr, brother of St Marchell, at Bodfari village. (Anne Robinson)
3 Fortified hill known as Gerrig Gwineu, the most likely location for Arthur's court Gelliwig. (Anne Robinson)
4 View from the summit of Gerrig Gwineu looking towards Northern Snowdonia. (Anne Robinson)
5 Former parish church of Llanfor possibly built on the site of a fortress belonging to Gildas' father. (Dee Blake)
6 The famous Llanfor Cavos (Caw) stone that marked the grave of one of Arthur's warriors mentioned in the old tradition. (University of Wales Press)
7 Scott Lloyd in the tiny interior of the Church of Rhos. (Steve Blake)
8 Exterior of Rhos chapel, which is linked to Maelgwn Gwynedd, in whose army Arthur may have been *penteulu*. (Steve Blake)
9 Castle mound at Deganwy where Maelgwn Gwynedd held court. (Steve Blake)
10 Upper reaches of the River Conwy. (Anne Robinson)
11 Steve Blake in the Arthurian Collection at Flintshire Library in Mold. (Dee Blake)
12 Arthurian texts in the Arthurian Collection of over 3,000 volumes at Mold. (Dee Blake)
13 Tremeirchion formerly known as Dinmeirchion (the Fortress of Meirchion). (Dee Blake)
14 The Maen Huail in the town of Ruthin in North Wales. (Anne Robinson)
15 Mountain pass named Camlan between Dolgellau and Mallwyd, the traditional site for Arthur's final battle. (Anne Robinson)

16 Possible location of a Dark-Age cemetery near to a farm called Trebeddau (the town of the graves). (Anne Robinson)

Colour Plates

1 Famous battle list from §56 of the *Historia Brittonum* in Harleian MS 3859, the earliest surviving manuscript to mention Arthur. (The British Library)

2 Seventeenth-century manor house on the summit of Caer Gai, the site that Welsh tradition associates with the childhood of Arthur. (Dee Blake)

3 Remains of Roman walls and earthworks that once fortified the site at Caer Gai. (Dee Blake)

4 Morfa Rhinaedd, namesake of Penrhyn Rhianedd – one of Arthur's courts in the Triads. (Steve Blake)

5 Dinarth hillfort, the most likely site for Arthur's court. (Steve Blake)

6 Llanderfel, one of the many churches dedicated to the warriors of Arthur. (Dee Blake)

7 The remains of an effigy of Derfel Gadarn at Llanderfel. (Dee Blake)

Maps

1 Sites associated with Arthur's relatives   98
2 The lands of Cunedda's Sons   101
3 Sites associated with Arthur's mistresses   105
4 Arthur's battle sites   159
5 Areas ruled by the Kings of Gildas   177
6 Sites linked to people associated with Camlan   194
7 Sites associated with Arthur's Burial   203
8 Sites linked to people associated with Arthur in two or more sources   215
9 Sites in North Wales associated with the family of Caw   232

Charts

1 Connections between the Sources   77
2 Arthur's Family Tree According to Geoffrey of Monmouth   82
3 Arthur's Family Tree According to *Brut y Brenhinedd*   83
4 Arthur's Family on his Father's Side According to Welsh Tradition   86
5 Arthur's Family on his Mother's Side According to Welsh Tradition   87
6 Arthur's Children According to Welsh Tradition   102
7 Descendants of Caw   231

INTRODUCTION

HE valley stretched out beneath us in the early morning light, the dew still fresh on the grass, and a misty haze hanging over the ancient battlefield gave a surreal atmosphere to the landscape. We were sitting on the high ground, only a few miles from civilisation, yet we could have been many miles away. With this panorama before us it was not difficult to summon up vivid images of ancient battles – of loyalty, honour and betrayal amid the clashing of shields. This was where the traditions of Arthur's own people placed the final act of the world's greatest legendary figure. The mountain pass from Dolgellau to Mallwyd appears on old maps which name the location as Camlan, and the land around the Dyfi river, a few miles to the south, preserves the same name. In the surrounding countryside can be found churches dedicated to Arthur's men who escaped from the battle, and the burial sites of warriors named in ancient Welsh poetry. The truth behind the location of Arthur's last battle is, like much of the original Arthurian legend, quite simple when the centuries of foreign accretions are stripped away and Arthur is returned to the landscape to which he belongs.

However, this is to some extent the end of our story rather than the beginning, for we began far from that desolate and haunting place, in a world made of antique letters and ancient manuscripts, where legend and history meet. The figure of Arthur known to most people today is a creation of the quills of clerics and of the authors of romances written from the twelfth century onward; the best-known stories of Arthur were originally political or ecclesiastical propaganda used to navigate the ever changing currents of medieval politics. We wanted to find what lay behind these enigmatic stories and, more importantly, what, if anything, remained of the original Arthurian tradition.

Trying to trace the evolution of Arthur and explain the complex material that makes up the original Arthurian tradition is rather like a murder investigation, the only trouble being that the crime scene itself is well over a thousand years old and its original location is uncertain. Also, the investigation records kept at the time have all but disappeared, and the body itself cannot be found. Coupled to this, those records that have survived are copies of third-hand accounts, with not a single eyewitness statement among them. Previous investigating officers, unable to get a conviction and pressurised by the politicians of the time, have fabricated evidence in an attempt to secure a conviction. In order to solve the mystery of Arthur, we had to cut through the centuries of misinformation and deliberate manipulation of the evidence until we arrived at a point where what was left was the best evidence possible – only then could we hope to identify the scene of the crime.

Many books have been written about Arthur, discussing the sites of his battles, his courts and his burial, and locating them in widely separated places across the island of Britain. However, this book will travel into what for many people is unfamiliar territory:

into a language, culture and landscape far removed from the contents of Arthurian volumes. You will find no Glastonbury, no Tintagel or Winchester, and no Camelot in this book, for these have little, if anything, to do with the real origins of Arthur. Nor will you find any mention of the famous Merlin, for this ancient Welsh figure had nothing to do with Arthur before the twelfth century. Instead you will be led through the traditions and poems of a time before the Norman invasion of Britain, to the very origins of the story of Arthur and a landscape that has remembered the passing of its heroes in the names of its hills, valleys and rivers.

It has long been known that the earliest Arthurian material can be found written in Welsh, yet much of this is unaddressed outside the pages of academic journals and is unknown to the world at large. Within the following pages you will be introduced to the lost sagas of Arthur's last battle, Arthur's feud with Huail the son of Caw, the death of Cai, Arthur's mistresses, and sources that name battles, enemies and events otherwise unknown. Visitors throng to see the supposed site of Arthur's grave in Somerset, but few know that there exists a manuscript detailing a different site for Arthur's grave. Written in a windswept monastery overlooking the Irish Sea, it places Arthur's last resting place at a remote chapel in the Welsh hills, a long way from the visitors and their cameras. In this book we will lead you there.

1

THE QUEST FOR ARTHUR

'... there appeared a star of great magnitude and brilliance, with a single beam shining from it. At the end of this beam was a ball of fire, spread out in the shape of a dragon. From the dragon's mouth stretched forth two rays of light, one of which seemed to extend its length beyond the latitude of Gaul, while the second turned towards the Irish Sea and split up into seven smaller shafts of light.

This star appeared three times, and all that saw it were struck with fear and wonder.'[1]

THE extract above, although not actually naming Arthur, is the foundation upon which Geoffrey of Monmouth built his legend of the great British king, the most famous character in his hugely influential *Historia Regum Britanniae* – The History of the Kings of the Britons – written between 1136 and 1138. It was this book that introduced the figure of Arthur to the world at large, and all later authors used it as the foundation upon which they built the figure of Arthur known today. Geoffrey cleverly puts these words into the mouth of Merlin, a figure whom an earlier book of his, *Prophetiae Merlini* – The Prophecies of Merlin – had already taken from obscure British origins as a mere wildman of the woods and had refashioned as the greatest prophet and wizard known to the medieval world.

The star appears to Merlin while he is accompanying the forces of Uthyr, brother of the ruler of Britain, Ambrosius, on their march to fight the Saxon invaders from the Continent. When Uthyr demands an explanation of this celestial message, Merlin, his eyes stained with tears, declares that it signifies that Ambrosius has just died and that calamity will befall Britain because of this. He urges Uthyr to continue to battle against the Saxon invaders, for if he is victorious he will become king of the Britons. He explains that the star itself and the fiery dragon originating from it symbolise Uthyr, and that the beam of light towards Gaul signifies Uthyr's son, Arthur, who will be a most powerful man whose dominions will encompass all the kingdoms over which the ray shines.[2] The most important part of the prophecy – often overlooked because of a focus on Geoffrey's Arthur – is that Merlin also explains the meaning of the second ray, which 'turned towards the Irish Sea and split up into seven smaller shafts of light'. Geoffrey tells the reader that this represents Uthyr's daughter, 'whose sons and grandsons shall hold one after the other the kingship of Britain'.[3]

After his inevitable victory in the ensuing battle and following the burial of his brother, Ambrosius, Uthyr is made king. Mindful of Merlin's explanation of the star, he orders two dragon effigies to be forged in gold in the likeness of the dragon seen in the rays of the star. One of these he sends to his court at Winchester; the other becomes his personal battle standard, to be carried before him and his men in the fights that follow. 'From that moment onwards he was called Utherpendragon, which in the British language means "a dragon's head". He had been given this title because it was by means of a Dragon that Merlin had prophesied that he would become King.'[4] (In the context of this work, 'British language' and 'Britons' refer to those people residing in the British isles in the sixth century who were not Saxon, Pictish (from northern Britain) or Irish. In modern terms this would place the Britons of this period in the area known today as Wales and its border regions, and the 'British language' was the ancestor to modern Welsh.)

The title 'Pendragon' has become synonymous with the heroic kings of the Dark Ages, and the above extract contains the first explanation of it. As the name attached to Arthur's father it is a creation of Geoffrey of Monmouth, who by means of Merlin's elaborate prophecy created a title known throughout the world today – a title that evokes images of double-headed comets blazing across the night sky, predicting both doom and salvation, and ancient conflicts fought out on mist-shrouded battlefields. In fact the title can be traced back beyond Geoffrey's generation, to the time in the early sixth century when Arthur rode into battle with his warriors at his side, defending the ever-shrinking territories inhabited by the Britons. Geoffrey, however, interprets the British word 'Pendragon' as 'Dragon's Head', and uses this image in the prophecy he attributes to Merlin to set the scene for Arthur's arrival. Arthur himself, however, is never referred to as Pendragon in any source, and the life story generally associated with him is primarily the work of Geoffrey, from his deceitful conception at Tintagel – when Uthyr had Merlin change him into the shape of his ally Gorlois so that he could sleep with Gorlois's wife – his rise to power at the age of fifteen and his many battles in which he is victorious, to his campaigns in Continental Europe, his final battle at Camlan and his resting place on the Isle of Avalon. This is the basis of the Arthurian legend known to both the medieval and modern world, but how much of it – if any – can be relied upon?

Geoffrey's explanation that the British word 'Pendragon' means 'Dragon's Head' is based on a translation that, though literal, is not correct. A better understanding of the title can be gained by other references to it, in Welsh literature. As well as meaning 'head', '*pen*' is also used in the sense of 'chief' or 'supreme'. '*Dragon*' or '*draig*' is a term often applied to great warriors in Welsh poetry, so the title 'Pendragon' is probably better translated as 'Chief of Warriors' or 'Foremost Leader'.[5] The earliest post-Roman Latin source regarding Wales uses the term '*insularis draco*' – 'dragon of the island' – to describe Maelgwn Gwynedd, who was the most powerful ruler in Wales in the sixth century.[6] In twelfth-century Gwynedd (a kingdom of North Wales) the court bard Gwalchmai in praising his patron Rhodri ap Owain referred to him as '*pen draig a phen dragon*' – 'foremost dragon and chief of dragons'.[7] It is clear, therefore, that Geoffrey did not invent the title 'Pendragon', but his understanding of the term as 'Dragon's Head' rather than 'Chief of Warriors' added colour to Merlin's prophecy.

THE ONCE AND FUTURE KING

King Arthur is undoubtedly the greatest legendary figure produced by the western world. He is the hero of a thousand stories, the catalyst for a million childhood dreams, and the icon of a nation –

albeit the wrong one. Arthur has indeed fulfilled the prophecy of the once and future king attributed to him by romance – the legend that he is not dead but sleeping in a cave with his men, ready to awaken when his people are in their hour of need, when he will rush forth with his army to defeat the enemy. He has been reborn to the world century after century from the pen, brush and imagination of numerous writers, artists, poets and politicians. For almost a thousand years the present general perceptions of his story have been developing, and yet the fundamental questions regarding Arthur's origins still remain unanswered. Did Arthur ever exist as a historical figure, and, if he did, where was his sphere of activity? Was he a king, a general or a warlord? Or was he purely a legendary figure for which any geographic quest is completely in vain? These are the questions that we set out to answer.

The present work explores the mystery that surrounds the origins of the figure of Arthur and returns to what little is known of the original traditions concerning him within the legends and poetry of his own people – traditions that developed long before Geoffrey of Monmouth, the greatest of medieval spin doctors, crowned him as the all-conquering Christian monarch of Europe. In the period in which Arthur lived there were no knights in shining armour, no large stone castles dominating the landscape, and no single king ruling the whole of the island that we now know as Great Britain. All these things were several centuries in the future. If your understanding of Arthur involves his being an English Christian sovereign, Tintagel, Cadbury Castle, Glastonbury, Round Tables, medieval courts, ladies-in-waiting and knightly derring-do then we respectfully suggest that you empty your mind of these romantic ideas and prepare to be transported back to the real age of Arthur – an age when Rome was in decline and had abandoned the provinces of Britannia to their fate; a time when the true Britons, retreating from the Saxon onslaught, stood pinned with their backs to the western sea with nothing between them and oblivion. It is from this background that the figure of Arthur emerged into history and legend, and it is from the traditions of his countrymen that his story developed.

Although it was Geoffrey of Monmouth who introduced Arthur to the world at large, he was not the first of the Anglo-Norman ecclesiastics to mention him. The name of Arthur was arousing the interest of Norman intellectuals several years before Geoffrey wrote his work, and had been mentioned briefly by two earlier historians: William of Malmesbury and Henry of Huntington. Both of these shared something in common with Geoffrey: they were all patronised by Robert of Gloucester, the half-brother of Matilda, whose right to succeed her father, King Henry I, had been usurped by her cousin Stephen.

In the early twelfth century the legends known collectively as 'The Matter of Britain' had become an important part of the political scene. An integral part of the myths that they contained was that Britain had once been conquered by Brutus, the son of the Trojan hero Aeneas – thus bringing Britain into line with other cultures throughout Europe in claiming a classical origin. 'The Matter of Britain', which also made mention of the hero Arthur, gave the new Norman dynasty an origin myth that it otherwise lacked, and Geoffrey's work set out to prove that Britain had a great pedigree among the nations of Europe, with a classical origin and a history of defiance against the Roman Empire. The figure of

Arthur was used as the primary symbol of this power – comparable to Charlemagne's status among the Normans' great rivals the Franks – and propaganda based upon 'The Matter of Britain' dominated British politics for centuries to come. The success and influence of the *Historia* were undisputed and unparalleled in medieval literature. Geoffrey's imaginative account of the fate of the Britons following the departure of the Romans at the beginning of the fifth century became the core of the Arthurian legend that subsequently dominated the royal courts of Europe, and can be briefly summarised as follows.

In AD 410 the Roman legions left Britain, to defend their empire from the invasions of the Goths. They never returned, and the Britons were left unprotected from frequent attacks by the Picts and by the Scots from Ireland. Amid this chaos the British king, Constantinus, was killed. As his two sons, the rightful heirs, were too young to rule, they were sent to safety abroad. Meanwhile a noble called Vortigern usurped the throne through treachery and invited a small number of enemy Saxons into Britain to act as mercenaries against the Picts. In return for this help the Saxons were given a small piece of land in Britain, and supplies. Having beaten back the Picts, the Saxons then brought over more of their countrymen and started to attack their hosts. After many battles a peace conference was held between nobles from both sides, but the Saxons arrived with knives hidden in their boots and slaughtered all the British nobles except Vortigern.

By this time Constantinus's sons, Ambrosius and Uthyr, were old enough to return to Britain, fight the Saxons, and take their rightful places on the throne. Many great victories were won, Ambrosius took the throne, and Britain regained some of its stability. But the Saxons were not yet totally vanquished, and when Ambrosius was poisoned by a Saxon disguised as a doctor his replacement was his brother Uthyr. During his reign, Uthyr, with the help of his magician adviser Merlin, changed his form and slept with the wife of his ally Gorlois. Subsequently Gorlois died and Uthyr married the widow, Eigr, and together they had two children, named Arthur and Anna. After the death of Uthyr, Arthur was made king – at the age of fifteen – and after many battles he defeated the Saxons and the Picts. He then set up a court renowned throughout Christendom, and was confirmed as King of Britain in a special coronation ceremony.

After many years of peace a messenger arrived from Rome saying that Arthur had to pay homage to the Pope. This angered Arthur and his men, so they set out to attack Rome. The Continental campaign of Arthur saw him take most of modern France and cross the Alps towards Rome, but as he did so he heard that Medrod – his nephew, whom he had left in charge – had taken the throne and Arthur's wife, Guinevere. Arthur returned to Britain and met the armies of Medrod (which included the Picts and the Saxons) at a place called Camlan. A great battle took place in which Medrod was killed and Arthur was mortally wounded. In his fragile state Arthur was taken to the Isle of Avalon, and there disappears from Geoffrey's pages.

The immense popularity of Geoffrey's work has been ascribed mainly to its being 'a very good book in an age when such works were rare'.[8] Anyone who reads works from the twelfth century will find most of them to be rather tedious by modern standards, whereas Geoffrey's work has a good narrative and keeps the reader interested. It shares these qualities with the highly influential eighth-century *Historia Ecclesiastica Gentis Anglorum* (Ecclesiastical History of the English People) of Bede, which is still very readable today – something that very few works of its period can claim. The fact that Geoffrey had produced a good read probably contributed as much to the book's popularity as did its contents, and these two factors together made his work unstoppable. The dissemination of the Arthurian legend was thus assured. The *Historia Regum Britanniae* spread the Arthurian story far and wide, and its manuscripts were copied, translated and altered to meet the specific needs of the day. The little-known hero of the Britons quickly became the most famous figure in Christendom, his story told from Iceland to Palestine, and other writers of the day were soon reworking and adding to his legend in a variety of ways.

In 1154 Henry II succeeded Stephen to the throne of England, and in the following year a Norman cleric called Wace dedicated a chronicle to the King's wife, Eleanor of Aquitaine. This work, entitled *Roman de Brut* – The Romance of Brutus – was a translation of Geoffrey's work into Anglo-Norman verse, but with some important additions. Wace added the concept of courtly love – barely present in his original – and was the first to introduce the idea of the Round Table, later to become a central image in the Arthurian legend. 'King Arthur, of whom the Britons tell many stories,' Wace wrote, 'established the Round Table. There sat the vassals, all of them at the table-head, and all equal. They were placed at the table as equals. None of them could boast that he was seated higher than his peer.'[9]

The *Roman de Brut* was one of the first works to transform Arthur from a British warrior into a medieval knight following the code of chivalry, but other works pursuing this ideal soon followed.

Between 1160 and 1180 Chrétien de Troyes wrote four long romances, *Erec et Enide*, *Cligès*, *Yvain* and *Lancelot*. His name suggests that he was either from Troyes in northern France or spent some considerable time there. At least two of these hugely popular poems were dedicated to Marie de Champagne, the daughter of Wace's patron Eleanor of Aquitaine, whose court was based at Troyes. The patronage of this powerful family with lands in England and France was an important factor in the spread of the Arthurian legend. At this point in the evolution of the Arthurian romance Arthur is relegated to a supporting role: it is his court, the Knights of the Round Table and their adventures that figure most prominently. And Chrétien de Troyes is notable for three important Arthurian innovations. In the eponymous hero of his poem *Lancelot* we are introduced for the first time to this famous Arthurian character who in later romances is the other member of a love triangle with Arthur and Guinevere. He is also one of the knights who quest after the Holy Grail, the most sacred of holy relics, which later writers identify with the cup used by Christ at the Last Supper. Second, Chrétien is the first writer to give a court of Arthur the name 'Camelot' – a name so intertwined with Arthur that it is difficult to imagine that it is such a late addition to the story. But the most important addition that Chrétien de Troyes made to the Arthurian legend – indeed to the whole of European literature – is his introduction of the Holy Grail in his poem *Perceval* (sometimes known as *Le Conte de Graal* – The Story of the Grail), so adding yet another aspect to the Arthurian legend, later to be used as a vehicle for ecclesiastical politics. The religious aspect of the quest for the Grail predominated, and Arthur and his knights became another step removed from their pseudo-historical origins.

In 1190 a cleric from Worcestershire named Layamon translated Wace's *Roman de Brut* into English, and in doing so produced a work closer to the style of the eighth-century *Beowulf*, with its emphasis on conflict and heroism, than to the French romances with their emphasis on courtly love and chivalry. Layamon expands upon the Round Table, giving details of its construction, and is the first writer to make Arthur the saviour of specifically the English race, rather than the British one, as had been the case in the sources up to this point.

At some point between 1193 and 1199 Giraldus Cambrensis, a Welshman of Norman descent, wrote in his work *De Principis Instructione* of the supposed discovery of Arthur's grave at Glastonbury in Somerset by the local monks in 1191. From this little acorn of mistruth took root the mighty oak of the Glastonbury Arthurian legends, its canopy eventually enveloping the tales and traditions of other peoples and places, including stories borrowed from Continental romance, Celtic folklore and Welsh legend.

Giraldus's work was the origin of one of the most famous yet least reliable Arthurian traditions: the identification of Arthur's last resting place, Avalon, as Glastonbury. It was not long before there became localised in the area the legend that Joseph of Arimathea – the rich man who had asked for Jesus's body from Pilate, according to the Gospels – had brought Christianity to Britain within a few years of the Crucifixion. The popular version of the Glastonbury legend – with Joseph of Arimathea and his followers arriving tired on the summit of Wearyall Hill, Joseph planting his staff in the ground where it can still be seen today as the Glastonbury thorn, and the hiding of the Holy Grail in the Chalice Well which still runs red with the blood of Christ – can be shown to have developed at Glastonbury over several centuries. In the sixteenth century this legend played an important part in the arguments between Henry VIII and the papacy that led to the formation of the Church of England. Henry argued that Joseph of Arimathea had established Christianity in Britain before Paul had taken it to Rome; therefore England's Church had superiority over that of Rome and the King did not have to follow Rome's rules. The version of the legends told to the throngs of visitors that have undertaken the Arthurian pilgrimage to Somerset is a compendium of tales, many originally from other parts of the country, that became attached to Glastonbury over the centuries. With two different strains of propaganda, ecclesiastical and romance, now melded together, the Arthurian legend became more influential than ever, and Glastonbury became a focal point for much of the Arthurian material written from the thirteenth century onwards.

At the beginning of the thirteenth century the *Merlin* romance of Robert de Boron was the first to mention the tale of the sword in the stone. A sword had been plunged deep into a stone by Merlin, and whoever could withdraw it would be proclaimed the rightful king. Many nobles tried and failed, until finally the sword was removed by Arthur, thereby proving his right to the throne. This tale was given greater emphasis by later writers, and became one of the best-known parts of the Arthurian story.

By 1225 the Cistercian monks of northern France had

compiled a five-volume work that told of the history of the Holy Grail from the time of Christ until the death of Arthur. This composite Vulgate Cycle, as it later became known, began with Joseph of Arimathea, included the romance of Merlin, the adventures of Arthur and his knights in search of the Grail and the love affair of Lancelot and Guinevere, and finished with the *Morte d'Arthur*, which told of the last days of Arthur and finally the disappearance of the Grail. This huge work appeared less than a century after Geoffrey's *Historia* and soon became the standard version of the Arthurian legend among the storytellers of Europe, but had little in common with its ancestor.

Versions of the Arthurian legends began to appear in German, Dutch, Italian and Scandinavian languages throughout the rest of the thirteenth century, and the Arthurian myth was now at its peak. Courts all over Europe were living the Arthurian ideal, and tournaments became popular, with jousting and swordplay entertaining the crowds. Its concept of chivalry became an important aspect of the Arthurian legend and was a fundamental part of high society in the medieval age.

By the fourteenth century, aspects of the Arthurian legend were being used to justify military conflict, and when, in 1301, Edward I wrote to Pope Boniface VIII to justify his right to invade Scotland he included several quotes from the pages of Geoffrey's *Historia*.[10]

The true resting-place of Arthur had always been a mystery, but the first mention of the phrase 'the once and future king' appeared in *The Alliterative Morte Arthur*, an anonymous poem from the late fourteenth century (not to be confused with the later and better-known work *Le Morte d'Arthur* by Thomas

Malory). Arthur had now become not only the epitome of chivalric society, but also a very important propaganda tool, and it seemed inconceivable that his reputation and importance would diminish.

One of the most important events in the evolution of the Arthurian legend was the arrival of the printing press in the latter half of the fifteenth century and William Caxton's publication of Thomas Malory's *Le Morte d'Arthur* in 1485. It was long thought that Malory had written his manuscript specifically for printing by Caxton, but in 1934 a manuscript copy was found in the library of Winchester Cathedral that differs in many places from the final printed version. The widespread fame and accessibility of this work in the modern period has led to it becoming the most popular version of the Arthur's story. Within the pages of *Le Morte d'Arthur* the motifs now most popularly associated with Arthur are brought together in one wonderful piece of romantic literature. Malory's retelling has everything: the sword in the stone, Merlin, the enigmatic Lady of the Lake, from whom Arthur recieves his magical sword, Excalibur, and the otherworldly Ship of Maidens appearing out of the mists to carry Arthur away to the Isle of Avalon. In order to make his magical mixture work, Malory changes the geography of the tale's setting. It is Malory that identifies Winchester as Arthur's court of Camelot, although William Caxton, his publisher, contradicts this geographic blunder in the introduction by telling the reader that Camelot was really a town in Wales.[11]

The site of Arthur's court of Camelot has been claimed by several places apart from Winchester, most notably by Cadbury Castle in Somerset. The association of Cadbury with Camelot first appeared in 1542, when the antiquarian John Leland recorded a supposed piece of folklore: that the local people believed that the Cadbury hill fort was Camelot. The 1970s saw huge excavations there that made use of the Camelot connection to obtain publicity. The site did show evidence of occupation in the sixth century, but so do many other places, and apart from Leland's dubious reference there remains nothing to link it with Arthur.

Sadly, Winchester's prestigious Arthurian relic, the eighteen-feet diameter, solid-oak Round Table fares no better. Scientific examination has shown that the table was constructed in the fourteenth century during the reign of Edward III – a king with a great interest in the Arthurian legends – and it is many years since this pseudo-Arthurian relic has seriously been taken to be genuine, if it ever has.[12] But, as far as the creation of Malory's new English Arthur was concerned, it was far better that he be located in a place that was once the royal seat of the kings of Wessex, rather than in the obscure courts of earlier Welsh tradition. Unfortunately, in the quest for Arthur, Malory's popular rendition is as far away from the Arthurian genesis as it is possible to go, yet *Le Morte d'Arthur* epitomises what most people think of as the Arthurian legend, even though it was really the end result of 350 years of evolution. In fact all attempts to find a Camelot contemporary with Arthur are in vain, for the Arthurian Camelot is an invention of the Continental writers of the twelfth century. Indeed, when studied closely, one by one all the great Arthurian sites tumble into the footnotes of history, useless in the search for the true origins of the legend.

That publication of *Le Morte d'Arthur* took place in the same year as the accession to the throne of the Tudor Henry VII is unlikely to be a coincidence. The Tudors came from a Welsh background and found it very convenient to make use of the Arthurian propaganda put in place by the Norman and Plantagenet dynasties that preceded them. Henry VII's naming his first-born son and heir Arthur was a move that captured the public's imagination, and it seemed possible that the hope that Arthur would return would now be realised. Unfortunately, however, Prince Arthur died, aged fifteen, in 1502. But it should not be taken for granted that the use of the Arthurian legend is completely consigned to the past, for both the current heirs to the throne of Britain, Prince Charles and Prince William, have Arthur as one of their middle names, and precedent allows them to use any of their given names on acceding to the throne.

Following Malory, little or no new Arthurian material (if we can truly describe Malory as new) was written, and the Arthurian legend entered a new phase. During the previous centuries Arthur had become widely known as an English king – much to the disgust of the Welsh, who had talked of Arthur before the Normans had arrived in Britain, and the Scots, who had been invaded by Edward I under the pretext that the *Historia* recorded Arthur's supposed conquest of their land. In 1534 Polydore Vergil, an Italian historian under the patronage of Henry VIII, dismissed Arthur and the rest of 'The Matter of Britain' as little more than a fairy tale. As the Tudor dynasty drew heavily on the Arthurian legend, Vergil was thus questioning the claims of the royal house. His attack provoked huge disapproval from antiquarians such as Humphrey Llwyd and, most importantly in the development of the Arthurian legend, John Leland, both of whom regarded Arthur as a historical character.[13] Between 1534 and 1543, in his role as the King's antiquary, Leland undertook a journey around the kingdom looking for old manuscripts in the last days of the great monasteries. During this journey he kept a series of notes now known as the *Itinerary*, and in these he identifies Cadbury Castle in Somerset as Camelot, reiterates the claims of Glastonbury, and supposedly finds an inscribed stone at Slaughter Bridge on the river Camel in Cornwall, claimed by Geoffrey to be the site of Camlan. In 1544 he wrote a work entitled *Assertio Inclytissimi Arturii Regis Britanniae* (A Worthy Assertion of Arthur King of Britain), which defended Arthur and 'The Matter of Britain'; but, as a recent writer has noted, this 'depended on enthusiasm rather than any tangible evidence'.[14]

Despite Leland's advocacy, during the mid sixteenth century the Arthurian legend began to lose some of its power, and the last time it was used at a high level was by the court astrologer and mathematician Dr John Dee in 1580, when he presented Queen Elizabeth with a book stating that Arthur had conquered America in his day and so Britain was now justified in seeking to colonise the country. Otherwise, the role of Arthur changed from one of historical ancestor and propaganda tool to one of literary inspiration. The first three books of Edmund Spenser's huge poem *The Faerie Queene*, containing a great deal of Arthurian material, appeared in 1590, and several plays with Arthurian themes appeared during the early part of the seventeenth century. Historical works dealing with 'The Matter of Britain' continued to appear throughout the seventeenth century – both for and against its authenticity – but the tide of its influence had turned.

The arrival on the throne of the German Hanoverian dynasty, in the person of George I in 1714, brought a new view of history, with emphasis on the Saxon origins of the monarchy; the once influential British origins were now forgotten or deliberately ignored. Little Arthurian material was published or performed during the eighteenth century, though one of the few places where Arthur was still discussed widely was in Wales. By the end of the century the Welsh were beginning to publish some of their lesser-known manuscripts, and by 1810 the three-volume *Myvyrian Archaiology* had put into print most of the major texts of the Welsh poets and chroniclers, many of which included Arthurian material. This availability of texts, together with the first new edition of Malory's influential text since 1634, in 1818, provided the impetus for a revival of interest in Arthur, and from this point on new works appeared regularly. Alfred, Lord Tennyson's *The Idylls of the King* was published to great acclaim in 1842, and in 1867–8 was reprinted with the illustrations by Gustave Doré which almost 150 years later remain among the most enduring images of Arthurian romance. William Dyce's murals in the House of Lords (1846) and the work of the Pre-Raphaelite painters, most notably that of Dante Gabriel Rossetti (1828–82), further popularised Arthurian subject matter in the world of fine art. Wagner wrote his huge operas *Lohengrin* (1850) and *Parsifal* (1882) on pseudo-Arthurian themes, bringing such material to a new audience in the opera houses of Europe. The pioneering early photographer Julia Margaret Cameron (1815–79) used Arthurian images, with models dressed in armour and lying on boats in scenes from Arthurian romance. The fast-developing nation of America joined in, with Mark Twain's classic novel *A Connecticut Yankee in King Arthur's Court* (1889) and the retellings of Malory illustrated by Howard Pyle in 1903–10. Aubrey Beardsley illustrated a new edition of Malory in 1893, bringing Arthur into the modern era of art nouveau. Whatever new fashion arose, Arthur could be, and was, adapted to fit.

The end of the nineteenth century had seen important work on the Arthurian legend by people with a background in Celtic studies, like Sir John Rhys, and the first serious work was being done on Welsh manuscripts, long inaccessible in private libraries but now being printed to an academic standard for the first time. In 1911 W. Lewis Jones published a serious study of the origins of the Arthurian legend, followed by E. K. Chambers in 1927. (Chambers's study is still in use today.) After the Second World War, The International Arthurian Society was founded in 1948, and its annual bibliographies of works published on Arthur and related subjects are still issued today and are a great help to Arthurian studies.[15] The Arthurian novel came back into vogue, with T. H. White's *The Once and Future King* (1958) and Rosemary Sutcliff's *Sword at Sunset* (1963) selling hundreds of thousands, and popular adaptations continued unabated – including Walt Disney's film *The Sword in the Stone* (1963), Rick Wakeman's musical homage *The Myths and Legends of King Arthur and the Knights of the Round Table* (1975), and John Boorman's *Excalibur* (1981), probably the finest film on the Arthurian legend (though an adaptation of Malory).

The first of Geoffrey Ashe's numerous works on the Arthurian legend appeared in 1958, and his publications during the next two decades, together with those of Leslie Alcock concerning his excavations at Cadbury, shaped the public's view of a possible historical Arthur. Shortly after, two books appeared that attempted to write a history of Dark Age Britain utilising sources with Arthurian content, namely Leslie Alcock's *Arthur's Britain* (1971) and John Morris's *The Age of Arthur* (1973). This approach went down very well on the high street, but in academic circles a new view was gathering pace and in 1977 an important essay by David Dumville, 'Sub-Roman Britain: History and Legend', discounted writing the history of the Dark Ages in this manner and was very critical of these sources.[16] Dumville argued that the Arthurian sources are not strictly historical texts: they are compilations of earlier material, not contemporary with their subject matter, and are therefore of debatable value.[17]

Different theories and ideas have come and gone over the centuries, but, once the later romantic material is removed, all scholars have to rely on the same handful of sources to support their ideas. There are as many theories as there are historians, and the history of Arthurian scholarship is almost as interesting as the man himself. Since the 1980s dozens of works have been published which purport to identify Arthur's sphere of activity as Scotland, Yorkshire, Cumbria, Wales, Somerset, Cornwall, Brittany and places further afield again. The interesting thing about all these works is that, on the whole, they use the same historical and literary sources to support their identifications.

The current framework within which these early sources are understood has been arrived at over centuries of scholarship, yet many points regarding the Dark Ages are far from certain and debate still rages over several fundamental issues. The nature of academia discourages radical ideas that change the way in which a subject is viewed: it prefers minor changes to pre-existing theories in order to improve them. But what if the original theory is seriously flawed? No amount of revision will make it work, and when generation after generation of students have been taught the same flawed theory it becomes even more difficult to correct it.

In our opinion, there is one aspect of the history of this period that is in dire need of revision, and that is the geographical context in which the available sources are understood. The current orthodox understanding has Welsh rulers giving land to Saxons in Kent and Welsh armies defending cities in Scotland. These ideas have in many cases been so skilfully argued that their absurdities have been overlooked and students have been taught theories as fact for far too long. Such modern academic legends bear little relation to the original manuscripts or the archaeological record.

Although much of the original tradition has been lost to us over the centuries, there remains a corpus of material that holds clues to answering some of the most fundamental questions regarding the figure of Arthur. What will probably surprise the reader is the extent of the evidence that can be gleaned from these early traditions: about Arthur's family, his courts, his battles and his war-band, and about a geography quite different from that commonly associated with his legend. Many will be heartened to learn that glimpses of the real Arthur are still available to us at the beginning of the twenty-first century. Even when the Normans were changing and adapting his story for their own needs, the British were still recording the original traditions in their poetry and stories. Thus two different versions of the legend ran side by side for the best part of 300 years. The English version of events with its origins in the work of William of Malmesbury and Henry of Huntington is well known, but who is familiar with the Welsh version from the pens of twelfth-century bards such as Meilyr Brydydd and Cynddelw? These Welsh bards – the inheritors of an ancient tradition – were continuing to record references to a much older and more authentic Arthurian tradition in one of the oldest languages in Europe.

The enigma of Arthur has its origins in the contents of a handful of old manuscripts: in essence Arthur is a textual problem, and in order to understand this problem we must study these manuscripts closely. The period of British history from the withdrawal of the Romans (*c.* AD 410) to the arrival of the Normans in 1066 is commonly known as the Dark Ages, but there is more manuscript and historical evidence about it than this term would have us believe. At this point it is important to differentiate between the date when a work was first written or composed and the date of the earliest manuscript in which it has survived to the present day. Before the arrival of the printing press in the fifteenth century, manuscripts had to be copied for circulation and to replace those suffering from wear and tear. A work first written in 1100 would probably have been recopied once every fifty years, so by 1400 it could have gone through six different copyists, each of whom may have introduced mistakes or added material to 'improve' the text. By 1400 it is unlikely that the 1100 manuscript would be still in use, as later copies would be in better condition, and the original manuscript may have been stored or simply discarded. By the year 2000 we may have copies from the 1400s, before the printing press arrived, but the original from 1100 is long gone – and with it the original version of the text.

For the period of Arthur we know of only one text that was

written in Britain at that time – by a monk called Gildas – although the work doesn't actually mention Arthur (a point of major importance to which we will return later). The composition of Gildas's work, *De Excidio Britanniae* (The Ruin of Britain), has been dated to *c.* 540, but the earliest manuscript dates from the eleventh century, 500 years later. The earliest manuscript that has survived which mentions Arthur dates from *c.* 1100 and records material first written in *c.* 830. In the strictest sense of the term, no primary source material exists, only later copies of it – mistakes and all – and therefore the only material we have to go on is not written in the hand of the original author. (This situation is not unique to British history: the Roman history of the British Isles is also preserved in manuscripts many stages removed from the original works. The *Agricola* of Tacitus, for example, is a funda-mental work for Roman Britain, but the earliest complete manuscript to have survived dates from the fifteenth century, 1,400 years after the work was first written.)[18] Moreover, for the people of Dark Age Britain, history was intermingled with prophecy, heroic poetry and sagas, in which historic and mytho-logical characters walk side by side. This legendary mindset was a reflection of an age when the merging of the real word with that of the supernatural was a common belief – a concept so deeply rooted that it was still being recorded in Celtic countries early in the twentieth century.[19] As the idea of immaculate written historical records did not exist in Arthur's day, we have to deal with legendary history, myth, folklore and oral traditions handed down over centuries. This results in plenty of room for interpre-tation and error – which is one of the main reasons why the understanding of Arthur is so varied.

The contents of the British manuscripts, originating in the oral tradition, contain references to people who were obviously important, even though the events attached to them have seldom survived. But what we have of this native oral tradition is minimal, as most of it never survived to take written form – though variants of some lost stories have survived in the folklore that has been recorded. Nevertheless, within the oldest traditions attached to Arthur there are many clues to place names, church dedications and settlements that point to the original Arthurian landscape, forgotten and neglected by recent generations, but known and recorded by the bards, historians and chroniclers of Wales. Within the original tradition, Arthur was not a king; there was no Lancelot, Galahad or association with places such as London (historically under Saxon control). And of course to his own people there was no Arthur sleeping in a cave awaiting the call to come to his country's aid – this privilege being reserved for more deserving figures such as Cynan and Cadwaladr, the traditional saviours of the Welsh. Furthermore, following his final battle, Arthur was considered to be dead and buried not in some fairy island or English monastery, but within a particular area of his native land.

If Arthur had not had the dubious honour of being adopted as a figurehead by the Norman invaders, from the brief references to his name in early chronicles and annals he would no doubt be regarded as merely an obscure minor historical figure and most of the world would have never heard of him – to the benefit of several forests. If this adoption had not taken place, there would be no King Arthur, no great Christian monarch, no Round Table, no Glastonbury legends, and no Camelot, Tintagel or Winchester –

just Arthur the warrior. If all that remained was the material found in Welsh sources, without the influence of the later Anglo-Norman propaganda, the classification of Arthur would be much easier and he would probably be mentioned only in passing along with other Welsh warriors of the period such as Urien Rheged. Arthur will not be found buried in the grounds of an abbey in Somerset. If any vestige of him remains it must be looked for in the histories and traditions of his own people; if it is not found there, then all trace of the real figure of Arthur has been lost.

Before searching out the realm of Arthur in the ancient landscape of Britain we must first journey through a different landscape – a landscape formed from ancient texts, lost sagas and heroic traditions. This is a landscape in which the mountains, hills and valleys were born from antique parchment and vellum, the seas, rivers and lakes flow with multicoloured pigments and faded inks, and the forests, fields and cities were etched with the tip of a long-broken quill. We must return to the traditions of Arthur in the period before Geoffrey of Monmouth – the material independent of Anglo-Norman influence – to examine the history and legends of Arthur's own people and unearth the geography that gave birth to his legend. This task will be as problematic and difficult as those undertaken by Arthur's warriors in the quest for Olwen, but its outcome may be just as satisfactory.

Below is a chronology of the additions to the Arthurian legend that developed from the time of Geoffrey of Monmouth. It can be seen that most of the well-known Arthurian incidents are from later romantic tradition.

1136–8 Geoffrey of Monmouth writes *Historia Regum Britanniae* and has Arthur fighting on the Continent.

1155 Wace is the first to mention the Round Table.

1165 Chrétien de Troyes writes an Arthurian poem naming Lancelot for the first time. This is also the first mention of Camelot as Arthur's court.

1180 Chrétien de Troyes introduces the Holy Grail for the first time, and uses Arthur's court as a backdrop for its quest.

1193–9 Giraldus Cambrensis notes the exhumation of Arthur and Guinevere at Glastonbury in Somerset and thus identifies the site as Avalon.

c. 1200 Robert de Boron is the first to mention that the Grail was the cup used by Christ at the Last Supper.

c. 1200 Robert de Boron is the first to mention the sword in the stone.

1225 The Vulgate Cycle is the first attempt to provide a cohesive story of Arthur and the Grail from beginning to end.

c. 1330 The Round Table now at Winchester is made.

1380 The first use of the phrase 'the once and future king' appears in the anonymous *Alliterative Morte Arthur*.

1470 Malory finishes his manuscript of *Le Morte d'Arthur*, which translates and combines the available French and Latin sources into one long telling of the Arthurian legend.

1485 William Caxton revises Malory's text and prints it. The Arthurian legend becomes standardised.

2

THE BIRTH OF A LEGEND

THE small group of clergymen stand patiently in silence, awaiting the attention of the new Bishop of Lincoln, Robert de Chesney. Though it is only three in the afternoon, the perpetual gloom that envelops the monastery makes it necessary to have candlelight, and the scent of the burning tallow candles permeates the air, warming the atmosphere of the cold stone room. Eventually the Bishop's attention returns to the parchment on the large oak table before him, and he motions the robed brothers forward. One by one the monks take the goose quill in hand and add their signatures to the document. Finally the statue-like figure that had spent the last twenty minutes silhouetted against the arched windows that overlook the gardens turns and walks to the illuminated area around the centre of the table. As he approaches it can be seen that he is a distinguished man, his hair beginning to grey and with lines etched around his eyes from years squinting under candlelight, scratching letters on to vellum parchment. He pulls back the sleeve of his robe, takes the quill in his right hand, and adds his signature to the charter of Bishop Robert: 'Galfridus Arturus, Episcopus

Sancti Asaphi. 1151' – 'Geoffrey son of Arthur, Bishop of Saint Asaph. 1151.'[1]

Geoffrey son of Arthur is much better known by the name he gives himself in his most famous work, the *Historia Regum Britanniae*: 'Galfridus Monemutensis' – 'Geoffrey of Monmouth'. The impact of his work on the medieval world and the subsequent Arthurian romances that grew out of it mean that 'Geoffrey of Monmouth' will be found in every book written about the Arthurian legend. Despite this, very little is known about Geoffrey himself, and the earliest records to mention him place him not at Monmouth, in Wales, but in the city of Oxford in England. It is here that his name is first found as a witness to the foundation charter for Oseny Abbey, *c.* 1129, and it appears on later charters on several occasions during the next twenty-five years.[2] Although the famous university had yet to be founded, in Geoffrey's time Oxford was already considered a seat of learning, and it seems that he was something of a teacher, as twice in earlier documents he is styled *magister* (teacher). His connection to Walter, the Archdeacon of Oxford and provost of the secular College of St George, has led scholars to believe that he was probably a canon of this college.[3]

The motives behind Geoffrey's masterpiece, which he finished sometime between 1136 and 1138, at first seem relatively clear. Following the Norman conquest of Britain in 1066, the chroniclers of the new monarchy found little information available about the pre-Roman history of the island, or of the Britons, the original inhabitants. Geoffrey of Monmouth filled this gap with a work which purported to give a complete history of Britain from the arrival of Brutus, the son of the Trojan hero Aeneas, in 1200 BC until the death of Cadwaladr, the last British king, in AD 688. Geoffrey claimed in his introduction that he had long searched for some information about the early history of Britain, but it wasn't until his friend Walter, Archdeacon of Oxford, gave him an ancient book written in the British tongue that he found what he was looking for. The identity of this mysterious book has been the cause of much debate over the centuries, and the *Historia* is today considered as only pseudo-history – more a piece of political propaganda than a serious study of the history of Britain.

The dedications in the text enable us to establish the real motives behind this literary highlight of an otherwise minor career which Geoffrey spent courting favour from his masters. At different times, according to the flow of political events, the dedications in the *Historia* change. In most of the surviving manuscripts the dedication is to Geoffrey's patron, the powerful Robert, Earl of Gloucester, and some also add Count Waleran of Worcester. Further manuscripts mention King Stephen and/or Alexander, Bishop of Lincoln (Geoffrey's ecclesiastical superior), to whom he dedicated his earlier work *Prophetiae Merlini* (The Prophecies of Merlin), included in the *Historia*, and his final work, *Vita Merlini* (The Life of Merlin).[4]

The *Historia* was finished after the death on 1 December 1135 of Henry I, who had named his daughter, Matilda, as his rightful heir. In the chaotic period that followed, Matilda and her cousin Stephen (Henry's nephew) vied and fought, often violently, for possession of the English throne. Geoffrey's dedications to Robert of Gloucester strongly link him to Matilda's cause, as Robert was Matilda's half-brother, chief ally and most powerful supporter. Indeed he was probably the most powerful lord in the country at that time. Unfortunately for Geoffrey, however, it was eventually Stephen who won the crown, and following this shift of power in English politics Geoffrey rewrote his dedication accordingly. Robert died in 1147, followed by Bishop Alexander in 1148, and from then on Geoffrey looked to Stephen for his advancement. His efforts were not in vain. Documented within the Canterbury records for February 1152 are not only the ordination of Geoffrey to the priesthood by Archbishop Theobald, but also his consecration to the bishopric of St Asaph in North Wales, following his election in the previous year.[5] There is no evidence to suggest that Geoffrey ever managed to visit his see – indeed, the rebelliousness of the Welsh under Owain Gwynedd would have made this a dangerous, if not virtually impossible, task. In fact the only act that Geoffrey ever performed in his newly confirmed episcopal role was to witnesses one of the most important historical documents of Stephen's reign, namely a charter issued from Westminster in December 1153 confirming the requirements of the Treaty of Wallingford. This document paved the way for Henry of Anjou (Matilda's son) to accede to the English throne, as Henry II, in the following year, 1154.

The political problems of the day did not just affect the dedications within the *Historia*: they also dictated much of its content and the geographical emphasis of the work. Lands held by Geoffrey's patron Robert of Gloucester and other powerful figures among Robert's supporters are the main focal points of the *Historia*, especially Caerleon in South Wales.[6] This site had been important in Roman times, but there is no evidence that it was ever the seat of a Dark Age royal court or the see of an archbishopric, as Geoffrey claimed. It is unlikely to be coincidence that some of the most glorious events within the *Historia* take place at a site under the control of Geoffrey's patron. The bishopric of Llandaf was already manufacturing an ancient past for itself, as can be seen in the contemporary *Book of Llandaf*, in which a collection of saints' lives and forged ancient charters was being used to claim land throughout South Wales. Robert and his supporters owned land in the Cardiff area only a few miles away, so Geoffrey was probably happy to play a part in the see of Llandaf's claims. The list of politically motivated relocations and creations within the *Historia* could fill a volume, but that is not the purpose of this work.[7] Instead, we are concerned with the sources that Geoffrey used for the figure of Arthur, and it is to these that we must now turn.

THE ANCIENT LOST BOOK

In order to understand the true source of the Arthurian legend as commonly portrayed today, it is imperative to understand where Geoffrey found the information he used to create the heroic character of Arthur and to examine how much of it, if any, still survives.

In the introduction to his *Historia* Geoffrey helpfully names his sources, when he bemoans the lack of information about the pre-Christian kings of Britain and the acts of Arthur in the works of the earlier historians Bede and Gildas.[8] The passages he used from these works can be identified quite easily, as he often quoted them in their exact form or changed them only enough to keep his narrative coherent.[9] The three major sources for our knowledge of pre-Norman Britain are Gildas's *De Excidio Britanniae* (The Ruin of Britain – usually known simply as *De Excidio*), written *c.* 540,

Bede's *Historia Ecclesiastica Gentis Anglorum* (The Ecclesiastical History of the English People), finished in 731, and the *Historia Brittonum* (The History of the Britons), a composite text based upon even earlier sources gathered together in the earliest version (*c.* 830) left to us today. Several quotations can also be found from such classical sources as Virgil and Ovid, and from the Vulgate text of the Bible.

The other major source that Geoffrey refers to is a mysterious book that he mentions on three separate occasions. He obviously wishes the reader to be well aware of this source, since he refers to it explicitly both in the introduction and in the closing section of his work. The introduction describes the mysterious source as 'a very ancient book in the British tongue' ('*quendam Britannici sermonis librum uetustissimum*').[10] The end of the *Historia* reveals the source to be 'the book in the British tongue which Walter the Archdeacon of Oxford brought from Britannia' ('*librum istum Britannici sermonis quem Gualterus Oxenfordensis archidiaconus ex Britannia aduexit*').[11] The remaining reference to the mysterious book concerns the story of Arthur's final battle at Camlan, and Geoffrey tells the reader:

> About this particular matter, most noble Duke [Robert of Gloucester], Geoffrey of Monmouth prefers to say nothing. He will, however, in his own poor style and without wasting words, describe the battle which our most famous King fought against his nephew, once he had returned to Britain after his victory; for that he found in the British treatise already referred to. He heard it, too, from Walter of Oxford, a man most learned in all branches of history.[12]

The claim that Geoffrey translated this mysterious book – 'At Walter's request I have taken the trouble to translate the book into

Latin'[13] – should not be taken literally, but should be understood in the context that Geoffrey himself supplies: i.e. he used the book to supply the story where gaps were left by the earlier sources of Gildas, Bede and the *Historia Brittonum*, which provide a definite historical framework for his *Historia*.

It is not always realised that there are a number of manuscripts – known as the Variant versions – that contain different texts of the *Historia* from that in the modern printed version.[14] These Variant manuscripts are notable for a number of things: there is no mention of Walter, Archdeacon of Oxford, and his mysterious ancient book; there is no dedication to a patron; and the texts differ so dramatically that some scholars have thought that the Variants represent an early draft put together from original sources or an early version of the *Historia* by another hand entirely.[15] Could these be a version of the *Historia* before Geoffrey received his mysterious ancient British book from Walter of Oxford?

So what did Geoffrey mean by a book being written 'in the British tongue' and brought 'from Britannia' ('*ex Britannia*')? This question was dealt with in our book *The Keys to Avalon*, but a brief recapitulation of some of the evidence will be useful at this point. The origin of Geoffrey's source material has been the cause of much heated debate between scholars since the twelfth century. Some believe that Geoffrey made everything up and was using a technique known as 'the lost-book typos' – common in medieval times – whereby he claimed some ancient source in order to give his book authority.[16] The historians who take this view thereby absolve themselves of all responsibility to address any of the questions surrounding the origins of Geoffrey's influential work and leave numerous questions unanswered. Unfortunately, this is the sceptical approach taken by many modern scholars. However, there are equally strong opinions that oppose this view. In 1970, for example, R. W. Southern stated that 'Personally I am convinced that the source which he [Geoffrey] claimed to have received from Walter, archdeacon of Oxford, really existed.'[17]

Those scholars who do believe that Geoffrey made use of an ancient book have argued for years about its origin. Was it a now lost text from Brittany, or a mysterious ancient book from Wales? This confusion arises from the exact meaning of the word 'Britannia', as it was used for both Wales and Brittany in the twelfth century. One of the most important clues as to which is meant comes from one of the earliest texts to mention a book dedicated to Robert of Gloucester, the poem *L'Estoire des Englies* (The History of the English), written by Geoffrey of Gaimar *c.* 1140:

Robert li quens de Gloucestre	Robert, the earl of Gloucester
Fist translater icele geste	Had this history translated
Solum les liveres as Waleis	According to the books of the Welsh
Kil aveient des Breton reis.	Which he had, about the British kings.[18]

As Professor E. K. Chambers pointed out in 1927, Geoffrey of Gaimar – writing for an Anglo-Norman audience in the early 1140s – considered the book dedicated to Robert of Gloucester (almost certainly the *Historia*) to have been taken from the Welsh.[19]

The debate still goes on today, though a close study of the contents of the *Historia* reveals that Geoffrey undoubtedly had access to Welsh insular traditions – written, oral or more likely both. The fact that Geoffrey was writing in Oxford and refers to Britannia as a separate region indicates that, unlike classical historians, he did not use the term to denote the whole of the isle of Britain. In conjunction with the quote above and the evidence detailed below, the authors agree with the opinion of John J. Parry, who wrote several important books on the subject: 'The name [Britannia] was used in a third sense to denote a British part of the island. Geoffrey, writing in England, could have meant by ex Britannia "out of Wales", and this is the sense, surely, which he intended.'[20]

The correspondences between the *Historia* and insular Welsh tradition add weight to the argument that Geoffrey's mysterious ancient book was of Welsh origin. It is possible to isolate parts of Geoffrey's narrative that derive from earlier sources almost all of which are either in Welsh or in Latin written by Welshmen. These sources includes such key works as the *Annales Cambriae* (The Annals of Wales), the *Historia Brittonum* and the tale of *Culhwch and Olwen*, all of which we will be looking at in detail in the next chapter. Below is a précis of the events in the Arthurian legend that can be shown to exist in earlier sources. It soon becomes clear that Geoffrey did not invent Arthur, as some claim, but simply pieced together earlier traditions and then added some material of his own.

Arthur is crowned at Caerleon by Dubricius the archbishop

Dubricius – known as Dyfrig in Welsh – is mentioned in the seventh-century *Life of St Samson*; the fullest version of his life, however, can be found in *The Book of Llandaf* (*c.* 1140), which also contains five charters that mention his name. All the sites associated with him are located in south-east Wales and Hereford-shire. Dyfrig is also mentioned in the *Lives of St Illtud and St Gwynllyw*, which are also set in south-east Wales. The *Annales*

Cambriae state that he died in 612, but evidence from the material mentioned above suggests a more likely date of *c.* 530. His body was buried on Bardsey Island, off the coast of the Lleyn Peninsula in North Wales, but was translated to Llandaf in South Wales in 1125.[21]

Arthur's battle on the river Douglas

In the famous battle list of Section 56 of the *Historia Brittonum* this site is found as Dubglas, where Arthur is recorded as fighting his second, third, fourth and fifth battles against the Saxons. The site of these battles will be looked at in more detail in Chapter 6.

Arthur's battle at Kaerluideoit

The only other source to mention this name as a site of one of Arthur's battles is *The History of Gruffudd ap Cynan*, a biography of a ruler of Gwynedd who died in 1137. This site will also be looked at in more detail in Chapter 6.

Arthur's battle at Coed Celyddon

Coed Celyddon was the site of Arthur's seventh battle according to the battle list in the *Historia Brittonum*. It is also mentioned in passing in other Welsh sources such as *The Black Book of Carmarthen* and *The Book of Taliesin*. The site of this battle will also be described in Chapter 6.

Arthur's weapons named Pridwen, Caliburn and Ron

These are based on the names given to Arthur's possessions in *Culhwch and Olwen*, and will be dealt with in detail in the next chapter.

Arthur fights at Badon and carries an image of the Virgin Mary on his shield

Badon is one of earliest recorded names for a Dark Age battle site in British history, being mentioned by Gildas in his *De Excidio*. It is discussed in detail in Chapter 6.

The sixty islands in Lake Lumonoy

These are taken directly from Section 67 of the *Historia Brittonum*.

The square lake with four different types of fish in each of the four corners

This comes directly from Section 70 of the *Historia Brittonum*.

The lake named Lin Ligua that swallows the sea and then belches it back out again

Again this comes straight from the *Historia Brittonum* – in this case Section 69.

Samson, Archbishop of York

St Samson was a well-known character in Wales before Geoffrey used his name for a fictitious archbishop of York. *The Life of St Samson* dates from the seventh century and is the oldest of the saints' Lives to have come down to us. The *Life* relates that Samson was the son of Amon of Dyfed in south-west Wales, and at an early age was sent to school at Llanilltud Fawr, where he was later ordained by Dubricius (another name used by Geoffrey, as we have seen). Samson travelled to Ireland and Cornwall before ending his days at Dol in Brittany. Samson is also mentioned in the

Lives of the Welsh saints Cadog, Illtud, Padarn and Teilio, which were all in existence before Geoffrey wrote his *Historia*. The south-east Wales provenance of the material regarding Samson and the other saints' names used by Geoffrey shows that the source of his ecclesiastical names was the hagiographical school of Llancarvan and Llandaf in the vicinity of Cardiff.

Arthur marries Guinevere

Gwenhwyfar is the name given to Arthur's wife in *Culhwch and Olwen*. See page 92.

Arthur crosses over the sea to fight the Irish king Gillamuri

A similar event is told in *Culhwch and Olwen*, where Arthur sails over to Ireland to fight with Diwrnach for his cauldron – see Chapter 5.

Cai and Bedwyr are his two closest companions during his Continental campaigns

Both these characters are Arthur's closest companions in early Welsh material – especially *The Life of St Cadog*, *Culhwch and Olwen*, and the poetry of *The Black Book of Carmarthen*.

Gawain is said to be the nephew of Arthur

This relationship is first attested to in *Culhwch and Olwen*.

Churches are built in honour of the martyrs Aaron and Julian at Caerleon

Gildas's *De Excidio* mentions the shrines of Julian and Aaron as being in Urbes Legiones (City of Legions). In Welsh this would translate as 'Caerleon' ('*Caer*' is 'city' and '*leon*' or '*lleon*' is 'legion'). Two Roman cities were known by this name in Wales: Chester and Caerleon on the River Usk. Bede copied this information directly from Gildas, and traditions regarding these martyrs can be found in *The Book of Llandaf* localised in south-east Wales.[22]

Names found in the long list of nobles present at Arthur's coronation

This long list of names can be divided into two sections: names which have been used previously in the *Historia* or are about to be introduced in the section following Arthur's death and names not mentioned elsewhere in the manuscript. The first section contains the names of some historical people such as Cadwallon Lawhir and Urien Rheged that can be found in the *Historia Brittonum* and early Welsh poetry. In the second section, consisting of fifteen names, five names can be positively identified with names from a collection of Welsh genealogies in the British Library manuscript Harleian MS 3859, dating from *c.* 950.[23] Below are the names found in the *Historia* and those found in the earlier source (with the number of the section in which they appear), side by side for easy comparison:

Historia Regum Britanniae	*Harleian genealogies*
Donaut map Papo	Dunaut map Pappo (11)
Cheneus map Coil	Ceneu map Coyl Hen (9)
Grifud map Nogord	Gripiud ap Nougoy (15)
Gorbonian map Goit	Garbaniaun map Coyl Hen (10)
Run map Neton	Run map Neithon (16)

The resignation of Dubricius and the appointment of new bishops

Dubricius is replaced by St David, the patron saint of Wales, who is a cult figure throughout the south-west of the country with his main centre at St David's in Pembroke. A cleric called Tebaus (a Latin equivalent to the Welsh Teilio) is made the bishop of Llandaf, and as a *Life of St Teilio* is found in *The Book of Llandaf* the South Wales provenance of this ecclesiastical material is obvious.

Macsen and Elen gain the crown of Rome

This story is told in more detail in the Welsh tale *The Dream of Macsen Wledig*.

Arthur tells of the time he fought the giant Retho, who wanted to make a cloak from the beards of kings, on Mons Aravius

Exactly the same story is found in Welsh tradition regarding a giant called Rhita, who is also mentioned in *Culhwch and Olwen*. This is dealt with in more detail on page 124.

Arthur fights Medrod at Camlan

In the *Annales Cambriae* both Arthur and Medrod are said to have died at Camlan, although it is not clear that they actually fought each other. Medrod appears on several occasions in Welsh sources, although he is never referred to as Arthur's nephew, as in the *Historia*. The battle of Camlan is a common theme in Welsh tradition, and will be discussed in some detail in Chapter 8.

THE BIRTH OF A LEGEND

The death of Arthur in 542

This date corresponds closely with the date 539/40 given to the battle of Camlan in the *Annales Cambriae*.

The details above show how much of the Arthurian story Geoffrey found in earlier Welsh sources, either oral or written, making it all but certain that his mysterious book written in the British tongue was Welsh. The *Historia* also contains further evidence of a Welsh source in the material not associated with Arthur.[24] At this point it is important to draw attention to the seventy surviving manuscripts of a Welsh version of Geoffrey's *Historia*, known today as *Brut y Brenhinedd* (The Chronicle of the Kings). These texts have had a chequered career which has seen them labelled both as mere translations of Geoffrey's Latin and as the original Welsh copies of Geoffrey's source book. The earliest manuscript in Welsh dates from *c.* 1200 and is itself a copy of an earlier text, as evidenced by scribal errors; therefore it cannot be Geoffrey's source, and we have no way of knowing if he worked from an earlier manuscript that is now lost.[25] In fact the truth is likely to lie somewhere in the middle, as, although many of the Welsh manuscripts are simply translations of the Latin, some do contain information not found in Geoffrey's text. *Brut y Brenhinedd* restores the Latinised names of Geoffrey to their original Welsh forms and in some cases adds patronymics known from other Welsh manuscripts. The Welsh place names mentioned in the *Historia* remain the same, but the Latin explanations of Geoffrey are omitted and additional details are included from insular Welsh traditions. The Welsh texts are often more brutal in their description of battles and place more emphasis on the ecclesiastical aspects of the narrative, rather than the courtly. In one of the few articles on the subject, Charlotte Ward summarises the situation thus: 'All of the MSS give details and Welsh equivalents not found in the Latin and they are independent of one another in many cases.'[26]

The *Historia Regum Britanniae* was written at a time when the Normans were keen to expand their sphere of influence further into Wales and Scotland – a political agenda clearly identifiable in Geoffrey's work. Geoffrey made use of the sources he had available to him, either historical or legendary, and filled in the gaps from his imagination to make a work that is very readable even today. All the evidence points to his mysterious claimed source as being a Welsh text – in all likelihood something similar to the manuscript known as Harleian MS 3859 mentioned above. This manuscript contains one of the earliest versions of the *Historia Brittonum*, a series of early Welsh genealogies and the *Annales Cambriae*, all three of which were clearly used by Geoffrey. It is to be hoped that further research or a lucky manuscript find will shed more light on the problem.

It seems strange, if not a little sad, that, given his contribution to the literary and political life of the medieval world, Geoffrey's death apparently did not warrant even a mention in the records or chronicles of his political masters. The only people to record Geoffrey's death were the very people whose traditions he stole, and in the *Brut y Tywysogion* (The Chronicle of the Welsh Princes) one simple and inaccurate entry (he was actually Bishop of St Asaph) brings the curtain down on one of the most influential characters of the medieval world: '1155 . . . In that year died Geoffrey, bishop of Llandaf.'[27]

3

THE KEEPERS OF TRADITION

HE surviving fragments of British antiquity from which Geoffrey of Monmouth borrowed are of great interest in our quest to uncover the origins of Arthur. Whereas the best-known stories of Merlin and Arthur's Continental campaigns are the work of a creative storyteller writing for a powerful political patron, the earlier traditions record, in a semi-legendary form, the figure of Arthur as known to his own people. As can be seen from the previous brief overview of the development of the Arthurian legend, the trail of literary evidence leads back to the Arthurian traditions born in the land now known as Wales. As Thomas Jones put it in 1958, 'The existence of traditions and stories about Arthur in the period before 1136 is restricted to Welsh texts and a few Latin texts, which are for the most part the work of Welshmen.'[1] These traditions constitute the earliest and most authentic corpus of Arthurian material that survives, despite their making no mention of such places as Glastonbury, Tintagel and Cadbury that are associated with Arthur in romantic fictions and modern myths (both scholarly and popular).

For many years there has been an important ongoing debate as to whether or not there was ever a fully developed Welsh Arthurian tradition, comparable in structure to the life developed by Geoffrey of Monmouth. In assessing the evidence of the Welsh sources, it becomes very clear that a distinct and decidedly different tradition existed among the remnant of Arthur's own people long before Geoffrey took up his quill and for ever changed the face of the Arthurian legend. All the earliest and most authentic Arthurian references emerge from a Welsh context. Moreover, despite the centuries of Norman subjugation and propaganda, the early traditions of the original Britons appear to have survived in the hills and valleys of Wales to a very late date, despite the ever-increasing popularity of Geoffrey's 'medieval best-seller' elsewhere. But what of the recorders of those traditions, the monks and bards of Wales? What exactly did they leave to posterity, and why is their testimony so important?

THE WELSH BARDS

The great stone hall fell silent as the bard Gwalchmai ap Meilyr entered the court; the warriors turned their attention from their feast, and boasts of valour toasted in mead, to the serious business of the bard and his songs. Here, amid the warriors of twelfth-century Powys, Gwalchmai was to sing the praise of Madog ap Maredudd and his retinue, following yet another successful raid. Gwalchmai took centre stage before the head table and waited for the general clatter and final murmur of unfinished conversation to cease. The hall awaited his words with expectation, and he slowly turned to meet the gaze of his audience; then he began to sing. As was customary, the eulogies the poet heaped upon the lord and his war-band were comparisons to the great warriors and warlords of the Welsh past. During his paean, among the names of the great warriors he evoked was that of Arthur – not only comparing the strength of Madog to that of Arthur himself, but also comparing the shout of Madog's war-band to that of Arthur's: '*mal gawr torf teulu Arthur*' – 'like the shout of the host of Arthur's war-band'.[2]

The Welsh bards of the twelfth century were the inheritors of a literary tradition born in the mists of antiquity, and that tradition has continued unbroken to the present day. Along with the Greeks and the Romans, the Welsh have one of the most ancient literatures surviving in the modern world. The earliest references to the poets within what are now commonly referred to as the Celtic peoples are found in the works of classical writers, who talk of the '*bardoi*' or '*bardi*' in Celtic Gaul. The word 'bard' was in use in both Wales and Ireland in the early Middle Ages and comes from an Indo-European root word, '*bardos*', meaning 'a singer of praise'.[3] These figures in Celtic society appear to have had a somewhat esoteric nature, judging by the testimony of classical sources such as Julius Caesar and the geographer Strabo. In discussing the Celtic social hierarchy these early sources refer to three important intellectual classes among the Continental Celts: bards, seers/poets and druids. The evidence establishes that the bards were the panegyric heroic poets (singers of praise), the seers or poets (*vates* or *manteis*) were philosophers, and the druids (*druidai*) appear to have been the pre-eminent educated class, taking both a religious and a judicial role. Of these three classes, only the bards seem to have survived the Roman occupation and the introduction of Christianity, and such anonymous figures of antiquity were the forerunners of the praise poets that flourished in Dark Age Ireland and Wales.

The bardic classes of Wales and Ireland committed to memory a vast catalogue of native material in the form of stories, poetry and genealogies, preserving the triumphs and tribulations of their rulers and sometimes those of neighbouring regions. This material was not recorded as we would record history today, arranged by subject and chronology, but often consisted of stories linked by themes and similar events, regardless of the chronology involved. If you judge it by the strict criteria applied by present-day historians to more recent periods, then it contains little that can be considered as historical fact. If, however, you understand the type of records that we have for the period in question and the background to their development, then these sources become more and more informative and remarkable. The distinction between history, literature and legend was not clear-cut to the authors of the material we are about to look at.

Within the bardic poetry preserved in Welsh manuscripts, as in virtually all Celtic heroic literature, you will find numerous personal and place names mentioned. Some of these have been firmly identified; many others as yet have not and belong to tales now lost. A good example is provided by a collection of Welsh stanzas known as 'The Stanzas of the Graves'. These are thought to date back to the ninth century, or perhaps even earlier, and take the form of an index or catalogue that records the burial places and stories of over a hundred once famous warriors, with further material that has been added from other sources during transmission, such as stanzas from Welsh saga poetry. Some stanzas refer to known stories, places and people; others contain only an otherwise unknown personal name and rather vague allusions to the site of a grave.

One of the most interesting points in regard to this and other traditional material is the significance laid upon *what* and *where* things happened, rather than when. Patrick Sims-Williams has pointed out that 'place-lore is in fact central to Celtic heroic literature'.[4] It is the reassessment of place-name lore in the remaining fragments of the native tradition that offers the most productive way to improve our understanding of the early traditions – including those concerning Arthur. Even though it was at an early period that Arthur achieved legendary status, the surviving sources do provide place-name evidence from the earliest traditions that can help us identify the area originally associated with him. Needless to say, the picture of Arthur obtained from these sources is quite different from that usually found in books on him.

When we ask what these sources can tell us about the historical Arthur the answer is complicated, not because of the apparent lack of material, not even because of the layers that have been added to the original material during century after century, but because of the nature of the historical documents that have survived. In Wales, history was handed down via oral tradition, and, from their many references to what were obviously well-known people, stories and events within them, the existing manuscripts make it clear that the vast majority of this history never survived to take written form. The conclusion of Dr Rachel Bromwich was that 'various converging lines of evidence serve to show beyond reasonable doubt that the incomplete fragments which have come down in Welsh were once part of a very much larger body of tradition ... The *Four Branches*, *Culhwch and*

Olwen, and the Welsh romances, represent relatively late literary adaptations of what must be regarded as a mere fragment of the cycles of narrative to which they belong.'[5]

The records of the original Britons appear in the history and literature of Wales and, although the earliest manuscripts date from the twelfth century, these contain valuable evidence for the earlier period. There has been excellent work done on many of the Welsh manuscripts, and dates of composition have been assigned based on linguistics, content and the orthography of the texts.[6] These dates of composition can be used to chart the development of certain themes, stories and characters in the written form, as again outlined by Dr Rachel Bromwich: 'The advance in knowledge of the historical development of the Celtic languages which has taken place during the present century may enable us to establish the date of a text in its earliest written form as several centuries earlier than the oldest manuscript in which it is contained.'[7]

In Wales, the poets of the Dark Ages are known as the *Cynfeirdd* or 'Early Poets', and their line of tradition came down to the *Gogynfeirdd*, literally the 'not so Early Poets' – also known as *Beirdd y Tywysogion*: the Poets or Bards of the Welsh Princes, the official court bards of the princes of the independent areas of Wales from 1100 to 1300. This bardic tradition continued, in one form or another, down to the sixteenth century. Until *c.* 1250 allusions in their work show that the bards were still very aware of their traditional inheritance. However, the poets of the mid thirteenth century onwards seem slowly to lose touch with this earlier material: their references to the past are mainly of a comparative nature, and elements from the later Continental romances and the influence of Geoffrey of Monmouth slowly impact upon their work. The poems of the *Gogynfeirdd* 'indicate that this oral literature was still in some degree familiar and in current circulation down to the end of the twelfth century; [as] to a lesser extent [do] references by the cywydd poets [bards writing in a poetic style used from *c.* 1300 onwards] of the succeeding period.'[8] From this period onward the bards gradually became less and less central to Welsh aristocratic society, and with the loss of Welsh independence and the introduction of printing, coupled with the decline of patronage caused partly by the dissolution of the monasteries, the function of this ancient class eventually became obsolete by the middle of the sixteenth century.[9]

As we said earlier, Arthur is essentially a textual problem, and it is in the manuscripts that contain the vestiges of the earliest British tradition that we continue our search for this elusive figure. Though the Welsh sources for Arthur have been studied for centuries, they are still little known in comparison with Geoffrey of Monmouth and the later romances. By using them it is possible to uncover the names of Arthur's companions and family and the geography in which they lived, enabling us to locate the earliest point of origin for the Arthurian tradition. Though many of the handful of early Welsh sources contain little more than obscure fragments, enough survives for us to be able to piece together a tradition in existence long before the Normans landed on these shores. The sources described below contain this pre-Norman tradition of Arthur. First, however, we turn to the point where the two cultures first meet: the Latin material that first makes Arthur a king and utilises him in the quest for Anglo-Norman domination of South Wales.

THE LIVES OF THE WELSH SAINTS

The first link back to the earlier Welsh material is found in the epilogue appended to Geoffrey of Monmouth's *Historia Regum Britanniae*:

> The task of describing their [the Britons'] kings, who succeeded from that moment onwards in Wales, I leave to my contemporary Caradoc of Llancarfan. The kings of the Saxons I leave to William of Malmesbury and Henry of Huntingdon. I recommend these last say nothing at all about the kings of the Britons, seeing that they do not have in their possession the book in the British language which Walter, Archdeacon of Oxford brought from Wales.[10]

The only text definitely written by Caradog of Llancarvan is *The Life of Gildas*, written at about the same time that Geoffrey was writing his *Historia*.[11] This text details the events of Gildas's life and relates the story of Arthur fighting a king called Melwas, who has abducted his wife, at a place called Glastennin, which has long been understood to mean Glastonbury in Somerset – in which case Caradog's is the earliest text to link Arthur and this town of his later fame.[12] The Lives of several Welsh saints, mentioning the exploits of Arthur, had been composed in South Wales by 1090, and at least one of them was written at Llancarvan, the later home of Caradog.[13]

The earliest manuscript containing these lives dates from *c.* 1200; it is housed in the British Library, and is known as Cotton Ms. Vespasian A. xiv. It is believed to have been written at Monmouth, and many of the lives contained within it are of South Wales origin.[14] The geography of the events depicted in the saints' lives is focused upon the boundaries of lands owned by the church dedicated to a particular saint – arguments over lands owned by certain churches played a very important part in the everyday life of religious houses in South Wales at the time. The depiction of Arthur in these Lives is very different from that in other early Welsh sources: Arthur is accompanied by Cai and Bedwyr, his companions in the earliest traditions, and is depicted as the local king or tyrant whom the saint must defeat in order to gain land. It appears in these Lives that the character of Arthur exists solely to fill this role of opponent of the saint and he is little more than an empty figure, although there are occasional elements that suggest some form of pre-existing tradition. Maelgwn Gwynedd, a historical North Wales king of the sixth century, undertakes the same role in some of the other saints' lives. The writers of these lives were obviously aware of the existence of Maelgwn Gwynedd from chronicles such as Gildas's *De Excidio*, but how did they become aware of Arthur? In his excellent article on this matter, Jeff Rider summarises the situation thus:

> The six Welsh Lives in which Arthur appears may . . . all be connected with the Norman Conquest and expansion into Wales between 1067 and 1135 and are part of the sudden and urgent increase in historiographical activity which this expansion provoked: when late eleventh- and early twelfth-century scholars turned to an investigation of the written and oral materials available to them concerning the British past, we may conclude, one of the figures they found there was Arthur.[15]

Not only do the Lives of the Welsh saints depict Arthur as a king – something not found in earlier Welsh sources – they also depict him as the King of Britannia, which within the saints' lives only ever means Wales, not the whole of Britain or Brittany.

Geoffrey was obviously aware of the hagiographical school centered upon Llandaf and Llancarvan, as indicated by his use of South Wales saints and reference to Caradog in the epilogue to his *Historia*. Was it among these saints' lives that he found material that inspired him to create the figure of Arthur the king of all Britain? Jeff Rider adds two very important points in relation to these sources:

> In sum then, the saint's Lives in which Arthur appears suggest two conclusions. First, that the creation of an Arthurian literary tradition in the twelfth century received its initial impetus from the strong Anglo-Norman and Cambro-Norman historiographical reaction to the Norman occupation of England and Wales: William the Conqueror was in some sense as responsible as anyone for the development of Arthurian literature. Second, that Geoffrey of Monmouth did not by any means invent the figure of Arthur, but gave an existing, rather malleable and fluid figure a shape and definition it had previously lacked.[16]

But, although the story of Arthur may have lacked definition, it was by no means as hazy as we are often lead to believe.

The *Historia Brittonum*

The *Historia Brittonum* is a compilation of native and traditional material found in over thirty different manuscripts. Although the different manuscripts all contain the same basic core of material, there are many additions in particular manuscripts and variations between them.[17] It is generally accepted that most of the material was collected together *c.* AD 830, and the material is often credited to its most famous editor, Nennius (writing in the first half of the ninth century), although he is only one of several claimed editors whose names appear on different manuscripts.[18] In his introduction he states, 'I have therefore made a heap of all that I have found, both from the Annals of the Romans and from the Chronicles of the Holy fathers, and from the writings of the Irish and the English, and out of the tradition of our Elders.'[19]

Some of the sources he used are named, such as *The Book of St Germanus* and *The Book of St Patrick*, but much of the material is untraceable and its age and authenticity are uncertain. The chronicle deals with the origins of the Britons, the Roman invasion, and then the fights between the Welsh, Picts, Scots and Saxons. There are two sections concerning Arthur: the first is the famous battle list of Arthur, which will be dealt with in detail in Chapter 6; the second, in a section known to scholars as the *Mirabilia*, deals with marvels found in Wales and contains some very early Arthurian folklore. From the following excerpt we can deduce that an Arthurian tradition which already regarded him as a semi-legendary hero was localised in South Wales by 830:

§73 There is another wonder in the country called Builth. There is a heap of stones there, and one of the stones placed on top of the pile has the footprint of a dog on it. When he hunted Twrch Trwyth Cafal [the great boar Trwyth], the warrior Arthur's hound, impressed his footprint on the stone, and Arthur later brought together the pile of stones, under the stone in which was his dog's footprint, and it is called Carn Cafal. Men come and take the stone in their hands for the space of a day and a night, and on the morrow it is found upon the stone pile.[20]

This place has been identified as a cairn which gives its name to Corn Gaffallt, a hill some 1,530 feet above the upper Wye in north Brecknockshire, between Rhayader and Builth Wells. Three more of the marvels mentioned in the *Mirabilia*, regarding lakes with fantastic properties, were used by Geoffrey in his *Historia*, as noted on page 41.

The *Historia Brittonum* is the earliest historical work to mention Arthur, and the oldest version of its text is found in the manuscript in the British Library known as Harleian MS 3859. This priceless manuscript contains the earliest and most comprehensive collection of historical material concerning Wales before the Norman invasion, as well as a series of Welsh genealogies that Geoffrey may have used to create the list of people present at Arthur's coronation, as we saw on page 43. The manuscript itself dates from *c.* 1100, but the contents were originally written far earlier: the *Historia Brittonum c.* 830, the Welsh genealogies *c.* 950 and the next source we will briefly look at, the *Annales Cambriae*, at around the same time.

THE *ANNALES CAMBRIAE*

These annals – sometimes and more accurately referred to as the Welsh Annals – were written *c.* 950 and consist of very short entries regarding the history of Wales and a few other important events from beyond Wales. The annals are laid out with the abbreviation '*An*" (for '*Anno*' – i.e. 'In the year') for each new year (454 of them), and every tenth year is marked by a Roman numeral ('I', 'II', etc.). Some of the years then have a short historical note added, whereas others are just left blank. One of the problems is that the first '*An*' has no entry, so we are unsure of the date at which to begin; however, scholars have narrowed down this first year to 444, give or take a year – an acceptable margin of error.

Despite this uncertainty, the annals are considered to be one of the primary sources for our historical understanding of early medieval Wales. Arthur is mentioned on two occasions: in relation to the battle of Badon and to his fight with Medrod at Camlan – see Chapters 6 and 8 respectively.

THE BARDIC INHERITANCE

§62 Then Talhaearn Tad Awen was famed in poetry; and Aneirin and Taliesin and Bluchbard and Cian known as Gueinth Guaut, were also famed in British verse.[21]

The above quote from the *Historia Brittonum* is the earliest reference to the Welsh bards who wrote poetry in the sixth century. The works of two of them – Aneirin and Taliesin – have survived, and they both make reference to Arthur.

Although it is impossible to be precise, it is believed that Welsh poetry was first written down about the middle of the ninth century, though the earliest copies left to us today come from 400 years later. Gildas (*c.* 540) speaks in a derogatory tone of unnamed Welsh bards who celebrated his contemporary Maelgwn Gwynedd: 'Your excited ears hear not the praises of God ... but empty praises of yourself from the mouths of criminals who grate on the hearing like raving hucksters – mouths stuffed with lies and liable to bedew bystanders with their foaming phlegm.'[22] His objection, as an ecclesiastic, is that they praise an earthly king in terms that he believes should be reserved for the King of Heaven alone.

It was poets such as these who gave birth to a truly heroic tradition, recording the battles, events and heroes of their age in great songs and poems of both victory and defeat, accompanying the war-bands and immortalising the names of the great warriors who fell in the incessant fighting of the period – heroes who stood to the last with their chosen lords and kings, hurling back the overwhelming enemy, smashing shield walls, and cleaving paths through their opponents. Such was the ideal of sixth-century warrior society. It is in a poem of this type attributed to the above-mentioned Aneirin that one of the most important and possibly earliest references to Arthur is recorded.

THE BOOK OF ANEIRIN

This manuscript contains one of the most important early Welsh poems to have survived, known as *Y Gododdin*. The poem details the disastrous raid on a place called Catraeth by Mynydd Mynnyddog and his men, in which all but three of them are slaughtered. The battle can be dated to *c.* 600, although its location remains obscure, despite scholars' persistent identification of Catraeth with Catterick in Yorkshire.[23] The passage concerning Arthur tells us little about him, except that he was perceived as a great warrior, to whom a person called Gwarddur could not compare:

Gochore brein du ar uur	He fed black ravens on the rampart of a fortress
Caer ceni bei af arthur	Though he was no Arthur
Rug ciuin uerthi ig disur	Among the powerful ones in battle
Ig kynnor guernor guaurdur	In the front rank, Gwarddur was a palisade.

The Book of Aneirin has been dated to *c.* 1275 and is the sole source for *Y Gododdin* and four other short poems known collectively as the *Gorchanau*.[24] Two different versions of the poem exist in the manuscript, written in two different hands, and are known as A and B. Version A has been dated to *c.* 1100 and is the longer of the two; version B is shorter, but appears far older – possibly ninth century. Both versions relate the same basic narrative. The scribe of hand B also wrote another early Welsh manuscript, *The History of Gruffudd ap Cynan*, a ruler of Gwynedd who died in 1137.[25] This evidence has led to the suggestion that *The Book of Aneirin* was written by a scribe with an interest in the House of Gwynedd and was therefore written at one of the two important monasteries in North Wales at the time: either Basingwerk or Aberconwy.[26] The mention of Arthur, if contemporary with the earliest version of the poem, is the first extant reference to him anywhere in world literature.

THE BOOK OF TALIESIN

This medieval manuscript, dating from *c.* 1325, contains some of the earliest and most obscure poetry written in Welsh, and a full translation of its contents has yet to appear. Some of the poems have been identified as twelfth-century compositions, but others go back to the tenth century and possibly further.[27] Arthur is mentioned in five different poems in all, although only one of them is actually about him. This poem is called *Preiddeu Annwn* (The Spoils of Annwn) and describes Arthur and his men sailing across the sea in Arthur's boat *Prydwen* to a place called Annwn. The purpose of this journey was to steal a magical cauldron, but the final line of some of the verses – 'Apart from seven, none came back'[28] – suggests that all did not go to plan. The poem contains many fantastical images, such as glass towers rising from the sea and pearl-rimmed magical cauldrons, which, combined with its obscure and difficult language, make it one of the most enigmatic sources concerning Arthur.

The remaining brief references to Arthur appearing in *The Book of Taliesin* are given below:

Kat Godeu (Battle of the Trees)

Derwydon doethur	Druids of the wise one
Darogenwch y Arthur	Prophesy Arthur.[29]

Kadeir Teyrnon (The Chair of a Prince)

Treded dofyn doethur	The third profound [song] of the sage,
Y vendigaw Arthur.	To bless Arthur.
Arthur vendigan	Arthur the blest
Ar gerd gyfaenant.	With harmonious art.
Arwyneb yg kat,	The defender in battle,
Ar naw bystylat.	The trampler on nine.[30]

Marwnat Uthyr Pen (Elegy of the Terrible Head)

Neu vi arannwys vy echlessur	I have shared my refuge,
Nauetran yg gwrhyt Arthur.	A ninth share in Arthur's valour.[31]

Kanu y Meirch (Poem for the Horses)

A march Gwythur, a march Gwardur	Gwythur's horse, Gwarddur's horse
A march Arthur, ehofyn rodi cur.	Arthur's horse, fearless in giving battle.[32]

Arthur is depicted in these extracts as someone who was remembered for his prowess in battle, not as a king who pulled a sword from a stone and quested for the Holy Grail in a series of chivalric adventures. The final extract is also interesting as it links

Arthur with Gwarddur, who is compared to him in the poem *Y Gododdin* mentioned above, and with Gwythur, who is mentioned alongside Arthur in a poem from the next Welsh manuscript we will look at, implying that some tradition linking these characters together was very strong in the early material.

THE BLACK BOOK OF CARMARTHEN

As the oldest manuscript written in Welsh (*c.* 1250), *The Black Book of Carmarthen* is a very important source for many different aspects of Welsh tradition, including Arthur. It was written at the priory of Carmarthen in south-west Wales, and at the dissolution of the monasteries in the 1540s it passed into the hands of the antiquarian Sir John Price of Brecon. It has been well known in Welsh circles ever since, and is one of the most widely discussed and studied of the early Welsh manuscripts.[33] The manuscript contains forty poems, some dating from the twelfth century and others which are a lot older. The poems vary in their subject matter: some are religious in nature or in praise of a patron, whereas others concern the prophet Myrddin, better known as Merlin – though the place of Merlin in Continental romances bears no relationship to the early Welsh traditions found in *The Black Book of Carmarthen*. Arthur is named in four poems, only one of which concerns him at any length.

The most substantial and important Arthurian poem found in the *Black Book* is known as *Pa Gur?* (Who is the Porter?). In ninety lines, this describes Arthur and his men asking for entry into a hall called Awarnach. In order to gain entry, Arthur has to name his men and detail their achievements:

Pa imda genhid	What band goes with you?
Guir gorev im bid	– The best men in the world
Ym ty ny doi	Into my house you will not come
Onys guaredi	Unless you vouch for them
Mi ae guardi	– I shall vouch for them.[34]

Arthur proceeds to list his warriors and detail their exploits, whether fighting lions on Anglesey or battling with dog-headed people on the mountain of Eidyn. This list of warriors is the earliest that has come down to us in Welsh tradition, and many of the names found in this poem can also be found in *Culhwch and Olwen* from *The Mabinogion* (the name given to a collection of eleven Welsh tales) and other Welsh traditions that are not associated with Arthur. The geography attributed to Arthur's warriors is very important, and will be dealt with in Appendices 1 and 2.

The three remaining references to Arthur in the *Black Book*, although brief, are fundamental to our understanding of the Welsh traditions about him. A poem concerning Geraint the son of Erbin makes a reference to Arthur being at a battle known as Llongborth:

En llogporth y gueleis e. y arthur	At Llongborth I saw Arthur,
Guir deur kymynint a dur.	Brave soldiers would hew with steel,
Ameraudur llywiaudir llawur.	The emperor, the leader (in the) toil (of battle).[35]

This reference has been the focus of many articles and discussions since it was first printed in 1801, and the location of this battle will be dealt with in Chapter 6.

In a poem called *Ymddiddan Rhwhg Gwyddneu Garanhir a Gwyn ap Nudd* (A Conversation Between Gwyddneu Garanhir and Gwyn ap Nudd) Arthur is named only by default, as the subject of the poem is the death of his son Llacheu. Arthur is the father of a number of children in Welsh tradition – a fact that will be dealt with in the next chapter.

Mi a wum lle llas llacheu	I have been where Llacheu was slain,
mab arthur uthir ig kertev.	Son of Arthur, terrible in songs,
Ban ryreint brein ar crev.	When ravens rushed to gore.[36]

The final mention of Arthur in the *Black Book* is found in '*Englynion y Beddau*' or 'The Stanzas of the Graves', which, as mentioned above, lists the burial places of over a hundred Welsh warriors. The mention of the grave of Arthur in this poem will be studied in detail in Chapter 8.

The Black Book of Carmarthen also contains the earliest versions of a collection of bardic lore, known as the Triads, that preserve material not found in any other source.

THE WELSH TRIADS

The Welsh Triads consist of the grouping together of lines of information in sets of three. It is thought that these groupings were used as mnemonic devices to help the bards remember the finer points of traditional lore and tales that they had to relate, bringing together events from the traditional histories, legendary histories and mythological material. Such material was probably once far more extensive than the contents of the earliest surviving manu- scripts, as what remains contains references to stories and people now otherwise lost to us.[37] In her monumental edition of the Triads, Dr Rachel Bromwich identifies ninety-six individual triads – twenty-four of which mention Arthur – from various manuscripts that date back to 1225. Of those twenty-four triads that mention Arthur, only ten contain information that adds to our knowledge of the Arthurian tradition that existed in Wales before the arrival of the Normans.

The later manuscripts of the Triads show a process that, for want of a better term, is known as the 'Arthurianisation' of material. The earliest manuscripts use the formula 'The three x of Ynys Prydein' (i.e. 'The three x of the realm of Prydein' – see Chapter 5), but later ones change this to read 'The three x of Arthur's court', showing the influence of the Continental romances upon native tradition.

Only two triads in the earliest manuscript are specifically about Arthur; the rest, found in either one of the two great Welsh compilations *The White Book of Rhydderch* and *The Red Book of Hergest*, which preserve the *Mabinogion* tales, cannot be relied upon as evidence of the earliest traditions. The later triads can be split into two groups: those that contain earlier Arthurian traditions not found elsewhere and those that have been influenced by the *Historia* of Geoffrey and its Welsh translations, by making Arthur and his court a mere setting for the triad rather than integral to it. The earliest triad to name warriors of Arthur is given below, and the three names mentioned also appear in the huge list of Arthur's warriors found in *Culhwch and Olwen*:

Tri Vnben Llys Arthur:	Three Chieftains of Arthur's Court
(Gobrwy) mab Echel Vordwytwll,	Gobrwy son of Echel Mighty Thigh,
a Chadr(i)eith mab Porthavr Gadw,	Cadrieth son of Portawr Gadw,
a Fleudur Flam.	And Fleudur Fflam.[38]

The true worth of the Triads is best summarised by Dr Rachel Bromwich, the scholar who has spent a lifetime studying them:

The Triads provide ample corroborative evidence for a fact which is clearly demonstrated by certain early Welsh poems preserved in *The Black Book of Carmarthen* and *The Book of Taliesin:* it is that at a period earlier than any at which the possibility of external literary influence need be considered, the name Arthur was already beginning to act as a luminary into whose orbit were drawn the heroes of a number of independent cycles of Welsh narrative: characters both of mythology . . . and of heroic tradition who really belong to different periods and perhaps also different parts of Britain from the historical Arthur.[39]

THE GOGYNFEIRDD

As mentioned earlier in this chapter, the *Gogynfeirdd* is the collective name given to the bards of the Welsh princes from 1100 to 1300 – from the reign of Gruffudd ap Cynan of Gwynedd to the fall of Llywelyn ap Gruffudd, the last native ruler of Wales. One of the earliest of the *Gogynfeirdd* was Meilyr Brydydd, *pencerdd* (chief poet) of Gruffudd ap Cynan. Meilyr Brydydd flourished in the first half of the twelfth century, dying around the time that Geoffrey of Monmouth's *Historia* first reached the world at large.

In 1135 King Henry I of England had died, and the removal of his strong hand over Welsh affairs created something of a rebellion and a literary renaissance in Wales. The fact that the English then busied themselves with a civil war between Stephen and Matilda meant that they were powerless to control Wales, and the outcome of this civil war left England with a feeble monarch. Because of these events a new independence gripped the Welsh psyche and, as Sir John Lloyd points out in his seminal *A History of Wales*, 'Everywhere the foreign yoke was cast off, the powers of the new settlers was dauntingly challenged, and a new spirit of daring and independence seemed to have seized the whole Welsh race.'[40]

Of the thirty-four poets of the *Gogynfeirdd* whose names have survived, seventeen (possibly eighteen) of them were from Gwynedd, eight or nine from Powys, three from Deheubarth, and one from Brecon. This shows that the literary revival was strongest in Gwynedd, which was also where the Welsh put up the most resistance to the advancing English armies, and it was from this background that the re-emergence of the bardic tradition in Wales and the rebirth of the old ancestral traditions began.

In the poetry of the *Gogynfeirdd*, Arthur is mentioned on several occasions – being compared to the patrons of the poets – and was evidently regarded as having been a historical person, stories about whom were well known to the bards' audience.[41] There are also many references to his companions, and to the place names attached to them from the pre-Norman traditions. The *Gogynfeirdd* were writing in a time for which we have detailed historical records, which can be used to check the events that the poets depict, and they record place names that would otherwise have been forgotten or remained unidentified. The study of these place names has not received the attention it deserves and, as we will see in later chapters, the information contained in this little-known poetry holds the key to unlocking several Arthurian mysteries. Among these poems is a reference that completely contradicts the legend of Arthur's return.

It is often said that the Britons believed that Arthur was not dead, but would return to his country's aid in times of need. This is frequently supported by the use of references from non-Welsh sources, quoting folklore traditions from Cornwall or English and

Continental sources. Even as late as 1530, Elis Gruffydd tells us within the pages of his chronicle, 'And yet they [the English] talk more about him than we [the Welsh] do; for they say and firmly believe that he will rise again to be king.'[42] Within the Welsh bardic tradition there is no evidence of such a belief in connection to Arthur; in fact the exact opposite can be shown to have been the case, for references in the poetry of the bard Cynddelw (1155–95) establish that Arthur was considered dead along with such heroes as Caesar and Alexander, and a statement in the poetry of Llywarch ap Llywelyn (1160–1220) states clearly, 'Maredudd also is dead, as is sovereign Arthur.'[43] This and other evidence led T. Gwynn Jones to the conclusion that 'There is no evidence whatever in these poems that the bards believed the tradition that Arthur was not dead, and that he would one day return to free his people from bondage.'[44]

To put the *Gogynfeirdd* into a literary perspective, during the period when they were composing and still drawing on the earliest Welsh traditions, their English contemporaries such as Henry of Huntington, William of Malmesbury and Geoffrey of Monmouth were writing the histories of the English, Glastonbury and in Geoffrey's case the mighty *Historia* and the *Vita Merlini*. Continental authors such as Wace and Chrétien de Troyes were writing the romances of the Grail and the Round Table. For at least a hundred years their works were running side by side, but dealing with two distinctly different traditions, until slowly the romantic tradition – so popular in England and on the Continent – began to take over and Arthur lost his traditional form as he became a propaganda tool for the Welsh and English alike. According to J. E. Caerwyn Williams, the Welsh literary renaissance of which the *Gogynfeirdd* poets were a major part 'coincided with the golden age of medieval Welsh prose, for it is broadly speaking the age of *Culhwch and Olwen*, The Four Branches of the Mabinogi, *Breuddwyd Macsen* [*The Dream of Maxen Wledig*] ... and *Breuddwuyd Rhonabwy* [*The Dream of Rhonabwy*]'.[45]

It is to this material that we turn next.

CULHWCH AND OLWEN

The tale of *Culhwch and Olwen* is found among the collection of tales known as *The Mabinogion*, and is the earliest and longest Arthurian narrative to have survived in Welsh – a fact that has led many to attribute it with more value as a source than is perhaps justified. A more critical approach soon shows that the tale is a composite of earlier traditions with the reworkings of the author who wrote it down in its current form. Several passages are obvious later additions, for example a possible mention of William the Conqueror and a further reference to another French lord incorporated in place of the original figure who probably had a similar name;[46] other clues to the date of composition lie hidden in the geography of events depicted in the tale.

Scholars date the composition of the tale in its current form to *c.* 1100 and, because of the geographical bias of the text, locate its point of origin as an ecclesiastical site in South Wales – possibly St David's. The date of this composition is very close to that of the Lives of the saints, one of which, *The Life of St Cadog*, shows several parallels with *Culhwch and Olwen*.[47] The tale should therefore be viewed as another product of the South Wales school

THE KEEPERS OF TRADITION

of authors who created the Lives of the saints and later influenced Geoffrey of Monmouth. Nevertheless, this cannot detract from the fact that *Culhwch and Olwen* is a major repository of early Welsh Arthurian material.

The tale is extensive, and includes literally hundreds of personal names and several place names linked to Arthur, a thorough survey of which is beyond the scope of this book. Instead we will look at the most important and identifiable names and places linked to Arthur, especially those that correspond to the other early traditions preserved in early Welsh poetry. The tale may be summarised as follows.

Cilydd ap Celyddon Wledig and his wife, Goleuddydd, the daughter of Amlawdd Wledig, pray for a child and their prayers are answered, although Goleuddydd goes mad during the pregnancy and refuses to go near any dwelling. When the birth is imminent she comes to the home of a swineherd and gives birth to her son, whom she names Culhwch (Pigsty), because he was born in a pig-run. Despite this, the boy is of gentle lineage as he is a first cousin to Arthur. Goleuddydd dies and Culhwch is put out to nurse, until many years later his father remarries. His new wife has Culhwch brought to court and asks him to marry her daughter, which he refuses to do, so she places a curse on him that he will never have a wife until wins the heart of Olwen the daughter of the giant Ysbaddaden Pencawr. In order for him to achieve that, his father tells him to go to the court of his cousin Arthur.

On arrival at the gates of Arthur's court, Culhwch has to explain himself to the gatekeeper to try to gain entrance; after the gatekeeper has spoken to Arthur, he agrees to let him in. Culhwch arrives in the court and Arthur asks him to explain who he is and what he wants. Culhwch states his lineage, proving his relationship to Arthur, and explains that he must win the heart of Olwen. He then invokes the help of Arthur's warriors, and names all of them – over 260 of them.

Arthur agrees to help, and sends his warriors Cai, Bedwyr, Cynddylig, Gwalchmai, Gwrhyr and Menw to assist Culhwch in the search for Olwen. After many months they meet a shepherd called Custennin, who gladly helps them to find Ysbaddaden as the giant has killed twenty-three of his sons. The shepherd's wife knows Olwen and calls her to their house, where she meets Culhwch for the first time. Olwen tells Culhwch that she can marry only with her father's blessing, as he will die when she takes a husband. In order to gain his blessing, Culhwch must do everything that Ysbaddaden asks, no matter how difficult. After Culhwch has visited Ysbaddaden three times and foiled his tricks to kill him every time, Ysbaddaden finally agrees to name the challenges which Culhwch must undertake. He names forty tasks, many of which sound impossible.

Arthur and his men undertake to help Culhwch in these tasks, which contain names and places from the earliest Welsh traditions, and the rest of the tale details the fulfilment of ten of them; the others are not mentioned. Finally Ysbaddaden agrees to let Culhwch marry Olwen, and at this point Goreu, one of Arthur's men, chops off Ysbaddaden's head and takes over his fort. Culhwch and Olwen become man and wife, and Arthur and his men disperse back to their homes.

The tale contains many fantastic events – such as fighting with giants and hunting giant boars – but Arthur is not present at all of them, and Cai and Bedwyr undertake many of the tasks along with

Culhwch in Arthur's absence. Although *Culhwch and Olwen* is the earliest tale to have survived concerning Arthur it is not solely about him, hence he is not always centre stage. However, within the tale are three sections which are specifically about Arthur: a list of warriors at his court, a list of his possessions, and descriptions of the tasks that he does undertake. The list of his possessions is dealt with below; the tasks he undertakes will be looked at in Chapter 5, and the warrior list in Appendix 1.

On their first meeting, Arthur tells Culhwch that he will give him everything he has in order to complete his task, 'save only my ship and my mantle, and Caledfwlch my sword, and Rhongomyniad my spear, and Wynebgwrthucher my shield, and Carnwennan my dagger, and Gwenhwyfar my wife.'[48]

The giving of names to important objects appears to have been a widespread practice in Celtic culture, and some of the possessions of Arthur are also mentioned in other Welsh material, but more importantly they also appear in the *Historia Regum Britanniae*, providing direct evidence that Geoffrey of Monmouth was using Welsh material among his sources.

Arthur's Ship

Although not given a name in the quotation above, later on in the tale the ship is named *Prydwen*, which translates as 'Fair Form'. It is also mentioned in the poem *Preiddeu Annwn* in *The Book of Taliesin*, where Arthur and his men sail to the Otherworld to steal a cauldron. Geoffrey of Monmouth uses the same name for Arthur's shield in the *Historia*: 'And across his shoulders a circular shield called Pridwen'.[49]

Arthur's Mantle

The mantle of Arthur is not named in *Culhwch and Olwen* but is called Gwen in two later sources. *The Dream of Rhonabwy* – also found in *The Mabinogion* – is the earliest text to mention the mantle by name, and also gives the most detailed description of it: 'And he spread the mantle in front of Arthur, and an apple of red gold at each of its corners, and he set the chair on the mantle, and so big was the chair that three warriors armed might sit therein. Gwen was the name of the mantle. And one of the properties of the mantle was that no one would see him, whereas he would see every one. And no colour would ever abide on it save its own colour.'[50] It is also named as one of the thirteen treasures of Ynys Prydein, along with such objects as a hamper which, when food for one person was placed in it, produced food for a hundred, and a magical chessboard on which the pieces played by themselves.[51]

Arthur's Sword

This is the earliest reference to the famous sword of Arthur that has become known throughout the world as Excalibur. The Welsh name 'Caledfwlch' breaks down into two elements ('Caled'+ 'fwlch') and can be understood to mean 'Battlebreach' – implying a weapon of great power in the right hands. It is named on one other occasion in *Culhwch and Olwen*, but rather surprisingly never appears again in early Welsh literature. Attention has been drawn to a sword named Caladbolg that belonged to the Irish hero Fergus mac Roig, and the similarity of names is obvious. It has also been suggested that the name was given to a specific type of sword rather than an individual weapon.[52]

Geoffrey probably knew the Welsh name, as he names Arthur's sword Caliburnus and adds that it was forged in the Isle of Avalon. It was only in 1180, in the poem *Perceval* by Chrétien de Troyes, that the name 'Escalibor' first appeared, and, of the many different variant spellings of the name that followed, it was 'Excalibur' that became the standard version that everyone knows today. Needless to say the romantic images of swords being drawn from stones and cast into lakes to be snatched from mid-air by the Lady of the Lake do not appear until the thirteenth century.

Arthur's Spear

Rhongomyniad, which translates as 'Spear Slayer', is only mentioned in this one instance in early Welsh tradition. The name was again used by Geoffrey in his *Historia*, where it simply becomes 'Ron' – 'A spear called Ron graced his right hand.'[53]

Arthur's Shield

The name of Arthur's shield, 'Wynebgwrthucher', translates as 'Evening Face', the meaning of which is very uncertain. Arthur's shield is also important in two other early sources, the *Historia Brittonum* and the *Annales Cambriae,* in both of which it is said to have borne the image of the Virgin Mary.[54] This will be looked at in more detail in Chapter 6. Geoffrey names Arthur's shield as 'Pridwen' – actually the name of his ship, see above.

Arthur's Dagger

The name of Arthur's dagger, 'Carnwennan', translates as 'Little White Shaft' and is never mentioned anywhere else in early Welsh tradition.

Arthur's Wife

Gwenhwyfar is discussed in the next chapter.

From the information above it is obvious that Geoffrey of Monmouth knew of this list or one very similar to it. Scholars have drawn attention to the fact that the element 'Gwen' appears in the names of a number of Arthur's possessions. 'Gwen' in everyday modern use means 'white', but in these tales it often has the alternative meaning of 'sacred' or 'holy', which suggests that the possessions had some ritualistic aspect attached to them, though it is not possible to say exactly what this may have been.[55]

THE DREAM OF RHONABWY

The Dream of Rhonabwy is unique in all the tales found in *The Mabinogion* in that an approximate date of authorship can be ascribed to it and it appears in only one manuscript, *The Red Book of Hergest*. The opening line states that 'Madawg ap Maredudd held Powys from end to end',[56] and this enables us to date the tale to some point between 1130 and 1160, when we know from historical sources that Madog ap Maredudd ruled over this kingdom.

The story is narrated in the form of a dream, and tells of Arthur and his men assembling before the battle of Baddon. With Owain, one of his warriors, Arthur plays a game of *gwyddbwyll* (a form of chess) that dictates the movement of soldiers on the battlefield and his eventual victory. The story contains many fantastic elements, and shows signs of material from the *Historia* of Geoffrey and traditional Welsh material having been woven

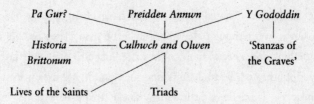

Chart 1 CONNECTIONS BETWEEN THE SOURCES

This chart shows how elements of the Welsh Arthurian tradition inter-relate between the different sources.

together. Two aspects of the tale are important in our quest for the origins of the Arthurian legend: the names of the forty-two counsellors of Arthur that find a parallel in the court list of *Culhwch and Olwen* and the geographical setting of the battle of Baddon – the Badon of the Saxon and Latin sources.

SUMMARY

Rachel Bromwich has pointed out, 'It has been long recognised that the prose narrative which has come down from medieval Ireland and Wales represents a mere fragment of an extensive literature which was developed, preserved, and transmitted over centuries by a highly-trained professional order of men of learning.'[57] The sources detailed above contain nearly all the information we have regarding the pre-Norman Arthur. Fragmentary and obscure though it may be, it is still possible to derive enough evidence from it to narrow down the locality in which the Arthurian tradition began. As we look closer at the names of people attached to Arthur we can begin to understand where the oldest Arthurian tradition originated, and in some instances can find it still intact in the landscape. The names in Wales have changed little since Arthur's day, although the importance of many sites has. It is something very special to uncover a site linked to one of Arthur's warriors through textual study and then find it still extant in the landscape. It might be little more than a stream or a stone, but occasionally such sites preserve some piece of folklore or tradition that correlates with what is written in the sources.

As can be seen, the original tradition of Arthur was not intended to be retold in the royal courts of Europe or used for propaganda purposes. It was much simpler in its origins – a fact that should not be forgotten. Even though many episodes from the Welsh tradition eventually found their way into the later romances, there are still episodes and stories that escaped use by Geoffrey of Monmouth and his counterparts on the Continent, and it is to this evidence that we now turn in search of Arthur's family and the places associated with them in the pre-Geoffrey tradition.

Many of the names and places we will come across in this book will probably be unfamiliar, but their beautiful language is descended from the language of the original British race – the language that would have been spoken by Arthur and the people who surrounded him. The battle cries from the throats of Arthur's war-band and the laments for the fallen Cai and Bedwyr would all have been sung and spoken in this ancient language, the ancestor of modern Welsh.

4

THE GENEALOGY
OF ARTHUR

ROM the evidence presented in the previous chapters it becomes clear that a distinct and decidedly different Arthurian tradition existed among the Welsh long before Geoffrey of Monmouth took up his quill and reworked British history to suit the purposes of his masters. Nearly all the earliest and most authentic references to Arthur originate in Wales, and this early tradition was preserved among the Welsh hills and valleys until as late as the sixteenth century, despite Norman subjugation and propaganda and the widespread popularity of Geoffrey's *Historia* across Europe. Although incomplete and fragmentary, the Welsh stories relating to Arthur contain a wealth of evidence in the form of place names, personal names and events connected to him. It is to this evidence that we now turn in search of Arthur's family and the places associated with it.

No doubt many readers will be surprised that a genealogy for Arthur can be constructed from the pre-Geoffrey tradition recorded in Welsh manuscripts. Both the Welsh and the Irish maintained their histories and genealogies in an oral form from ancient times, and they were first written down in the Middle

Ages, many centuries after the people they concern had died. So, although the genealogies that have survived to the present day are found primarily in manuscripts of the thirteenth and fourteenth centuries, the origin of the material is much older. Many of the famous figures of the later Arthurian romances, such as Gawain and Kay, have their origins in these sources.

Within the Arthurian sources detailed in Chapter 3 are a handful of references to people who are identified as 'the cousin of Arthur' or 'the uncle of Arthur'. From such allusions it is possible to start drawing up a family tree for Arthur, and more material is found in the genealogical tracts preserved in Welsh manuscripts. As far back as the twelfth century the Welsh were renowned for their love of genealogy, as Giraldus Cambrensis recorded in his *Description of Wales*, which he wrote while accompanying Baldwin, the Archbishop of Canterbury, around the country in 1188, gathering support for the Crusades: 'The Welsh value distinguished birth and noble descent more than anything else in the world. They would rather marry into a noble family than into a rich one. Even the common people know their family tree by heart and can readily recite from memory the list of their grandfathers, great-grandfathers, great-great-grandfathers, back to the sixth or seventh generation.'[1]

In our previous book, *The Keys to Avalon*, we constructed the family tree of Arthur including material from *Brut y Brenhinedd*. This material we have now removed, leaving a family tree based solely upon genuine Welsh tradition. Among the many manuscripts that preserve this genealogical information, the name 'Arthur' is not found very often; however, one particular collection of material, although not among the earliest manuscripts, contains information not found in any other source. The tract known as *Bonedd y Saint*, the earliest manuscript of which dates from *c.* 1250, preserves the genealogy of over a hundred saints from Wales, many of them obscure, and within this material are references to cousins of Arthur and also his children.

The relationships thrown up by our newly constructed family tree are surprisingly consistent throughout the whole gamut of Welsh sources, whether they date from the eleventh or the fifteenth century. The amount of detail that such sources provide and the agreement between different texts of different ages strongly suggest that there was a cohesive tradition regarding the family of Arthur long before Geoffrey put pen to paper in the 1130s. And the geography associated with these people is very enlightening about the source of the Arthurian legend, as will become apparent.

Below are two family trees derived from Welsh traditions: one focusing on the father of Arthur, the other on his mother. An alphabetical list of Arthur's cousins, nephews, uncles and aunts follows, detailing the locations attached to each of them. The accompanying map identifies these sites and enables us to identify the point of origin for the most famous character in British history.

THE FAMILY OF ARTHUR ACCORDING TO GEOFFREY OF MONMOUTH

Before looking at the Welsh tradition it is relevant to look at what Geoffrey had to say regarding the family of Arthur. One of the most fantastic parts of the *Historia* is the story of how, with the help of Merlin, Uthyr changes his shape into that of Gorlois, the husband of Eigr, the object of his desire. Thus disguised, Uthyr enters Gorlois's castle and spends the night with Eigr and Arthur is conceived. Gorlois is killed soon after, and Uthyr then marries Eigr, who is aware that she is pregnant by someone other than her husband. Uthyr and Eigr then have another child, Anna, who is Arthur's sister, and soon after this Uthyr is taken ill and dies. The next we hear of Arthur is at the age of fifteen, when he is made the leader of his men in the battles against the Saxons.

The *Historia* tells us the name of his wife, Guinevere, and of his nephews Gawain and Medrod, the sons of Anna, his sister; aside from this we are told nothing more about Arthur's relations – no children or other relatives are mentioned by Geoffrey. Geoffrey was obviously aware of the Welsh tradition, in which Arthur does have children, as we shall see below, so one has to wonder why he didn't give Arthur any descendants.

The two genealogies from the *Historia* and *Brut y Brenhinedd* show that the extent of Arthur's family is very restricted. When the Latin of the *Historia* was translated into Welsh, the translator used names familiar to him from the Welsh tradition outlined below.

Chart 2 ARTHUR'S FAMILY TREE ACCORDING TO GEOFFREY OF MONMOUTH

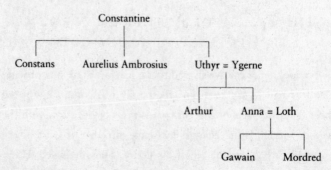

ARTHUR'S CHILDHOOD

The only source that details Arthur's upbringing is a section in the Vulgate Cycle of Grail romances known as the *Vulgate Merlin,* first published *c.* 1225. The text tells us that, after Arthur's birth, Merlin took the baby of Uthyr and Eigr to be fostered by a couple in the area. The husband of this couple was called Antor, and he had a son called Kay. It was this couple who christened the child Arthur, and they brought him up as their own. At the age of fifteen he was with Kay and Antor in London, where knights were trying to pull a sword from a stone to prove their worth and rule the kingdom. As so many knights were together in one place, competitions were held, and during one of these Kay broke his sword and ordered Arthur to get him another one. Unable to find Kay's spare sword, Arthur picked up the one nearest to him, which just happened to be embedded in a stone. The rest, as they say, is history (well, almost). See Appendix 2 for a discussion of this and an English translation of the Welsh tradition.

Chart 3 ARTHUR'S FAMILY TREE ACCORDING TO *BRUT Y BRENHINEDD*

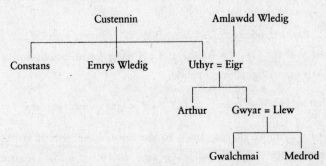

THE ORIGINAL WELSH TRADITION OF ARTHUR'S FAMILY

Arthur on his Father's Side

After many hours spent going through the earliest genealogical material, we were rather surprised to discover that Uthyr, Arthur's famous father, barely rates a mention and is *never* actually said to be the father of Arthur. According to Geoffrey of Monmouth, Uthyr Pendragon fathered Arthur on the night he changed his shape to look like Gorlois and slept with Gorlois's wife. All Arthurian literature from then on unquestioningly makes Uthyr the father of Arthur, but in the Welsh material no such association is made. The Arthurian poem *Pa Gur?* in *The Black Book of Carmarthen* contains the earliest Welsh reference to Uthyr Pendragon, in the lines

Mabon am Mydron   Mabon the son of Mydron
Guas uthir pendragon.   Uthyr Pendragon's servant.[2]

Uthyr Pendragon is associated with Arthur, as are the dozen or so other people named in the poem, but he is not said to be Arthur's father and one has to wonder where Geoffrey got his information from.

Another poem in *The Black Book of Carmarthen* contains a line that may be the source of Geoffrey's identification, and is given in its original form below:

Mab arthur uthir ig kertev The son of Arthur terrible in songs[3]

You will notice that '*arthur*' and the word '*uthir*', which in this context means 'terrible', appear next to each other in this line. Did

Geoffrey come across this line or one very similar and read it as 'Arthur mab Uthir ig kertev', which would then translate as 'Arthur the son of Uthir in songs'? Did this line give Geoffrey exactly the hint he needed to make Uthyr Pendragon the father of Arthur? Although impossible to prove, this possibility has been put forward as a possible source for Geoffrey's description of Arthur's paternity.[4] According to the *Historia*, Uthyr was the brother of Aurelius Ambrosius, but no other source confirms this point and the naming of Uthyr as Arthur's father must rest squarely on Geoffrey's shoulders.

Another reference to Uthyr in Welsh poetry gives him a son named Madog and a grandson named Eliwlod in a poem known as the *Dialogue of Arthur and the Eagle*, found in Jesus College MS 20, dated *c.* 1325. In this poem Eliwlod has taken the form of an eagle and is instructing Arthur about the Christian faith.[5] The poem contains material not found elsewhere and is thought to date from the twelfth century, although the existence of certain passages from the poem in the earlier *Black Book of Carmarthen* casts doubt on this dating. The passages in the earlier source concern the religious instruction of an unnamed person, but in the Jesus College manuscript they are reproduced in a more modern orthography and put into the mouths of Eliwlod and Arthur. It is possible that the narrative of Arthur and Eliwlod was created in order to deliver some pre-existing religious poetry in a form palatable to an audience familiar with the figure of Arthur.

No evidence has survived which enables us to place Uthyr in any particular region of Wales, and few references to him survive in the poetry of the *Gogynfeirdd*, further indicating that he was

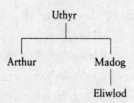

Chart 4 ARTHUR'S FAMILY ON HIS FATHER'S SIDE ACCORDING TO
WELSH TRADITION

not a very important character. The reasons why Geoffrey created
Uthyr as Arthur's father are examined at the end of this chapter.

Arthur on his Mother's Side

In contrast to his father, we have a much more detailed picture of the
mother's side of Arthur's family. All the earliest references to Arthur
can be associated with this branch of the family, and by studying the
locations attached to each person it is possible to build up a good
idea of where the traditions originated. Many of the people –
especially the little-known saints – are remembered only from a
place name or a church dedication, and it is often not possible to
provide any more information than that. The relationship of each
person to Arthur is shown in brackets after his or her name, and the
places mentioned below are shown on Map 1. (In the names listed,
'ap' means 'son of' and 'ferch' means 'daughter of'.)

Amlawdd Wledig (Grandfather)

A king of Wales according to *The Life of St Illtud*, Amlawdd
Wledig seems to have as his sole purpose the fathering of children
who become uncles or aunts to Arthur. Nothing definite is known
about him, and the only clue we have is that one of his sons,

The church below is dedicated to St Marchell at Whitchurch near Denbigh, and the church on the right to her brother Dehifyr at the nearby village of Bodfari. Both of these saints were children of Tywanedd, a sister of Arthur's mother, Eigyr, and therefore cousins to Arthur. Many church dedications to Arthur's cousins can be found in North Wales, showing that the oldest Welsh traditions concerning his family where localised in this area. Many of these churches were originally Celtic but have been rebuilt over the centuries.

The oldest sources place Arthur's court at a site called Gelliwig. The only place in Britain where this name survives is on the Lleyn Peninsula in north-west Wales. Looking over the site of Gelliwig is the fortified hill known as Gerrig Gwineu.

This view north east from the summit of Gerrig Gwineu looks towards the mountains of Northern Snowdonia. Remains of stone fortifications can still be found amidst the undergrowth here. Facing in the other direction, it is possible to see the Wicklow Mountains in Ireland. The tale of *Culhwch and Olwen* mentions that it was possible to see these peaks from Arthur's court.

The former parish church of Llanfor was once the great Minster of Penllyn. Llanfor was the most important ecclesiastical site in the Penllyn area just south of the Ediernion Valley – Caw's kingdom according to Welsh tradition. The church is built within the remains of a Roman fort that is possibly also the site of the fortress belonging to Gildas' father. *Inset:* The famous Llanfor Cavos (Caw) stone that once marked the site of the grave belonging to one of Arthur's warriors mentioned in the old tradition.

Above: Scott Lloyd in the interior of the Church of Rhos, now called Llan-rhos, situated one mile north east of Deganwy. The chapel is tiny, with room for six people at best, and is right next to the beach.

Left: Exterior of the little chapel which is associated with Maelgwn Gwynedd who, according to Welsh tradition, died here and was later buried on Ynys Seiriol (better known as Puffin Island). It is likely that Arthur was the *penteulu* (leader of the warband) for the armies of Maelgwn Gwynedd in the first half of the sixth century.

The castle mound at Deganwy where Maelgwn Gwynedd, the most powerful ruler in Wales in the first half of the sixth century, held his court. The castle was situated on the east bank of the River Conwy.

The information within the *Vera Historia* concerning the final resting-place of Arthur locates it near a chapel dedicated to the Virgin Mary in a remote part of Gwynedd. The Abbey of Aberconwy, where the text was composed, owned a chapel at Rhyd Llanfair (the ford of the sacred enclosure of Mary) on the upper reaches of the River Conway, shown here.

Above: Steve Blake in the
Arthurian Collection at the
Flintshire Library
Headquarters in Mold,
which contains over 3,000
volumes dedicated to the
Arthurian legend.

Left: The original Arthur can
be found in the pages of
books such as these, not in
the better known *Le Morte
d'Arthur* and continental
romances.

Tremeirchion (the Town of Meirchion), formerly known as Dinmeirchion (the Fortress of Meirchion). Meirchion was Arthur's uncle and this is one of many sites in North Wales named after Arthur's relatives and warriors who are mentioned in the old tradition.

An interesting Arthurian story concerning Arthur's feud with Huail, the son of Caw, can be found in the earliest Arthurian tale, *Culhwch and Olwen*, and also in the chronicle of Elis Gruffudd. This chronicle tells us that Huail was beheaded by Arthur upon this large stone known today as *Maen Huail* in the town of Ruthin in North Wales.

This mountain pass between Dolgellau and Mallwyd is named Camlan and it is the traditional site for Arthur's final battle. According to a thirteenth-century text known as the *Vera Historia De Morte Arthuri*, here the mortally wounded Arthur 'gives orders to be taken to Venedotia [Gwynedd] since he had decided to sojourn in the delightful Isle of Avalon'.

A Dark-Age cemetery containing over 40 graves from the early sixth century was discovered in the 1820s at a place called Trebeddau (the town of the graves). Today the site is impossible to locate with certainty, but it is probably situated beneath a T-junction near to a farm still known as Trebeddau. Is this Arthur's final resting place?

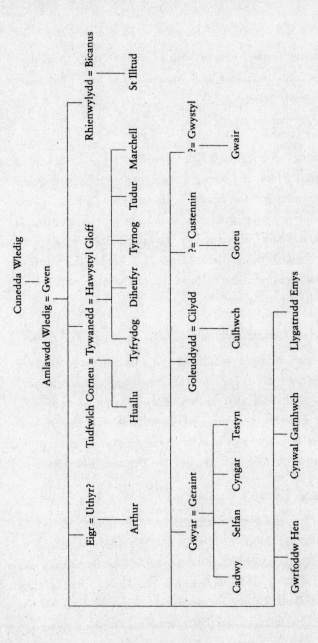

Chart 5 ARTHUR'S FAMILY ON HIS MOTHER'S SIDE ACCORDING TO WELSH TRADITION

Gwrfoddw, shares his name with a king of Erging in modern Herefordshire, suggesting that Amlawdd may have ruled there. This is very tenuous.[6]

Bicanus (Uncle)

According to *The Life of St Illtud*, Bicanus was a prince of Letavia (a Latinised form of Llydaw), a place that has long been understood to mean Brittany, though Welsh tradition is far from clear on this point and some scholars have thought it might be a region of South Wales.[7] References to Llydaw in the poetry of the *Gogynfeirdd* as being 'over the Severn Sea' suggest that a part of the south-west peninsula of England might be intended.[8] Nothing else is known about him.

Cadwy ap Geraint (Cousin)

It has been suggested that Cadwy ap Geraint should be identified with a person whom *The Life of St Carranog* calls Cato, who ruled from a place called Dindraethwy, apparently somewhere in South Wales or Devon, in the time of Arthur. Cadwy is mentioned in the warrior list in *Culhwch and Olwen* and is described as one of the forty-two counsellors of Arthur in *The Dream of Rhonabwy*.

Cilydd ap Celyddon Wledig (Uncle)

Cilydd ap Celyddon Wledig is the father of Culhwch, the hero of *Culhwch and Olwen*. After the death of his wife, Goleuddydd, his counsellors suggested he marry the wife of King Doged. The only place in Wales linked to Doged is Llanddoged, near Llanrwst on the River Conwy, suggesting that Cilydd's kingdom was somewhere in this vicinity. Nothing more is known of him.

Culhwch ap Cilydd (Cousin)

Culhwch ap Cilydd is the hero of *Culhwch and Olwen* and, as seen from the following extracts, a first cousin to Arthur by his mother.

Nonetheless the boy was of gentle lineage: he was first cousin to Arthur.[9]
Arthur is thy first cousin.[10]
Quoth Arthur 'My heart grows tender towards thee: I know thou art sprung from my blood.[11]
Quoth Arthur: 'True it is. Thou art then my first cousin.'[12]

Culhwch and Olwen is a composite tale whose events take place all over Wales, and it is not possible to assign any one specific location to Culhwch. See the notes above on Cilydd, his father.

Custennin ap Mynwyedig (Uncle)

According to *Culhwch and Olwen*, Custennin ap Mynwyedig was married to an unnamed daughter of Amlawdd Wledig and the father of Goreu, a cousin to Arthur. No localisation is possible.

Cyngar ap Geraint (Cousin)

Section 76 of *Bonedd y Saint* makes Cyngar ap Geraint the son of Geraint and Gwyar the daughter of Amlawdd Wledig, and the patron saint of Llangefni on Anglesey. Other dedications to him have been recorded at Trefilan in Ceredigion and Hope in Flintshire, and it also possible that his name is remembered at Ynys Gyngar, a small hill on the estuary of the River Dwyryd near Porthmadog.

Cynwal Garnhwch (Uncle)

A genealogical tract known as *Bonedd yr Arwyr* details the lineage of heroes from Welsh tradition and survives in several manuscripts, the earliest of which (*c.* 1475) is known to be a copy of something much earlier. According to Section 29 of this tract, Cynwal was the son of Amlawdd Wledig and the father of Gwen Alarch, a lady of Arthur's court according to *Culhwch and Olwen*. No localisation is possible.

Diheufyr (Cousin)

According to Section 43 of *Bonedd y Saint*, Diheufyr was the saint of Bodfari in Flintshire, where Edward Lhuyd recorded the existence of a well bearing his name *c.* 1695.[13] Diheufyr is also mentioned in *The Life of St Winefred* (*c.* 1150), as Winefred visited him on her way from Holywell to Henllan (in present-day Denbighshire) and then Gwytherin, where she died and her relics were revered until they were removed by Robert of Shrewsbury in 1136 to Shrewsbury Abbey (where they later became a mystery for Ellis Peters's fictional creation Brother Cadfael).

Eigr ferch Amlawdd Wledig (Mother)

As noted above, Eigr is the mother of Arthur by Uthyr Pendragon according to Geoffrey of Monmouth in one of the more fantastic sequences found in the *Historia Regum Britanniae*. Welsh tradition, however, knows nothing of this episode and never associates her with Uthyr. In *Culhwch and Olwen* we find the statement that Arthur's mother was also the mother of Gormant by Ricca, who is almost certainly Rhita Gawr – see below. Surprisingly, many of the Welsh sources refer to Arthur's mother as a daughter of Amlawdd Wledig but do not name her, and we can only assume that the name is correct. Rarely mentioned by the *Gogynfeirdd*, Eigr became popular with later bards, who drew more heavily from *Brut y Brenhinedd*. No localisation is possible.

Geraint ap Erbin (Uncle)

This relationship to Arthur relies upon the statement in Section 76 of *Bonedd y Saint* that Geraint married Gwyar the daughter of Amlawdd Wledig. Geraint ap Erbin is a very important character in Welsh tradition, and is connected to Arthur in a poem from *The Black Book of Carmarthen* that places his death at a place called Llongborth. Because some historians have identified Geraint ap Erbin with another ruler called Geraint who ruled in Devon in 705, the site of this battle has been identified with Langport in Somerset. According to Welsh tradition, however, the battle took place near Tresaith on the Ceredigion coast, and it will be discussed in more detail in Chapter 6.

Goleuddydd ferch Amlawdd Wledig (Aunt)

The tale of *Culhwch and Olwen* names Goleuddydd as the mother of Culhwch, the hero of the tale, and she gives birth to him in a pigsty. No location is associated with her, but see the notes above on her husband, Cilydd.

Goreu ap Custennin (Cousin)

According to *Culhwch and Olwen*, Goreu's unnamed mother was a daughter of Amlawdd Wledig, therefore making him a cousin to Arthur – a relationship also found in one of the triads concerning the 'Three Exalted Prisoners of Ynys Prydein': 'This exalted prisoner was Arthur. And it was the same lad, who released him from each of these three prisons – Goreu ap Custennin, his cousin.'[14]

In *Culhwch and Olwen* Goreu kills Ysbaddaden Pencawr and then takes over his fort and dominions. The exact location of these is never mentioned, but place-name evidence suggests a couple of sites in the area of Neath in South Wales.[15] The name 'Ysbaddaden' also means 'Hazel Tree', making it very difficult to identify place names specifically associated with the Ysbaddaden of the tale.

Gormant ap Ricca (Half-Brother)

Culhwch and Olwen mentions Gormant on one occasion as 'Brother to Arthur on his mother's side'.[16] This implies that Arthur's mother, Eigr, was at some point married to Ricca, who can be identified with Rhita Gawr – see below.

Gwair ap Gwystyl (Cousin)

A medieval Welsh manuscript concerning the knights of Arthur supplies the information that Gwair's mother was a daughter of Amlawdd Wledig.[17] Gwair is named as one of the forty-two counsellors of Arthur in *The Dream of Rhonabwy*, and the poets of the thirteenth century depict him as being of a dismal disposition: 'to become as Gwair ap Gwystyl' was to become miserable.[18]

Gwen ferch Cunedda Wledig (Grandmother)

Gwen appears as the wife of Amlawdd Wledig in three different sources, and is presumably the mother of his many children, although only two are certainly hers: Eigr and Cynwal Garnhwch.[19] No localisation is possible, but the geography connected to her brothers is very suggestive. See page 102.

Gwenhwyfar (Wife)

The wife of Arthur and famous in later romances for her infidelity with Lancelot, in Welsh tradition Gwenhwyfar is the daughter of

Ogrfan Gawr. His name is associated with the hill fort known as Old Oswestry on the Welsh border and with the site now occupied by Knucklas Castle. The only place to preserve her name is Groes Gwenhwyfar near Llangollen, which was first mentioned in 1697 by Edward Lhuyd, although it is impossible to be certain that the name refers to Arthur's wife, as Gwenhwyfar was a common name in Wales in medieval times.[20]

Gwrfoddw Hen (Uncle)

According to *Culhwch and Olwen*, Gwrfoddw Hen was an uncle of Arthur, being his mother's brother, and was killed by Llwydog Gofynniad, one of the piglets of the great boar Trwyth, in Ystrad Yw (near Crickhowell in South Wales).[21] Apart from Ystrad Yw, we do not know of any other sites linked to him, but the name 'Gwrfoddw' does appear in *The Book of Llandaf* as a king in Erging, a region just south of Hereford, and it has been proposed that the two are the same person, although chronology makes this unlikely.[22]

Gwyar ferch Amlawdd Wledig (Aunt)

Section 76 of *Bonedd y Saint* states that Gwyar was the wife of Geraint ap Erbin and the mother of Iestin, Selyf and Cyngar. See the notes on Cyngar for a possible location.

Gwystyl (Uncle)

Gwystyl is the father of Gwair by an unnamed daughter of Amlawdd Wledig. He is possibly to be identified with Gwystyl ap Nwython, mentioned as one of the warriors of Arthur in *Culhwch and Olwen*, but no location is possible.

Hawystyl Gloff (Uncle)

Section 43 of *Bonedd y Saint* makes Hawystyl Gloff the father of saints Tyfrydog, Diheufyr, Tyrnog, Tudur and Marchell by Tywanedd, a daughter of Amlawdd Wledig. Nothing else is known about him, but the locations of the church dedications to his children suggest that he came from north-east Wales.

Huallu ap Tudfwlch Corneu (Cousin)

A very interesting genealogical tract known as *Bonedd Gwyr y Gogledd* (The Lineage of the Men of the North) names Huallu's mother as Tywanedd, a daughter of Amlawdd Wledig, making him a cousin of Arthur. Nothing is known about him, but see the notes on his father, Tudfwlch Corneu, below.

Iaen, sons of (In-laws)

'Teregad son of Iaen, and Sulien son of Iaen, and Bradwen son of Iaen, and Cradawg son of Iaen (men of Caer Dathal were they, kindred to Arthur on their father's side).'[23] This piece of information in *Culhwch and Olwen* is very interesting, as it gives a place name which enables us to locate where this family came from, though nothing is known about them individually. The children of Iaen are mentioned in the later manuscript called *Bonedd yr Arwyr*, where, although some of the names differ, an extra line is added which explains why they were considered to be related to Arthur:

§2 7. *Elerich verch Iaen mam Kyduan ap Arthur.*
§2.7. Elerich the daughter of Iaen was the mother of Cydfan the son of Arthur.[24]

Could the fact that Arthur had a child by one of Iaen's daughters make Iaen's other children kin to Arthur and in effect his in-laws?

The place name Caer Dathal is also mentioned in the *Mabinogion* tale *Math fab Mathonwy* as being in Arfon. Arfon is the name for a part of west Gwynedd centred upon Caernarfon, and the few scholars who have tried to identify the site have agreed upon the impressive hill fort called Tre'r Ceiri overlooking the village of Llanaelhaearn.[25]

Iestyn ap Geraint (Cousin)

Iestyn is the son of Geraint in two different entries in *Bonedd y Saint*, and Welsh tradition records that he was the founder of two places called Llaniestyn – one on Anglesey and the other on the Lleyn Peninsula.

St Illtud (Cousin)

The Life of St Illtud, written *c.* 1100, contains a reference to St Illtud as a cousin to Arthur: 'In the meantime the magnificent soldier [Illtud] hearing of the magnificence of his cousin, King Arthur, desired to visit the court of so great a conqueror.'[26] This is of great interest as this predates Geoffrey of Monmouth. Arthur plays no further part in the Life, but it does show that the genealogy of his mother was widely known at this point. St Illtud is a cult figure right across southern Wales but his major cult centre was at Llanilltud Fawr (present-day Llantwit Major).

Llygadrudd Emys (Uncle)

Llygadrudd Emys was an uncle of Arthur, one of his mother's brothers, according to *Culhwch and Olwen*, which also states that he was present at Arthur's court. He was killed, along with his brother Gwrfoddw Hen, by the piglet Llwydog Gofynniad in Ystrad Tywi (Llandeilio, South Wales) while hunting the giant boar Trwyth.

Marchell ferch Hawystyl Gloff (Cousin)

Section 43 of *Bonedd y Saint* relates that Marchell was the daughter of Tywanedd ferch Amlawdd Wledig and the sister of Tyfrydog, Diheufyr and Tyrnog. She was the saint of Whitchurch near Denbigh and Capel Marchell near Llanrwst. No other traditions remain concerning her.

Rhienwylydd ferch Amlawdd Wledig (Aunt)

According to *The Life of St Illtud*, her son, Rhienwylydd was the wife of Bicanus and daughter of Amlawdd Wledig. Nothing more is known.

Rhita Gawr

See Chapter 5 for details.

Selfan ap Geraint (Cousin)

Selfan is closely associated with his brother Iestyn at Penmon in Anglesey according to one version of Section 76 of *Bonedd y Saint*.

Tudfwlch Corneu (Uncle)

Little is known about this person, husband to Tywanedd ferch Amlawdd Wledig. The tract *Bonedd Gwyr y Gogledd* calls him a prince of Cernyw, which has for a long time been identified as Cornwall, but in the next chapter we will see that this might not be the case. As his wife is linked to North Wales, is it possible that he is the same as the Tudfwlch Hir mentioned in *The Book of*

Aneirin, who is connected with the region of Eifionydd centred on Criccieth in North Wales?

Tudur ap Hawystyl Gloff (Cousin)

Tudur is another son of Tywanedd ferch Amlawdd Wledig according to Section 43 of *Bonedd y Saint*. His name is commemorated in a church dedicated to him at Darowen near Machynlleth and also at Eglwys Dudur at Llanwchllyn, near Bala, and at Ffynon Dudur, a holy well near Llanelidan in the Vale of Clwyd.

Tyfrydog ap Hawystyl Gloff (Cousin)

Tyfrydog is the brother of the above and the saint of Llandyfrydog on Anglesey.

Tyrnog ap Hawystyl Gloff

Tyrnog is another brother of Tudur ap Hawystyl Gloff, but this time commemorated at Llandyrnog in the Vale of Clwyd.

Tywanedd ferch Amlawdd Wledig

Tywanedd is the mother of Diheufyr, Huallu, Marchell, Tudur, Tyfrydog and Tyrnog, and from the locations attached to each of them we can suppose that she lived in North Wales.

Outside the two genealogies outlined above, three other references to relations of Arthur can be found in Welsh tradition: two in *The Dream of Rhonabwy* and one in *Culhwch and Olwen*. The people named below are important to Welsh tradition, and it is possible that their relationships to Arthur derive from later traditions trying to make them part of the Arthurian story. Whatever the case, we have thought it wise to include them here for the sake of completeness.

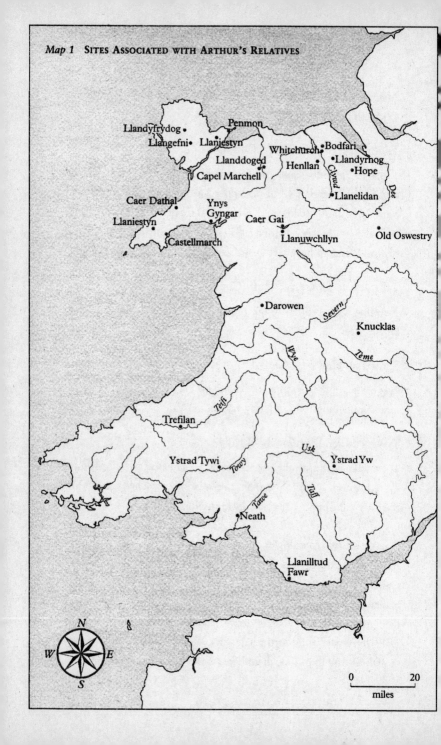

Map 1 SITES ASSOCIATED WITH ARTHUR'S RELATIVES

Llandyfrydog
Penmon
Llangefni
Llaniestyn
Whitchurch
Bodfari
Llanddoged
Henllan
Llandyrnog
Capel Marchell
Hope
Caer Dathal
Ynys
Gyngar
Caer Gai
Llanelidan
Llaniestyn
Castellmarch
Llanuwchllyn
Old Oswestry

Darowen

Knucklas

Teme

Severn

Wye

Teifi

Trefilan

Usk

Ystrad Tywi
Towy
Ystrad Yw

Tawe
Taff

Neath

Llanilltud
Fawr

N
W   E
S

0   20
miles

THE GENEALOGY OF ARTHUR

Caradog Freichfras ap Llyr Marini (Cousin)

According to a manuscript concerning the names of Arthur's knights, Caradog Freichfras's mother, Tywanedd, was a sister to Eigr, the mother of Arthur, thereby confirming Caradog Freichfras and Arthur as cousins.[27] The medieval tract *Bonedd y Saint* mentions Caradog Freichfras as the father of saints Cadfarch at Aberdaron on the Lleyn Peninsula, Cawrdaf at Llangorwda near Llanbadarn Fawr in Ceredigion, Abererch in Lleyn and Llangoed on Anglesey, Maethlu at Llanfaethlu on Anglesey and Tangwn at Llangoed with his brother Cawrdaf. The Triads state that Caradog Freichfras was one of the three 'Battle Horse-men of Ynys Prydein' and the 'chief elder of Cernyw' – for the location of these sites, see Chapter 5.[28] *The Dream of Rhonabwy* states in relation to Arthur that Caradog was his 'chief counsellor and his first cousin.'[29]

Caradog Freichfras found his way into the later French romances as Karadeues Briebraz, and the thirteenth-century *Livre de Carados* contains a story concerning the infidelity of his wife.[30]

Gwalchmai

Culhwch and Olwen tells us that Gwalchmai was 'Arthur's nephew, his sister's son, and his first cousin.'[31] Gwalchmai is better known by the name Gawain, given to him by Geoffrey of Monmouth and the Grail romances, but Welsh tradition has little to say about him. He appears in a triad as one of the 'Three Well-Endowed Men of Ynys Prydein',[32] and in 'The Stanzas of the Graves' his burial site is referred to:

Bet gwalchmei ym peryton. The grave of Gwalchmai is in Peryddon
Ir diliv y dyneton As a reproach to men.[33]

Peryddon is an old name applied to the River Dee,[34] suggesting that Gwalchmai was buried somewhere along its course – perhaps, as we suggested in *The Keys to Avalon*, at the place still known as Gwalchmai near Basingwerk Abbey in North Wales.

March ap Meirchion (Cousin)

March ap Meirchion is a character used extensively by the later Continental romancers – especially in the Tristan series of tales, as King Mark of Cornwall. *The Dream of Rhonabwy* lists him amongst the forty-two counsellors of Arthur and also refers to 'March ap Meirchion at their head. A first cousin to Arthur is he.'[35]

Several pieces of folklore concerning March in Wales survive in medieval manuscripts. One links him to Castellmarch near Abersoch on the Lleyn Peninsula, where a tradition exists that March is said to have had horse's ears.[36] And in 1540 the king's antiquary John Leland recorded the following at Henllan near Denbigh: 'Ther is a little Water caullid Merach Mirchion, whereby, as sum saie, was Lorde Marach a Mirch[i]ons Place. It is in Henellan [paroc]h.'[37] The village of Tremeirchion (Town of Meirchion) in Flintshire was originally known as Din Meirchion (Fort of Meirchion) and is only five miles away from Henllan.

March's relationship to Arthur can be explained in two ways: either Meirchion is a brother of Uthyr, as suggested by *Brut y Brenhinedd*, and this found its way into *The Dream of Rhonabwy*; or, as a later Welsh text suggests, he married yet another daughter of Amlawdd Wledig.[38]

As can be seen from Map 1, the geography of Arthur's family on his mother's side is confined primarily to the northern half of

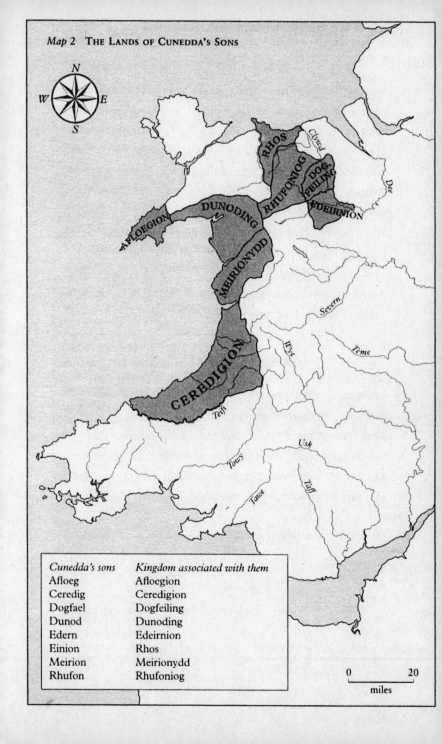

Map 2 THE LANDS OF CUNEDDA'S SONS

Cunedda's sons	Kingdom associated with them
Afloeg	Afloegion
Ceredig	Ceredigion
Dogfael	Dogfeiling
Dunod	Dunoding
Edern	Edeirnion
Einion	Rhos
Meirion	Meirionydd
Rhufon	Rhufoniog

0   20

miles

Wales. Eigr's mother was Gwen the daughter of Cunedda, and the regions of Wales named after her brothers offer another piece of evidence for the geography associated with the family of Arthur outlined above. The British Library's Harleian MS 3859, which also contains the earliest text of the *Historia Brittonum* and the *Annales Cambriae*, defines the region under the influence of Cunedda's children thus: 'This is their boundary: From the river which is called Dyfrdwy [Dee], to another river, the Teifi and they held very many districts in the western part of Britannia [Wales].'[39] This area is outlined on Map 2 and covers many of the places named in this chapter, showing that for two generations before Arthur was born his family was associated with North Wales.

ARTHUR'S CHILDREN

In the mass of Arthurian literature that survives it is surprising to find very little mention of any children that Arthur may have had. The romances that do make mention of a son of Arthur do so only in passing, whereas Welsh tradition names five children of Arthur and two grandchildren. But claims of direct descent from Arthur are rare in history, even in Wales. Arthur's famous wife,

Chart 6 ARTHUR'S CHILDREN ACCORDING TO WELSH TRADITION

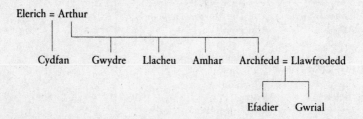

Gwenhwyfar, is not recorded as having had any children by Arthur – or anyone else for that matter.

Amhar

The earliest reference to a child of Arthur is found in the *Mirabilia* attached to the *Historia Brittonum*: 'There is another wonder in the country called Ergyng. There is a tomb there by a spring called Llygad Amr; the name of the man who is buried in the tomb was Amr. He was a son of the warrior Arthur and he killed him there and buried him.'[40]

Llygad Amr (Eye of Amr) has been identified with a cairn at the source of the River Gamber at Gamber Head near Llanwarne. Amhar's name survived through to the later Welsh Arthurian romance *Geraint mab Erbin*, where he is listed as one of the four servants who guarded Arthur's bed.

Archfedd

Section 85 of *Bonedd y Saint* preserves an interesting piece of tradition regarding a daughter of Arthur and her two sons, Arthur's grandchildren: '*Efadier a Gwrial plant Llawvrodedd varchoc o Archvedd verch Arthur i mam*' – 'Efadier and Gwrial children of Llawfrodedd the knight and Archfedd the daughter of Arthur was their mother'.[41] Llawfrodedd Farchog is found in the warrior list in *Culhwch and Olwen* and as one of Arthur's forty-two counsellors in *The Dream of Rhonabwy*.

Cydfan

Cydfan's mother was Elerich, as noted in the notes on Iaen above. Nothing else is known about him.

Gwydre

Culhwch and Olwen states that 'Gwydre son of Arthur'[42] was killed by the great boar Trwyth in the Preseli mountains of Dyfed in south-west Wales. Nothing else is known about him.

Llacheu

Two references to a son of Arthur named Llacheu can be found in *The Black Book of Carmarthen*:

Kei guin a llachev	Cai the fair and Llacheu
Digonint we kadev	They performed battles[43]
Mi a wum lle llas llachev	I have been where Llacheu was slain
Mab arthur uthir ig kertev	Son of Arthur, terrible in songs[44]

These extracts prove that Llacheu existed in the earliest strand of the Arthurian legend, but we have to rely on later references to his name to try to identify the region in which he was active. The thirteenth-century bard Bleddyn Fardd refers to Llacheu in the lines

Dewr a was ban llas, yn llassar—arfau,	He was a brave youth when he was slain in the blue-enamelled arms,
Fal y llas Llachau is Llech Ysgar;	as Llacheu was slain below Llech Ysgar;[45]

The location of Llech Ysgar is uncertain, but the context of this and other poems that mention it suggest that it was in the kingdom of Powys.[46]

Llacheu is the only one of Arthur's children who survived into the later romances, and he is mentioned as Loholt in *Erec et Enide* by Chrétien de Troyes and in the anonymous *Perlesvaus*.[47]

ARTHUR'S MISTRESSES

One of the triads found in the later manuscripts concerns the three mistresses of Arthur, which leads one to wonder whether any one of them could have been the mother of some of Arthur's children. Information regarding two of them is very enlightening in regard to the location of their traditions and is detailed below; any tradition regarding the third mistress seems to have been lost.

It should come as no surprise that a man of importance in the sixth century had mistresses: it was common practice in most parts of the world (and some would say that little has changed). But, as

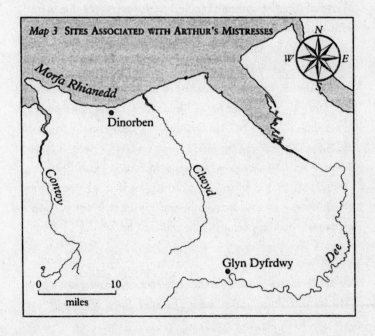

Map 3 SITES ASSOCIATED WITH ARTHUR'S MISTRESSES

Arthur later became the archetypal Christian king, any references to mistresses were ignored or suppressed, further enhancing the authenticity of this material.

A'e deir Karedicwreic oed y rei hynn:	And his [Arthur's] Three Mistresses were these:
Indec verch Arvy Hir,	Indeg daughter of Garwy the Tall,
A Garven verch Henin Hen,	And Garwen daughter of Henin the Old,
A Gvyl verch endavt.	And Gwyl daughter of Gendawd.[48]

Indeg

The first mistress, Indeg, appears often in poetry as a great beauty, and *Culhwch and Olwen* mentions her as one of the women of Arthur's court, thus proving that she belonged to the earliest phases of the Arthurian legend. A bard named Gruffudd ap Maredudd (early fourteenth century) refers to Arthur being in love with the daughter of Garwy Hir in the lines 'Mine is a participation in the care of Arthur of the highlands of Prydein . . . for the daughter of Garwy Hir, (for one of) the hue of snow.'[49]

No specific location is attached to Indeg, but her father was a popular figure among the bards. Tudur Aled *c.* 1500 refers to him in a poem as 'Garwy of Glyn Dyfrdwy' – a village on the banks of the River Dee midway between Llangollen and Corwen in North Wales.[50] As no other geographical information exists regarding either Indeg or her father, we must assume that she came from North Wales – an assumption supported by the geographical information surrounding Arthur's other mistress below.

Garwen

We are fortunate to have another reference concerning Garwen in 'The Stanzas of the Graves' from *The Black Book of Carmarthen*:

Y *beddeu yn y morua*	The graves on the Morfa,
Ys *bychan ay haelwy*	Few are they who mourn them;
Y *mae sanant syberw vun*	There lies Sanant the proud maiden,
Y *mae run ryuel afwy*	There lies Rhun, fervent in battle,
Y *mae earrwen verch hennin*	There lies Garwen daughter of Henin,
Y *mae lledin a llywy*	There lie Lledin and Llywy.[51]

The most easily identifiable name in the list is Rhun, whose father, Maelgwn Gwynedd, ruled from Degannwy and is said to have been killed by a plague that rose from Morfa Rhianedd (Sea Strand or Beach of the Maidens), which in all likelihood is the Morfa spoken of in this poem. This Morfa is situated on the North Wales coast between Llandudno and Colwyn Bay and is also named on several occasions in the *Ystoria Taliesin* (History of Taliesin), a composite life of Taliesin preserved in a manuscript from the mid sixteenth century.[52] Henin Henben, the father of Garwen according to another stanza from the same poem, was buried at Dinorben, a hill fort above the town of Abergele on the North Wales coast, only a few miles from Colwyn Bay.

CONCLUSION

One of the most notable aspects of the material detailed above is the total dominance of Arthur's mother, Eigr; by comparison, Uthyr barely rates a mention in Welsh tradition. This is at total variance with the Geoffrey of Monmouth-influenced romance tradition, which would have us believe that it was Uthyr who was the important parent. When and why did this emphasis change?

All the earliest material agrees upon the identity of Arthur's mother as a daughter of Amlawdd Wledig, but only one source implies that Uthyr was Arthur's father, and the date of that source is open to question. The first person clearly to state that Uthyr was Arthur's father was Geoffrey of Monmouth, but why did he create this link? The historical sources that Geoffrey used for the framework of his text make no mention of Arthur, but for the period concerned focus upon a person named Ambrosius Aurelianus of Roman descent. The Welsh traditions that Geoffrey had access to mention a warrior called Arthur, who fought many battles, but no Ambrosius. How was Geoffrey to bring these two traditions together?

We know that Uthyr is not the father of Arthur in Welsh tradition, but we do know that he was attached to Arthur in the poem *Pa Gur?* from *The Black Book of Carmarthen*. Another poem in this manuscript contains the words '*arthur*' and '*uthir*' next to each other, which, as mentioned above, may have been the hint that Geoffrey needed to use this name for the otherwise absent father of Arthur. The result of Geoffrey's introduction of Uthyr can best be described as follows:

1. By making Uthyr the brother of Ambrosius, Geoffrey connected Arthur with the historical material he found in the works of Gildas, Bede and the *Historia Brittonum*.
2. By making Uthyr marry a daughter of Amlawdd Wledig he linked the genealogy of Arthur from Welsh material to the historical material noted above.
3. In Arthur the Roman and Welsh bloodlines came together.
4. Welsh traditions made the mother the important parent, but, as this was not the rule of succession in the twelfth century, the father's line was emphasised and the mother's dominance in the earlier tradition was suppressed.

In essence this means that the story of Arthur as the son of Uthyr, related in every Arthurian romance, was the invention of Geoffrey of Monmouth. The story that Uthyr Pendragon was the brother of Ambrosius and killed the usurper Vortigern (see Chapter 1) is also an invention, as are the claims that Arthur was descended from Roman stock. The Arthurian tradition of the Middle Ages is so far removed from the earliest material and so corrupt as to be almost worthless in our search for the origins of Arthur. Since the twelfth century, the oldest genealogy of Arthur has been lost amid the romantic fictions of Geoffrey and the Continental romancers.

The geography associated with members of Arthur's family has survived until the present day, however, and the evidence shows that the northern half of Wales contains a majority of the locations and traditions attached to these people. The beginnings of the *literary* Arthurian tradition found in texts from South Wales at the turn of the twelfth century are also the beginnings of the geographical confusion about Arthur. Geoffrey of Monmouth continued this process in 1136 with the appearance of his *Historia*, which depicted Arthur as holding sway not just in Wales, but also over the whole of Britain from Cornwall to Scotland and in large parts of the Continent. Following Geoffrey, Arthur could be found as a character in romances written as far apart as Norway and the Holy Land; the warriors and saints of his extended family remembered in the hills of Wales were forgotten and replaced by the romantic characters of Lancelot and Perceval. This romantic figure of Arthur became the most popular figure of the medieval period, but his Welsh origins had become lost in the political propaganda for a united Britain (something which had never existed in history) and to a lesser extent for a united Wales (again, something that had never existed previously). The political power attached to the figure of Arthur became the most potent symbol of monarchy and heroism at the expense of the simple truth of his origins. In the next chapter we will explore how the misunderstanding of Welsh geographical terms and names obscured the origins of Arthur and led to his legend being spread across the whole of Britain.

5

SOME GEOGRAPHICAL PROBLEMS

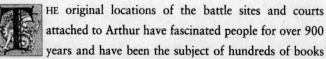HE original locations of the battle sites and courts attached to Arthur have fascinated people for over 900 years and have been the subject of hundreds of books and learned articles. Using the evidence put forward in the previous chapters, we must now try to identify the geographical region in which to search for Arthur and his warriors as dictated by early Welsh sources. We have already seen that the locations linked to members of Arthur's family are concentrated in a far smaller region of Britain than previously thought, and by looking at the original meaning of the place names in which their traditions exist we can begin to identify specific sites.

The historian Jurgen Spanuth has pointed out one of the fundamental problems in understanding ancient geography: 'It is a basic fault in historical method, but an extremely common one, to attribute to ancient peoples modern geographical knowledge and conceptions, and to equate the names and phrases used by the ancients with those of modern geographers.'[1] Over the centuries,

Welsh place names and geographical terms have often been understood in a Saxon context, or in terms of our modern understanding of names and regions, leading to certain sources appearing to be less worthwhile than they really are. It is important that we understand these place names and geographical terms from the point of view of the people who wrote the tales and the poetry. When this is done, the internal evidence of our sources is quite enlightening. Fortunately the one element that is consistent throughout the Welsh Arthurian material is the land in which events concerning Arthur take place.

YNYS PRYDEIN

In our previous book, *The Keys to Avalon*, we suggested that the geography of Britain had been corrupted through the misunderstanding of Welsh geographical terms, sometimes innocently and sometimes for political reasons. In that work we made use of evidence from *Brut y Brenhinedd* which, though useful in formulating ideas at the time, we now find to be too unreliable to use with confidence. Despite this, the basic idea that Welsh geographical terms have been misunderstood still stands, and in this chapter we will take a close look at this point by placing the emphasis on internal evidence from more reliable Welsh texts, especially the poetry of the *Gogynfeirdd*. In order to restate our argument it has been necessary to use a few pieces of evidence originally put forward in *The Keys to Avalon*, although we hope that the new material printed here will more than compensate for this repetition.

The earliest sources from Wales set Arthur's exploits in a land called Ynys Prydein in Welsh or Britannia in Latin. Both of these names have for centuries been interpreted as meaning the island of Britain as we envisage it today, from Cornwall in the south to Scotland in the north, and the information within the texts has been read accordingly. In Latin texts of an English provenance and in many later Welsh texts this identification is almost always correct; however, in Latin texts written in Wales and in earlier Welsh sources these terms appear to relate to a different definition of the land in question. If the early Welsh bards say that Arthur held sway in a land named Britannia or Ynys Prydein, where exactly did they have in mind? We will start with a look at the Welsh phrase 'Ynys Prydein'.

Before proceeding to study the exact definition of '*prydein*' we must first understand exactly what the word '*ynys*' meant in medieval Wales. In modern Welsh the word is used to denote an island or a land bordering water, whether on an estuary or on the coast, and many examples can be found on any large-scale map of Wales. This same usage also applied in medieval Welsh, but at this period '*ynys*' also had another derived meaning, which is very enlightening. *Geiriadur Prifysgol Cymru* (Wales's equivalent of *The Oxford English Dictionary*) defines this alternative meaning as 'kingdom, realm, province or region.'[2] Two instances from the bardic poetry of the twelfth century demonstrate this usage:

Llys lleuuer ynys, gwrys goruyndawd.	Light court of the realm, the feeder of ferocity.[3]
Teyrn teir ynys	prince of the three realms[4]

The continued usage of '*ynys*' in this way can be shown in the work of a bard from the fifteenth century, who refers to a region of the kingdom of Powys called Gwenwynwyn. Gutun Owain calls the region *ynys Gwenwynwyn* (the realm of Wenwynwyn), whereas a bard from a hundred years previously, Guto'r Glyn, calls it *gwlad Wenwynwyn* (the land of Wenwynwyn), showing that the terms '*gwlad*' ('land') and '*ynys*' (realm) were synonymous with each other.

The particular usage of the word '*ynys*' to mean 'realm' was widespread in the twelfth and thirteenth centuries, and continued to be current until the sixteenth century.[5] The fact that all the Welsh manuscripts which have preserved the early Arthurian material were written before 1400, and contain material from much earlier, means that we must consider the possibility that the term '*ynys*' was being used in the sense of 'realm or kingdom' rather than 'island'.

Armed with a better understanding of the medieval usage of the word '*ynys*', it becomes easier to understand the next part of this important phrase in its correct medieval context. 'Prydein' has long been understood to simply mean 'Britain', as we know it today, and all evidence in which it appears has been understood in a Britain-wide context. This interpretation is so well established that it was a little surprising to find that there are many instances where 'Prydein' does not denote the whole of Britain. The poetry of the *Gogynfeirdd* is an excellent source for the original meanings of place names, as the poems are linked to historical characters whose whereabouts we know from other sources. Many of the poems written in this period are praise poems for the head of society, which for Wales at this time means the princes of Gwynedd, Powys and Deheubarth, the three major divisions of Wales. The earliest poets of this era were writing at the same time as Geoffrey of Monmouth, and they often used the word 'Prydein' to denote the land we know today as Wales.

Meilyr Brydydd in his elegy to Gruffudd ap Cynan, the ruler of Gwynedd (d. 1137), calls him '*Pasgadur kynrein, Prydein briawd*' – 'Nurturer of Princes, rightful monarch of Prydein'.[6] Cynddelw in his elegy to Owain Gwynedd, Gruffudd's son (d. 1170), refers to him as '*priawdnen Prydein*' – 'chief ruler of Prydein'.[7] Pryddyd y Moch in an ode to Rhodri ap Owain (d. 1195) calls him the '*o Ynys Brydein, briawd ureint*' – 'Privileged ruler of Ynys Prydein'.[8]

These are just a few of dozens of examples in which rulers of Wales are called the rulers of Prydein.[9] These princes rarely, if ever, left Wales, and they were certainly too busy defending their own borders to be claiming ownership or sovereignty over the whole of Britain. In her excellent article on aspects of sovereignty in the poetry of the *Gogynfeirdd*, Rhian Andrews explains how some of the bards of the twelfth and thirteenth centuries were continuing 'to use the term "Prydain" despite the increasingly popularity of its successor "Cymry"'.[10] The term 'Cymry', the modern Welsh name for 'Wales', replaced 'Prydein', and there are even examples of the two words being used interchangeably. Bleddyn Fardd (fl. 1250) calls Rhys ap Maredudd by two different terms within six lines: '*Aryf Prydein*' – 'armed man of Prydein' – and '*Kymry ddiffreityat*' – 'defender of Cymry'.[11]

It is not only in poetry that we find 'Ynys Prydein' as a term used for Wales: it can also be found in the *Mabinogion* tale *Branwen ferch Llyr*. Composed in the eleventh century, this also contains an interesting use of '*ynys*' to refer to the total number of districts in Wales. The tale is set in North Wales, with major parts

THE LOST LEGEND OF ARTHUR

of the story taking place at Caernarfon, Harlech and Edeirnion, and at Aberffraw on Anglesey. During the tale, Bran travels over to Ireland to rescue his sister, but before doing so he calls upon the soldiers of his kingdom to help him: 'And there and then he began to have messengers dispatched, to muster the whole of the realm [*ynys*]. And then he had come to him the full levy of sevenscore districts and fourteen.'[12]

The most interesting aspect of this quotation is the number of districts attributed to the realm. The story gives the number as 154, and one of the earliest works to detail all the cantrefs (districts) of Wales gives the number as 156, which when we consider that some boundaries change and districts join together or divide up is remarkably consistent.[13] The total number of cantrefs in the *ynys* shows that the term should be used in the sense of realm – not island, as all modern translators have it, thereby distorting the geography of the tale.

The examples above show that the term 'Ynys Prydein' was often used to denote the kingdom of Wales, not the island of Britain. The effect that this has on the understanding of our sources is profound, for sources written in Welsh have been used by scholars to write the history of sixth-century southern Scotland, the Saxon invasion of England and the early history of the Saxon kingdoms of Northumbria and Mercia. The little-known fact that a provable alternative meaning for the geographical term 'Ynys Prydein' exists means that the Welsh sources used to write the history of the British Isles must be reconsidered, and neglected sources – especially the poetry of the *Gogynfeirdd* – should be looked at in a lot more detail by historians, both Welsh and English.

BRITANNIA

The Latin term 'Britannia' is the name assigned to the whole of Britain in the Latin texts of the classical historians Caesar and Tacitus, but we find a different understanding of the word in Latin texts written by Welsh authors. The earliest definite use of 'Britannia' in another sense by a Welsh author is found in the *Life of St Alfred* written by Asser, a monk from South Wales, *c.* 900: 'There was of late in Mercia a strenuous king . . . Offa by name, who ordered to be made between Britannia and Mercia, the great dyke from sea to sea.'[14] There is no doubt that in this instance the term 'Britannia' is used to denote Wales, as the earthwork known as Offa's Dyke still runs along the boundary between England and Wales.[15] But on other occasions in his work Asser uses the term 'Britannia' to denote the whole island, showing how changeable the usage of these terms was. The authors of the Latin *Lives of the Welsh Saints*, mentioned in Chapter 2, use 'Britannia' throughout to denote Wales. They refer to Maelgwn Gwynedd as the greatest king in all Britannia, whereas the Welsh refer to him as the most powerful ruler in Wales, and the term *'dextralis britannia'* ('southern Britannia') is also used to denote South Wales on several occasions. Another text of South Wales provenance, *The Book of Llandaf* (written *c.* 1135), contains a document called *The Privilege of St Teilio*, written in both Latin and Welsh, which shows that the terms 'Britannia' and 'Cymry', from two different languages, were clearly considered to denote the same region:

Latin: *aregibus istis & principibus brittannie*   The Kings and Princes of Britannia.[16]

Welsh: *Breenhined hinn hatouyssocion cymry*   The Kings and Princes of Cymry.[17]

From the evidence above it is easy to see how Latin texts of Welsh provenance may have been misunderstood over the ages. The use of 'Britannia' to mean 'Wales' by Welsh authors writing in Latin means that we should also take a closer look at such important texts as the *Historia Brittonum* and even the *De Excidio* of Gildas, the most important yet least understood of our early texts.[18] If Gildas was concerned primarily with Wales – and there is evidence to suggest that he was – then his references to the Saxon invasion and the two walls built by Roman legions in the fifth century must also be reassessed.[19]

The evidence above also shows that early Welsh manuscripts did not necessarily use the same geographical terminology as later Welsh manuscripts or sources from outside Wales. The identification of the term 'Prydein' with Wales, instead of Britain, does not apply to all Welsh texts, but the very fact that it existed at all means that we must reassess our understanding and interpretation of these valuable source materials. With this understanding in place it is possible to make better sense of the earliest sources regarding Arthur and narrow down his sphere of influence. As historians have always tried to identify sites attached to Arthur from the standpoint that he was ruling in the whole of Britain, we think it is a worthwhile exercise, based on the evidence above, to try to identify sites attached to him from the viewpoint that he ruled in Wales. The battle sites will be dealt with in the next chapter; other sites are discussed below.

THE COURTS OF ARTHUR

The most famous court of Arthur is undoubtedly that of Camelot, home to the Round Table and the most fantastic court that ever existed. The Knights of the Round Table would leave its gates to embark on their quest for the Holy Grail and would joust for the attention of fair maidens in its grounds: this is the image that is portrayed in the pages of the Arthurian romances. Its name is still used today to denote a powerful family or organisation: it was used to describe President Kennedy's circle in America, and is the name of the company that runs the national lottery in the UK. But, despite its widespread fame, the court of Camelot is an invention of the twelfth century, first appearing in the pages of the poem *Lancelot* written by Chrétien de Troyes in 1165 and taking its name from a river that flows beneath the castle of Montgomery on the Welsh borders.[20] In contrast, few are aware of the courts associated with Arthur in the early Welsh traditions, but within the Triads we find the names of the earliest known of them.

The first triad in the earliest collections concerns Arthur's courts, and is given in full below. We will look at each of the sites mentioned, in conjunction with the evidence of the previous chapters, and try to identify where it was located.

Teir Lleithiclvyth Ynys Prydein:
Arthur yn Pen Teyrned ym Mynyv, a Dewi yn Pen Esgyb, a Maelgvn Gvyned yn Pen Hyneif;
Arthur yn Pen Teyrned yg Kelli Wic yg Kernyw, a Bytwini Esgob yn Ben Esgyb, a Charadavc Vreichuras yn Ben Henyf;
Arthur yn Ben Teyrned ym Penn Ryonyd yn y Gogled, a Gerthmul Wledic yn Benn Hyneif, a Chyndeyrn Garthwys yn Benn Esgyb.

Three Tribal Thrones of the Realm of Prydein:

Arthur as Chief Prince in Mynyw [Caerlleon in some variants], and Dewi as Chief Bishop, and Maelgwn Gwynedd as Chief elder;

Arthur as Chief Prince in Celliwig in Cernyw, and Bishop Bytwwini as Chief Bishop and Caradwg Strong-arm as Chief Elder;

Arthur as Chief Prince in Penrhyn Rhianydd in the North, and Gerthmwl Wledig as Chief Elder, and Cynderyn Garthwys as Chief Bishop.[21]

Mynyw and Caerlleon

The first section of the triad indicates that Arthur had a court at either Mynyw (St David's) or, according to a variant, Caerlleon. Mynyw is mentioned in relation to Arthur in *Culhwch and Olwen*, but not as Arthur's court: it is merely a place where he spends the night during the hunt for the giant boar Trwyth across South Wales. Apart from this one reference, Mynyw has no part to play in early Arthurian traditions and its use here appears to originate in the ecclesiastical debate of the twelfth century as to whether or not Mynyw as the seat of the Welsh church should have independence from Canterbury. Making Mynyw the site of a court of Arthur would support its claimed pre-eminence over its rival in Kent. There is no record in Welsh history of Maelgwn Gwynedd having any connection with St David's, suggesting that there is a confusion of traditions and that the original court named may have been in lands under his jurisdiction. This possibility is further strengthened by another variant of this triad in a later manuscript, which replaces Mynyw with Aberffraw, the seat of the princes of Gwynedd on the isle of Anglesey.[22]

The mention of Caerlleon (i.e. City of Legions) also appears to be influenced by the later traditions of Geoffrey of Monmouth, who locates Arthur's court at Caerleon on the River Usk in South Wales. The court of Caerleon appears on many occasions in the later Arthurian literature from the Continent, but *never* in early Welsh tradition. The Welsh also used the name for the city of Chester on the current border between Cheshire and North Wales. Under its Latin name, Urbes Legiones (City of Legions), Chester is mentioned in the *Annales Cambriae* as the site of an important battle between the Welsh and the Saxons in AD 613 – something that we will discuss in Chapter 6. The fact that the name 'Caerlleon' was applied to two different cities on the border between Wales and England – one in the North and the other in the South – has led to much confusion over the years. Little is known about the history of either city during the sixth century, but it is unlikely that either site has any authentic links with the earliest phase of the Arthurian legend.[23]

GELLIWIG

Gelliwig is the oldest and most important of Arthur's courts named in two early Welsh texts: in the Triad quoted above and also on five occasions in *Culhwch and Olwen*. Both sources add that the court was in a place called Cernyw, and owing largely to the author of *Culhwch and Olwen* and to the Welsh versions of the *Historia* this has been widely understood to mean Cornwall. In many instances this is the correct interpretation, but again the internal evidence of the Welsh sources suggests that at one time an alternative meaning of the term existed. The fact that this court is the oldest one linked to Arthur means that it is of the utmost importance. In the words of Dr Oliver Padel, 'It demands identification, and there have been numerous attempts to do so.'[24]

In his article, Dr Padel reviews the various attempts over the last century to identify the court of Gelliwig with different sites in Cornwall – Calliwith, Callington and Killibury Castle being the major contenders, although none of the arguments for these sites is terribly convincing.[25] While generations of scholars have looked in vain for similar-sounding names in Cornwall, they have ignored the fact that the name 'Gelliwig' exists in Wales to this day. The only location still bearing this name anywhere in Britain is sited on the Lleyn Peninsula in north-west Wales, where the name is attached to an old hall and a nearby farm.[26] The existence of the name itself is insufficient to prove that this was the site of Arthur's court, but there is another piece of evidence from *Culhwch and Olwen* that might help us to identify the site. Within the list of warriors attached to Arthur is one who is named as 'Medyr the son of Medredydd (who from Celli Wig would hit a wren on Esgeir Oerfel in Ireland, exactly through its two legs)'.[27] The passage implies that it was possible to see a place named Esgeir Oerfel (the Ridge of Coldness) in Ireland from Gelliwig, but where exactly was this place?

In his excellent article 'The Irish geography of *Culhwch and Olwen*', Professor Patrick Sims-Williams links the Welsh name to a site called Seisgeann Uairbheoil found in medieval Irish manuscripts as an abode of famous heroes.[28] According to the evidence from several Irish sources, the site was situated in the Wicklow mountains on the east coast of Ireland, and Sims-Williams suggests that the actual site was Bray Head, a hill on the coast to the south of Dublin. This would have been a very useful landmark for sailors; indeed it still is, as anyone taking the ferry from Holyhead to Dublin will plainly see. Even with ideal conditions it is not possible to see the Wicklow mountains from Cornwall, but on a very good day they are visible from the west coast of North Wales.

The bards from as early as 1150 also mention the court of Gelliwig. Cynddelw, the bard of the court of Gwynedd, mentions it in an elegy to Owain Gwynedd:

Kyrt kertynt mal kynt kelliwyc   Songs flow as formerly at Celliwig[29]

Meurig ap Iorwerth, a bard from Powys, mentions it in a poem to Hopcyn Thomas:

I Arthur loyw deml wrth aur wledig	Like unto sovereign Arthur, whose temple shone with gold,
A'I lwysgall awen lys Gelliwig	He at Gelliwig, whose court was the cell of the muse.[30]

Iolo Goch, a poet who lived in the Vale of Clwyd in North Wales and had close connections to Valle Crucis Abbey near Llangollen, mentions Gelliwig on two occasions: the first in an elegy to two sons of Tudur Fychan of Penymynydd on Anglesey in 1382, and the second in a poem praising Ieuan ab Einion of Chwilog (north of Pwllheli). In this poem Ieuan is named Sheriff, an office he held at Caernarfon between 1385 and 1390, so dating the poem to this period.

Colli cun, cyllaig Gwynedd,	Losing a hero of Gwynedd,
Call a glew, cuall ei gledd,	Wise and bold, swift his sword,
Cellan ior, coll anwerys,	Lord of Cellan, terrible loss,
Cell y gler, celliwig lys.	Poet's chamber, court of Celliwig.[31]
Cwrt hynod is Llyn frodir	A prominent court below the land of Llyn,
Cell y dwin, Celliwig ir;	Wine cellar, fresh Celliwig.[32]

It is clear that the present site of Gelliwig on the Lleyn Peninsula is meant in these poems. A century later (*c.* 1480) Gutun Owain mentions Gelliwig in a poem concerning Huw Conwy of Bryn Euryn, near Colwyn Bay, and leaves us in absolutely no doubt as to where it is:

Lle Gawn Gelliwic Gwynedd	We find Gelliwig in Gwynedd.[33]

There remains one other source that clearly identifies the Gelliwig of Welsh tradition with the site still named Gelliwig today. A charter from 1209 for the Cistercian abbey of Cymmer near Dolgellau, founded in 1199, names several sites in or bordering the cantref of Neigwl on the Lleyn Peninsula, in which Gelliwig now stands.[34] The name given to the site in the charter is '*ynyskellywyc*' ('*ynys*' here being used to denote an isolated property). The charter is a reconfirmation of lands given to the abbey, meaning that the name '*ynyskellywyc*' existed before 1209. These references show that the bards of North Wales knew of Gelliwig as an important court on the Lleyn Peninsula: nowhere in the Welsh material is there any evidence to link the name to Cornwall, or anywhere else.

If we were looking solely for the name 'Gelliwig', the identification of the site of Arthur's court provided by the evidence above would be beyond doubt. But we also have to account for the name 'Cernyw'. For centuries people have tried in vain to find Gelliwig in Cornwall, but perhaps what we need to do is find Cernyw near Gelliwig. From the other references to Cernyw in Welsh sources, clues begin to emerge that the name was once attached to Gwynedd in some way.

In *Culhwch and Olwen* a character named Rhita Gawr, the father of Arthur's half brother Gormant, is referred to as 'the chief elder of Cernyw'.[35] What little else we know of Rhita Gawr can be found in a folk tale concerning a fight with Arthur for his beard, which Rhita Gawr wished to have in order to finish his cloak made from the beards of kings. This story was used by Geoffrey in the *Historia*, and he named the site of the fight as Mons Aravius. The Welsh version of this tale places the event on the Aran mountains to the south-west of Bala Lake, where a burial mound and valley bear names associated with this fight.[36] Bardic poetry also records that the cairn on the summit of Snowdon, the highest mountain in Wales, was known in the fourteenth century as Bedd Rhita, the Grave of Rhita. If Rhita was the chief elder of Cornwall, why do the only occasions in which he is mentioned in Welsh sources place him in North Wales?

Within Welsh manuscripts, other references to Cernyw suggest associations with North Wales rather than Cornwall. For example, a genealogical tract known as *Bonedd Gwyr y Gogledd* (The Lineage of the Men of the North) names the father of a person called Huallu as 'Tudfwlch Corneu prince of Cernyw'.[37] A prince of Cernyw can in no way be called a man of the north, which has led many scholars to consider this section to be a later addition to the text. However, if Cernyw is not Cornwall, an explanation is possible. The only other occurrence of the name 'Tudfwlch' is in *The Book of Aneirin,* as a ruler of the cantref of Eifionydd, a part of the Lleyn Penninsula – the same area in which we find Gelliwig. Could the two men called Tudfwlch actually be the same person?[38] Also in North Wales is a village called Llangernyw (the Sacred Enclosure of Cernyw), six miles south of Colwyn Bay. It is unlikely that this site has anything to do with Cornwall.

One question that must be asked is, What does the term 'Cernyw' actually mean? '*Cern*' in old Welsh was used to mean 'the side of the head' or an 'exposed slope', suggesting that 'Cernyw' could have been used to denote an exposed headland or peninsula. Could it be that in the earliest Welsh sources 'Cernyw' is a descriptive name for a landscape feature rather than the name of a region? That Cornwall and the Lleyn Peninsula are both prominent peninsulas could be more than just coincidence. Is it only later writers such as the authors of *Culhwch and Olwen* and the Welsh translators of Geoffrey's *Historia* who have associated Cernyw with Cornwall? Current scholarship identifies Cernyw with Cornwall, but can't locate Gelliwig. Our theory has located a place known as Gelliwig, from at least the twelfth century and also associated with Arthur in the poetry from this period, but has found only circumstantial evidence for the name 'Cernyw'. Which of the opposing theories is correct?

The site of Gelliwig that has survived today is situated on a low-lying coastal plain dominated by the nearby hill of Mynydd Rhiw (1,000 feet), home to a Neolithic axe factory. But is it on the site of a sixth-century court? The answer to this must be left to the archaeologists, but the final piece of evidence we can provide is on a hill close to Gelliwig, known as Cregiau Gwineu. On the summit of this hill, which slopes steeply down to the sea, are the remains of an unusual hill fort. The fort consists of a stone wall built around the summit of the hill except at the north-facing slope, which is guarded by a thirty-foot-high outcrop of rock – an ideal place to retreat to if threatened.[39] The identification of this hill fort as the court of Arthur referred to in the texts is impossible to prove, but on a clear day it is possible to see the Wicklow mountains in Ireland from its summit. Coincidence?

PENRHYN RHIANYDD

The last court mentioned in the triad has never been satisfactorily identified, with most scholars trying to identify it with a site in southern Scotland owing to a misunderstanding of the term 'Ynys Prydein'. The triad states that Penrhyn Rhianydd is in the north, but the north of where?

Much has been written over the centuries about the kingdoms of northern England and southern Scotland – often referred to as the north British kingdoms or simply the 'Old North'. All the works touching upon this subject would have us believe that the existence of these kingdoms is an irrefutable fact, but in reality this couldn't be further from the truth. The current theory can be summarised as follows. A number of kingdoms of Welsh-speaking Britons existed in the southern half of Scotland and northern England, with major centres at Dumbarton and Carlisle. The Welsh sources that mention these kingdoms refer to events that happen in the area as taking place in *Gogledd* – 'the north' – and from these sources it is possible to derive a handful of place names, events and people attached to these kingdoms. The ancestry of the rulers of this area is found in the genealogical tract known as *Bonedd Gwyr y Gogledd* (The Lineage of the Men of the North). The fate of the kingdoms known as Rheged, Gododdin, Elfed and Ystrad Clud is uncertain, but the general belief is that the English and Scots overran them until the final king of Ystrad Clud was killed in 1018. The people emigrated to North Wales as their kingdoms were overrun, and took their stories and traditions with them. The poetic and historical sources we have concerning *Gogledd* were written down in North Wales at this time, and many of them became grafted on to the landscape of their new home in the form of place names and folklore.

This theory has been current since the sixteenth century, and is now so well established that it is surprising to find that it still is just a theory – there has never been any archaeological evidence to confirm it. During our research it became apparent that there was a fatal flaw in this theory. The process of a people renaming their new land with names from their old home is known as secondary localisation, and can be proved to have occurred when the primary place names can be identified – for example, Perth in Australia is named after Perth in Scotland, and Birmingham in Alabama, USA, is named after Birmingham, England – and when we also know that people emigrated from the primary site to the secondary one. The biggest problem with the idea that Welsh kingdoms originally existed in southern Scotland is that none of the place names attached to *Gogledd* in the Welsh sources can be definitively identified with a site in southern Scotland. All the places mentioned in the sources that can be identified are found in North Wales – a fact which academia puts down to secondary localisation even though such a process can be shown to have taken place only when the primary sites have been identified. But if the names found in North Wales are not caused by secondary localisation, how can they be explained?

The evidence in Welsh material centres around references to *Gogledd* (the north). The question is, the north of what? The answer is Ynys Prydein, which as we saw above can be understood to mean the kingdom of Wales as well as the isle of Britain. With this in mind, would it not make more sense for the events connected to *Gogledd* to take place in the north of Wales rather than the north of Britain? This simple adjustment to the current understanding explains why all the places that can be identified are found in North Wales rather than Scotland. Is it not more likely that the people and places attached to *Gogledd* are remembered in North Wales for the simple reason that that is where they originally were? The misappropriation of this 'northern' material has come about because of a misunderstanding of the geographical term 'Prydein', and the theory of secondary localisation has then been adopted in order to make sense of this misunderstanding. The existence of the north British kingdoms is, in short, an academic legend.[40]

Our theory outlined above enables us to identify the site of Arthur's obscure court of Penrhyn Rhianydd. The term '*penrhyn*' simply means 'headland' and can be found as a place-name element all along the Welsh coast. The second part of the name, 'Rhianydd' is a variant spelling of 'Rhianedd' and is the clue to the whereabouts of the court. Among the Welsh traditions concerning the sixth-century king Maelgwn Gwynedd, a place named Morfa Rhianedd is mentioned on several occasions. The location of this site has been identified with the shoreline between Llandudno and Colwyn Bay on the North Wales coast (see page 107). The small town of Penrhyn Bay lies midway between these two towns. Positioned between the coastline and a hill fort, it is the only place in Wales where parts of the two place-name elements of Arthur's court can be found together.

The nearby hill fort that dominates the drive along the North Wales coast is today called Bryn Euryn, but was originally known as Dinarth, meaning Fortress of the Bear. It is also possible that its original name contains the first part of the name 'Arthur'. Gildas in his *De Excidio* refers to 'Bear's Stronghold' as the home of Cuneglasus, the King of Rhos, and scholars have thought that this is a reference to the fort of Dinarth.[41] This shows that the hill fort or another site in the immediate vicinity was the home of a prince within a few years of Arthur's lifetime. The Chief Bishop of Penrhyn Rhianydd according to the triad is Cynderyn Garthwys – better known as St Kentigern, the founder of the monastic establishment at St Asaph fifteen miles away from the site. Penrhyn

Rhlanydd is not mentioned in any other Welsh sources and is very obscure, but what little evidence we do have suggests that it was situated in the vicinity of Penrhyn Bay.

PLACES VISITED BY ARTHUR IN *CULHWCH AND OLWEN*

The central feature of *Culhwch and Olwen* is the forty *anoethau* (things difficult to perform) that Ysbaddaden demands that Culhwch must undertake in order to gain the hand of his daughter Olwen. The motif of the hero completing tasks in order to win the hand of someone's daughter is a common one in mythology: a prime example from the classical world is related in the story of Jason and the Argonauts. *Culhwch and Olwen* is a composite of earlier material, and it describes only ten of the forty tasks in any detail.[42] The figure of Arthur is present in only six of the ten tasks described, and only four of these contain any definite geographical information that can help us to identify regions associated with Arthur in the earliest traditions.

Task One

Arthur and his men set out to seek two men of Arthur's court who had been turned into the pups of the bitch Rhymhi. They come to the house of Tringad in Aber Deu Cleddyf, where they are told that Rhymhi is living in a cave near the river, from which she attacks the farmers' stock in the area. Arthur and his men go to find this cave in his ship *Prydwen*, and subsequently find Rhymhi and her two pups. When she was surrounded, 'God changed them back into their own semblances for Arthur.'[43]

The Welsh prefix '*Aber*' means 'the estuary of a river' or 'where two rivers join' and '*Daugleddyf*' (literally 'Two Swords') was mentioned by Giraldus Cambrensis in 1188 in his *Description of Wales*: 'From the same mountains [Preseli] come the two Cleddau streams. Between them is the region called Deugleddyf, which is named after them. One runs by Llawhaden Castle and the other through Haverfordwest, and so they join the sea.'[44] The two rivers named Cleddau meet to the south-west of Haverfordwest in Pembrokeshire and run together for several miles, until reaching the coast at Milford Haven. The exact location of the cave is uncertain.

Task Two

Arthur sends a message to Odgar, the King of Ireland, to ask for the magical cauldron of Diwrnach. The King asks Diwrnach for the cauldron, but he refuses to give it up, so Arthur sets off to Ireland in his ship *Prydwen* with a few of his men to take the cauldron by force. Llenlleog, one of Arthur's men, subsequently kills Diwrnach with a sword called Caledfwlch (the original Excalibur). They return to their ship and escape from Ireland with the magical cauldron, disembarking at the house of Llwydeu the son of Cel Coed at Porth Cerddin in Dyfed.

The exact location of Porth Cerddin in Dyfed is uncertain. The name translates as 'the Harbour of the Rowan Tree', and scholars have suggested that it might be Porth Mawr near St David's in Pembrokeshire, or Pwll Crochan five miles west of Fishguard, both of which fit the available evidence.[45] Before the source moves on to the next task there is a short line that states 'And Mesur-y-Peir is there.' The name means 'Measure of the Cauldron', and presumably the place that it refers to was situated at or very close to Porth Cerddin.

Task Three

The hunt for the giant boar Trwyth is the task described in the most detail in *Culhwch and Olwen*. To discuss every geographical place name in this section of the source would require many pages and would serve little purpose as the geography of this event has been carefully mapped in a variety of journal articles and is described in detail in the academic edition of the tale.[46]

Arthur and his men set out to Esgeir Oerfel in Ireland (discussed above), where the boar and his seven young pigs are living, to get the comb, razor and shears that are between the ears of the boar. After three days of fighting, Arthur sends Gwrhyr, his interpreter, to speak to the boar in order to try to put an end to the fighting. One of the piglets of the boar tells Gwrhyr that Arthur will not have what he wants until the boar is dead and that in the morning they will go to Arthur's country to cause as much mischief as possible. The following day the boar and his seven piglets 'set out by sea towards Wales',[47] arriving at Porth Cleis in Dyfed. This place is identifiable with the mouth of the River Alun five miles south-west of St David's, and was historically where Gruffudd ap Cynan landed when he arrived from Ireland in 1081 to reclaim his right to rule Gwynedd. This fact has led some to suggest that the route taken by the boar across South Wales might parallel the route taken by Gruffudd on his way to the decisive battle of Mynydd Carn, an unidentified site on the borders of Dyfed.

The rest of the section details places in South Wales, many of which are readily identifiable, until the boar plunges into the Severn estuary. Here Arthur's men wrestle the razor and the shears from his head, but the boar escapes by crossing the River Severn into Cornwall. Here 'from mischief to mischief the comb was won from him',[48] and the boar is forced into the sea off Cornwall, never to be seen again.

Apart from the narrative in *Culhwch and Olwen*, the great boar Trwyth is mentioned in *Y Gododdin* and the *Historia Brittonum*, and was obviously an important part of Welsh mythology. The author of this section in *Culhwch and Olwen* appears to have made use of these earlier traditions and seems to have created the boar's journey across South Wales in order to explain pre-existing place names. The most important aspect of this task is the antiquity of the tale, not the presence of Arthur.

Task Four

The final task undertaken by Arthur and his men in *Culhwch and Olwen* is to obtain the blood of 'y Widon Ordu merch y Widon Orwen' – 'the Very Black Witch, daughter of the Very White Witch'. Two of Arthur's servants enter her cave but are defeated by the hag, who 'drove them out squealing and squalling'. Two more of Arthur's men try to vanquish her, but they too are defeated and all four men are loaded on to Arthur's horse Llamrei and carried away from the site. Arthur approaches the cave and with his dagger Carnwennan 'struck her across the middle until she was as two tubs'.[49] Caw of Prydein then takes the hag's blood and keeps it with him.

The location of this cave according to the tale is in 'Y Gogledd' at 'Pennant Gouut yg gwrthir Uffern'. '*Gogledd*', as we have seen, means 'north' and, as we showed above, could in this context very well mean North Wales. '*Pennant*' is a common place-name element in Wales and means 'the head or the upper reaches of a valley'. '*Gouut*' is an old spelling for '*gofid*', meaning 'grief' or 'distress'; '*gwrhtir*' means 'uplands' or 'high ground', and '*Uffern*' is often used to denote hell in the Welsh language. The place name therefore translates as 'The Valley of Grief in the Uplands of Hell', which doesn't really give us much to go on. The name of the witch Ordu is found associated with a hill named Orddu between Bala and the Llangwm near Cerrigydrudion. The hill is first mentioned first mentioned as 'Yr Ordh Dhu' in Edward Lhuyd's 1698 *Parochialia*, and the similarity between the two names was noted in the Royal Commission for Ancient and Historical Monuments inventory for Denbighshire in 1914.[50] Could this place name preserve any knowledge of the Very Black Witch? In the village of Llangwm stands a church that was originally dedicated to Gwynnog and Noethon, two sons of Gildas, who was in turn the son of Caw of Prydein who collected the witch's blood and kept it with him.[51]

It is also interesting to note that a piece of Arthurian folklore, from a manuscript now lost, records an event in which Arthur is captured by a hag and her children and is forced to spend the night in their cave. In order to escape he must answer three riddles, which he does and duly escapes. Although it is impossible to make a clear link between these two pieces of tradition, it is interesting to note that the hag's cave in the lost manuscript is described as 'a cave in Denbighshire' – the very same county in which the hill Orddu is situated.[52]

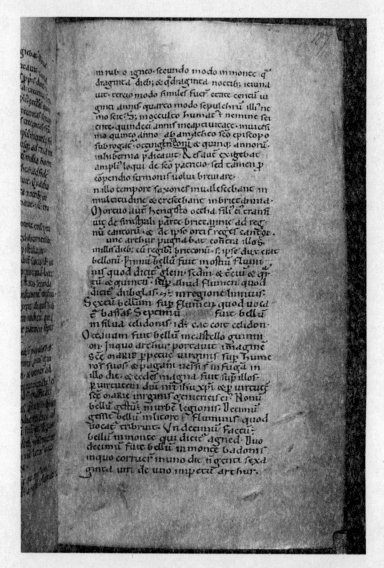

The earliest surviving manuscript to mention Arthur is kept in the British Library and is known as Harleian MS 3859. This manuscript dating from *c*.1100 contains copies of the *Historia Brittonum* and the *Annales Cambriae*, both of which mention battles associated with Arthur. The plate here shows the famous battle list from §56 of the *Historia Brittonum*.

Caer Gai, near the village of Llanuwchllyn at the southern end of Bala Lake, is the site that Welsh tradition associates with the childhood of Arthur and it is named after his foster brother Cai, who later became better known as Sir Kay. Today this seventeenth-century manor house occupies the summit.

Remains of the Roman walls and earthworks that once fortified the site at Caer Gai.

According to the Triads, Arthur held court at a place called Penrhyn Rhianedd, the location of which has not been identified before. The second part of the name 'Rhianedd' is also mentioned as the name of this section of the North Wales Coast between Colwyn Bay and Llandudno, known as Morfa Rhinaedd.

The first part of the name of Arthur's court Penrhyn Rhianedd is preserved in that of Penrhyn Bay, a small town found on this section of coast. Above Penrhyn Bay is a hillfort known as Dinarth (the fortress of the Bear) alluded to by Gildas in c.540. This is the most likely site for Arthur's court.

Llanderfel, one of the many churches dedicated to the warriors of Arthur. Derfel Gadarn (Derfel the Mighty) was one of the few recorded survivors of Arthur's final battle of Camlan.

The remains of an effigy of Derfel Gadarn can be found within the porch of Llanderfel. Depicting him seated on a stag and holding a staff, it shows that he was held in very high regard. On 22 May 1538 a separate effigy of St Derfel was burnt at Smithfield Market by the order of Thomas Cromwell as part of the execution pyre of a Friar Forest, who was convicted for refusing to recognise Henry VIII as the head of the Church.

One other place name attached to Arthur is the name of his hall, Ehangwen, mentioned in the list of warriors in *Culhwch and Olwen*. The location of this hall is unknown, and the only other information we have concerning it is that it was built by 'Glwyddyn Saer (craftsman) one of Arthur's men and his chief builder', who was slain by the boar in Dyfed.[53]

The South Wales provenance of *Culhwch and Olwen* is reflected in the majority of the place names mentioned in the text. There are no place names identifiable in North Wales, but several references to '*y Gogledd*' probably relate to this region. The author obviously had close connections with the same ecclesiastical school in South Wales that was responsible for the Lives of the Welsh saints, and the dialect of some of the words used in the text is very close to that still in use today in Pembrokeshire and Carmarthenshire. Historical events in South Wales – especially the landing of Gruffudd ap Cynan at Porth Cleis in 1081 and the visit of William the Conqueror to St David's in the same year – seem to be in the mind of the author.[54] The only task which takes place outside South Wales and has a place name attached involves the Very Black Witch, and it is interesting to speculate whether the author obtained this incident from an older corpus of Arthurian material.

PLACES ATTACHED TO ARTHUR
IN EARLY WELSH POETRY

In the Welsh poetical references to Arthur there are only two poems that mention any place names that we can attempt to identify. The first of them is *Preiddeu Annwn* from *The Book of*

THE LOST LEGEND OF ARTHUR

Taliesin, but the names there are so obscure that no identifications are possible.[55] The other poem concerning Arthur that provides place names is *Pa Gur?* from *The Black Book of Carmarthen*, and the lines from the poem that name these places are given below.

A thi ae gueli	And you will see them,
Vythneint elei	the vultures of Elei[56]

The name 'Elei' is often identified as the River Ely in South Wales, but it is more likely that it is connected with the town of Pwllheli, known in the fourteenth century as Portheli and Porthely – an identification that seems to be borne out by references in the poem to Anglesey and Gwynedd.[57]

Y guaed gouerei	He caused the blood to flow,
In neuat awarnach	in Afarnach's hall,
In imlat ew a gurach	fighting with a witch.[58]

The poem gives no clue about the location of Afarnach's hall, but in *Culhwch and Olwen* Arthur and his men travel to the fort of Wrnach the Giant, who is probably the same person as Afarnach. It is described as 'a great fort of mortared stone and as Bedwyr entered the castle he crossed three baileys [*catlys*]'.[59] The reference to mortared stone sounds more like a castle from the later period in which *Culhwch and Olwen* took its final form, but the three baileys mentioned could refer to any one of the many triple-ditched hill forts in Wales. Apart from this information nothing else is known.

Ew a guant penpalach	He pierced Pen Palach
In atodev dissethach	in the dwellings of Disethach.

The name 'Disethach' is not mentioned elsewhere in Welsh tradition, but the termination '-ach' is used in Welsh to denote something unpleasant. Two places in Wales might preserve a form of the name: Dyserth near the North Wales coast in Denbighshire and Disserth near Llandrindod Wells in Powys. Either one of these is a possible site for the piercing of Pen Palach – whoever he may have been.

Ar eidin cyminauc	At Dinas Eidyn on the border.[60]
Ym minit eidin	On Mynydd Eidyn
Amuc a chinbin	he fought with dogheads.[61]

The fort of Eidyn and the mountain of Eidyn are also mentioned in the poem *Y Gododdin,* the setting of which has long been identified with the north-east of England and southern Scotland, leading scholars to identify Eidyn with Edinburgh. As discussed above, the idea of British kingdoms in northern England is difficult to confirm, and the internal evidence of the poem suggests that the events of *Y Gododdin* have little to do with this area.

Dinas Eidyn is described as being 'on the border'. Which border is unclear, however, but it is unlikely to be the border between Scotland and England. The identity of the enigmatic dogheads is difficult to ascertain and provides no clues for the geography of this event. A place called Llech Eidyn (Slab of Eidyn) exists in Merionethshire, and it has also been suggested that 'Eidyn' might have survived as a place-name element in the names of Treuddyn (a village in Flintshire) and Creuddyn (better known as Great Ormes Head at Llandudno).[62]

| *Rac riev emreis* | Before the lord of Emrys.[63] |

The *Gogynfeirdd* often used 'Emrys' to denote the land of Gwynedd in their praise poetry to rulers of Gwynedd, who were often referred to as the dragons of Emrys.[64] This may have arisen from the legend of the two dragons at Dinas Emrys near Beddgelert in the mountains of Snowdonia, as recorded in the *Historia Brittonum*.[65]

Yguarthaw ystawingun   On the upland of Ystawingun.[66]

This site has defied all attempts at identification and remains unlocated.

Kei win a aeth von   Cai the fair went to Mon.[67]

This is the easiest place name to identify, as Mon has been used for over two thousand years and is still in use today as the Welsh name for the isle of Anglesey. Arthur is also associated with the island in the chronicle of Elis Gruffudd, written *c.* 1510: 'There was a causeway over the Menai around the place that is called today Bon y Don, at that place there were certain men in armour guarding it all the time. And the king of this island made many cruel battles against Arthur.'[68] The Menai Strait separates Anglesey from mainland Wales, and Bon y Don can be identified as the place found on modern maps as Moel y Don. Although this extract is a composite of Welsh traditions and later romantic material, it is interesting in that it places Arthur, and presumably his warriors, in Anglesey – as does the poem *Pa Gur?* from *The Black Book of Carmarthen*.

CONCLUSION

It is hoped that the evidence gathered together in this chapter has drawn attention to some of the problems regarding Arthurian geography. That the exact meaning of the geographical terms used by the Welsh bards in the twelfth century is not as clear-cut as we have been led to believe, and that alternative definitions can be shown to have existed, is fundamental to our understanding of the surviving sources. When reading the source materials from this alternative point of view, several place names become easier to identify and the sphere of Arthur's activities becomes clearer. All ideas of a sixth-century warrior fighting battles as far afield as Cornwall and Scotland must now be disregarded. The reason such ideas existed in the first place is that Welsh geographical terms were misunderstood by English historians as far back as William of Malmesbury – indeed this misunderstanding is one of the major factors that led to Arthur becoming such a fascinating historical enigma. Understanding that the elusiveness of Arthurian geography is due not solely to the fantastic stories told about him but also to the misappropriation of geographical terms over the centuries means that we must now look more closely at the handful of early Welsh place names that we have. If we spent as much time and effort trying to identify the locations of Ystawingun, Pennant Gouut and the dwellings of Disethach as we do Camelot, Badon and the Isle of Avalon, Arthur would not remain an enigma for long.

6

ARTHUR'S BATTLES

Then Arthur fought against them [the Saxons] in those days, together with the kings of the British; but he was their leader in battle (dux bellorum). The first battle was at the mouth of the river called Glein. The second, the third, the fourth and the fifth were on another river, called the Dubglas, which is in the country of Linnuis. The sixth battle was on the river called Bassas. The seventh battle was in the wood of Celidon, that is the battle of Coed Celyddon. The eighth battle was Castello Guinnion, and in it Arthur carried the image of the holy Mary, the everlasting Virgin, on his shoulders,[1] and the heathen were put to flight on that day, and there was a great slaughter upon them, through the power of Our Lord Jesus Christ and the power of the holy Virgin Mary, his mother. The ninth battle was fought in Urbes Legionis. The tenth battle was fought on the bank of the river called Tribruit. The eleventh battle was on the mountain called Agned. The twelfth battle was on monte Badonis, and in it nine hundred and sixty men fell in one day, from a single charge of Arthur's, and no one laid them low save he alone; and he was victorious in all his campaigns.[2]

ITHIN the whole of Arthurian studies there is probably no point discussed more among scholars than the locations attributed to Arthur's battles and their relationship to the historical existence of Arthur. This is not just a modern phenomenon: scholars of all periods have searched for these battle sites, and one of the earliest to do so was Henry of Huntington, who wrote in 1129, 'These wars and the places of these wars Gildas the historian [meaning the *Historia Brittonum* – quoted above] relates. But all the places are unknown in our age.'[3] This remains true to the present day, although we hope to offer some new insights and suggestions about this perennial subject.

The comment by Henry of Huntington – coming as it does from the mouth of an Anglo-Norman cleric writing a history of England – is interesting, for it shows how little was understood about Arthur in the years immediately preceding the *Historia* of Geoffrey of Monmouth. Henry's contemporary William of Malmesbury comments, 'It is of this Arthur that the Britons fondly tell so many fables, even to the present day; a man worthy to be celebrated, not by idle fictions, but by authentic history. He long upheld the sinking state, and roused the broken spirit of his countrymen to war.'[4]

Over the centuries, scholars have come up with locations for the twelve battles as far apart as Scotland, Cornwall, Cumbria and Yorkshire. Geoffrey of Monmouth, drawing on earlier Welsh material, created his own geographic context to suit the political aims of his patrons and then applied it wholesale to his newly created Arthurian epic. He appears to be in no doubt as to the locations of the battles, but when he relates them he mentions only Dubglas, Celidon and Badon from the battle list in the *Historia Brittonum* and then adds completely fictitious battles which expand Arthur's realm as far as Scotland and Continental Europe.

Geoffrey's use of only three battles from the *Historia Brittonum* is interesting: one cannot help but feel that if this master storyteller had access to other battle names from a version of this particular source he would have made use of them. As he apparently did not, this begs the question, What source for these battles was Geoffrey using?

Geoffrey's geographical reworkings of the place names of the earlier tradition were themselves changed over the generations by later writers all the way down to Malory, creating many of the popular Arthurian sites known today. Modern scholars and enthusiasts have continued this tradition, applying the names attributed to Arthur's battles in the *Historia Brittonum* to their personal understanding of the battle list and the general Arthurian context. What can now be added to any further discussion of Arthur's battles?

In any serious study of Arthur one has eventually to deal with the questions that are most often asked about him: Did he ever exist as a historical figure, or is he a fictional construct conjured from the imaginations of patriotic chroniclers and storytellers? And, if he did exist, what was he: a king, a tyrant, a general, a Romanised cavalry leader or a British warlord? Over the years, scholars addressing these questions have made extremely valuable contributions to the study of the Arthurian context. Things have developed, and the one-time fashion for dismissing Arthur as a purely mythic figure was said by Professor Thomas Jones in 1958 to be 'no longer acceptable'. Jones added that he accepted 'the idea that there was a historical person of the name of Arthur early in the sixth century, who may have been a leader of the Britons against their enemies, whoever they were, the Picts or Scots or Saxons, or a combination thereof'.[5] Such a view is still widely held among many of today's scholars and by ourselves, who belong to the 'no smoke without fire' school of Arthurian studies.

There *is* evidence to establish the existence of a historical Arthur, although he became legendary at a very early date and despite the many attempts to dismiss him from our history books. Arthur still refuses to be laid to rest. One of the main reasons for this is that there is a large hole in our knowledge of the late fifth and early sixth centuries – the period that tradition assigns to him – and, until there is a secure framework for the period in general, Arthur and numerous other figures assigned legendary status cannot be assigned their rightful positions, whether that is as purely legendary figures or as historical ones.[6]

One the most important points relating to Arthurian studies was made by Thomas Jones in his important article 'The Early Evolution of the Legend of Arthur' and could equally be applied to the early medieval period as a whole: 'from time to time many theories have been proposed which have been argued so skilfully that there is a danger that we may forget that they are only theories'.[7] We have taken this to heart, so in this present work you will find hardly any reference to many of the earlier hypotheses regarding Arthur – such as that he was a Roman cavalry leader who defended western Britain from Scotland to Cornwall, fighting one minute on Hadrian's Wall and the next in Devon, Lincolnshire or Cornwall, or that he had northern or Cornish origins. The idea of any Dark Age figure ruling from one end of the present country to the other cannot be seriously considered, while the battle sites are described by Rachel Bromwich as being 'in places which are too widely separated over Britain for it to be at all likely that they were victories won by single leader – or even that they were all fought against the Saxons, rather than (in some cases) against Picts, Scots and fellow Britons'.[8]

Also, little reference will be made to other Arthurian theories which periodically appear in regard to a schizophrenic Arthur made up of different historical figures merged together to try to accommodate the available evidence, or identifying as Arthur any person from the historical record who bears the letters '*Art*' or '*Arth*' anywhere in his name, regardless of his not fitting any of the known evidence from the early tradition or the right historical period.

This said, however, the name 'Arthur' in certain forms does appear attached to historical figures, mainly of the late sixth century. These figures are all unacceptable as the 'true' Arthur for many reasons, and have all been dealt with by various scholars over the years.[9] It has been suggested that this later popularity of his name existed because Arthur had already reached the status of a minor hero by the time of his death, and, as happened in modern times with the name 'Diana' after the death of the Princess of Wales, thereafter the name gained in popularity in succeeding generations – a fact pointed out by the Chadwicks in the 1930s: 'There is therefore good reason for believing that its wide currency towards the end of the sixth century must have been due to some famous person of that name in the near past. This would agree well enough with the dates given to Arthur in the *Annales Cambriae*.'[10]

The historical people named Arthur in question are

- *Arturius* son of Aedan mac Gabrain of Dalriada;
- *Artuir* son of Bicoir Britone;
- *Feradach hoa Artur* (Feradach grandson of Artur);
- *Arthur map Pedr* (*fl. c.* AD 560).

Various authors have tried to make one of the people named above fill the boots of Arthur, usually using much later evidence to prove their point. Historians from South Wales in the nineteenth century tried to identify Arthur with a person named Athrwys in the genealogies of the rulers of Glamorgan – yet another example of people seizing upon a similar-sounding name regardless of the lack of evidence. A recent resurgence of this particular theory now has two Arthurs separated by over 200 years, needlessly complicating matters even further.[11]

The Revd A. W. Wade-Evans neatly summed up the crux of the problem concerning the geography of Arthur's battles in 1956, when he wrote, 'Not one of the sites (so far as I know) has been satisfactorily identified and all attempts to place them would seem to be futile until Arthur's field of activities has been narrowed down within credible and probable limits.'[12] Today a majority of scholars agree on the identification of one of the sites named in the battle list (Urbes Legiones as Chester), but otherwise Wade-Evans's comment is still relevant, and we agree that the search for Arthur's battles has to start with a narrowing down of his sphere of activity.

The problem with the ancient sources is that the geography and stories portrayed within them are open to misunderstanding and in many cases appear to be in direct conflict with the present orthodox picture of the period and the current theories about Arthur. The key to solving the mystery of Arthur's battles is to understand the geography used within the early sources from the perspective of the author at the time he was writing, rather than applying later ideas to the geographical terms used. The geographic context of the early Arthurian tradition already outlined in the previous chapter appears to point to what is now known as Wales and the Marches and to North Wales in particular as the source of the legend. If the one battle site generally agreed upon – for Urbes

Legiones – is at Chester, near the present-day Welsh border, and the identifiable places from the earliest Arthurian tradition seem to be in North Wales, then surely there should be evidence for Arthur's battles within this geographical framework.

The history of the Dark Ages is a difficult subject: what little is known about this period is obscure in its overall context, and the sources can appear at first sight to be contradictory and difficult to interpret. Furthermore, there is very little contemporary evidence, and such as does exist seems to contradict important points in the modern historical framework applied to it. In fact it is often said that we have no reliable contemporary account at all for the events following the withdrawal of Rome from Britain's shores in the early part of the fifth century, and also no reliable contemporary account of the arrival of bands of Germanic invaders on these shores. There are, however, some basic accepted facts reconstructed from meagre and complex evidence for the events of this time.

The departure of the Roman legions *c.* AD 410 appears to have been followed by the native population reverting to pre-Roman Celtic tribal structures, creating small, independent kingdoms ruled by warlords, kings and petty tyrants. With no central control, these independent warlords and self-appointed kings appear to have warred incessantly among themselves, as of old. But an even greater calamity was to befall the Britons: following the Roman withdrawal and taking advantage of the Britons' lack of military organisation, the Picts, Irish and Scots launched continuous attacks from the north and the west. Meanwhile from the south and the east the Saxon tribes gradually arrived in ever greater numbers, establishing their first identifiable kingdoms in England in the late fifth century. (The general supposition that the

Germanic war-bands arrived suddenly on these shores – consti-tuting what is popularly termed the 'Saxon Invasion' – is open to question, as there is evidence that Saxons were present in England at a much earlier date, possibly as mercenaries employed by Rome.) The archaeological evidence shows a definite dividing line between British and Saxon culture from the Severn estuary across to the southern Pennines and the north-east of England. Although it impossible to determine an exact boundary between the two cultures, it is obvious that the Welsh borderland was a zone of conflict between them by the end of the sixth century.

This is the background to the figure of Arthur – a figure born from one of the newly emerging kingdoms of the late fifth century, a people beset on all sides by enemies, a race literally fighting for their very existence – and even this brief overview shows the difficulties faced by all historians of this period in the absence of reliable historical sources, contemporary or otherwise. The historical Arthur was a man who had to come to terms with the strong winds of change. His world was not that of the regal figure presented by Geoffrey of Monmouth, or the figure presented in the later romances. His was a time of warlords and tyrants, civil wars and invasions, with the Britons backed into the western reaches of the island, fighting to stem the ever increasing flow of invaders.

THE BATTLES OF ARTHUR IN THE *HISTORIA BRITTONUM*

Now we return to the most famous of the Arthurian texts: the *Historia Brittonum*, commonly referred to as Nennius, the name of one of the editors according to some manuscripts.[13] Nennius refers to himself in the following way: 'I, Ninnius, disciple of Elvodugus, have undertaken to write some extracts.'[14] Elvodugus is also known to history from another source, as the *Annales Cambriae* record his death under the year 809 and give him the title 'Chief Bishop in the land of Gwynedd'.[15] The same annals also state that in 768 he reformed the date of Easter among the Britons, to bring it into line with Rome.[16] The bard Einion ap Gwalchmai (*c.* 1220) notes the association of Elvodugus with the town of Abergele on the North Wales coast, where there was also a well that carried his name, and later tradition also associates him with Caer Cybi (Holyhead).[17] From this evidence we can assume that Nennius came from Gwynedd in North Wales, and that that was where his version of the text was compiled in the ninth century.

Opinions differ greatly about the worth of the *Historia Brittonum*, and this is especially true in regard to Arthur's battle list. Some consider it to contain possibly the most important information available regarding Arthur; others consider it so elusive that no theories about a possible historical Arthur can be based upon the evidence contained within its pages. The importance of the *Historia Brittonum* in the quest for Arthur lies in the early date of the original text and of the earliest manuscript and in the uniqueness of the traditions contained within it.

The names of the battles ascribed to Arthur in the *Historia Brittonum* have lain behind many a scholar's quest for him, but they pose very difficult questions – such as, Where did these names of battles come from, and how genuine are they? The most likely answer to the first of these questions was put forward some years ago and suggests that the source used by the author was an earlier

Welsh bardic battle poem.[18] This suggestion is supported by evidence of translation from Welsh to Latin within the text and by what appears to be part of the original rhyme scheme of just such a poem in the battle names 'Dulas', 'Linnius', 'Bassas', 'Legionis' and 'Badonis'.[19]

There are many examples of poems listing the victories of a great leader or king within Welsh poetic tradition, from the earliest days through to the poetry of the *Gogynfeirdd*. The earliest known example of this practice comes from a short section within a praise poem to Cynan Garwyn of Powys in *The Book of Taliesin*, in which Cynan's victories are recorded: 'Cynan host-protector . . . a battle was fought on the Wye . . . a battle in fair Anglesey . . . a battle in Crug Dyfed . . . a battle in the land of Brachan.'[20] Other early examples of this apparently widespread practice include poems about the battles of Gwallawg and of Urien Rheged and his son Owain. But probably the best example of a battle poem is the one that concerns the victories of Cadwallon and recounts sixteen battles for Ynys Prydein by location and mentions in passing a further sixty encounters. The style of each of the entries follows the formula below:

Lluest gatwallawn glotryd	The Camp of Cadwallan the famous,
Yggwarthaf digoll uynyd	On the uplands of Mynydd Digoll,
Seithmis aseithgat beunyd.	Seven months and seven battles each day.[21]

Numerous theories have been put forward about the battle list in the *Historia Brittonum*, and it is not our intention to cover all these in detail. Instead we will give a brief synopsis of the main points for each site and what can be discerned from the known evidence.

The locations given for Arthur's battles in the *Historia Brittonum* can be summarised as follows, and each will be dealt with in its own section:

1. At the mouth of the River Glein.
2,3,4,5. On the river Dubglas in the region of Linnuis.
6. On the river Bassas.
7. In the wood of Celidon (Coed Celyddon).
8. In Castello Guinnion.
9. In Urbes Legiones – the City of Legions.
10. On the shore of the River Tribruit.
11. On the mountain called Agned. (A variant contained within another manuscript gives the site as Mons Breguoin.)
2. On monte Badonis.

The Mouth of the River Glein

This is one of the most obscure references in the list. The river mentioned is sometimes identified as the River Glen in Lincolnshire, owing to the identification of the region Linnius in the following entry as Lincolnshire. This seems a most unlikely place for a battle of a Welsh warrior in the sixth century. The name 'Glein' is, however, preserved in Wales: the village of Gleiniant (the Valley of Glein) is just north of Llanidloes in mid-Wales, and a stream called Nant y Gleiniant (Brook of Gleiniant) flows into the River Trannon, near the village of Trefeglwys. At this site are the remains of the Roman road that ran from Caersws over the hills to Pennal near Machynlleth. This Roman road would have been of obvious strategic importance, and is therefore a likely site for a battle – unlike a river in Lincolnshire.

The River Dubglas in the Region of Linnius

The exact meaning of the region of Linnius in this context is uncertain, although many have tried to identify Linnius with Lincolnshire. A possible explanation may be that 'Linnius' is a Latinised form of a Welsh name in a region that contains one of the many rivers named Dulas in Wales. The exact site of this battle has never been identified, although the River Derwent in Yorkshire has been put forward as a possibility – though it is not one that seems to fit the evidence. The name 'Dubglas' is a Latinisation of the Welsh 'Dulas' and can be found *c.* 1200 in a monastic charter of Abbey Cwmhir (north of Llandrindod Wells), which refers to the River Dulas as *Duglas*.[22] 'Dulas', meaning 'Black Water', is quite a common river name in Wales: the Afon Dulas flows into Liverpool Bay at the town of Llanddulas, and there are two further rivers with this name near Machynlleth and another in Anglesey. Any one of these is a plausible location for Arthur's battle.

The River Bassas

No river of this name is known to have survived anywhere in Britain, and no identification has been convincingly argued for this. The 'Bas' element of the place name, however, has survived at Bassaleg near Newport in South Wales, Baschurch in Shropshire and Basingwerk Abbey near Holywell. Basingwerk is known in Welsh as Dinas Basing (the Fortress of the Descendants of Bassa), and the 'werk' element derives from the old English word 'weorc', meaning an earthwork or fortification – probably in relation to the earthen dyke known as Wat's Dyke nearby. Could this have also lent Bassa's name to stretch of the nearby River Dee? The area around Basingwerk has been the site of several battles over the centuries, situated as it is on the border between England and Wales, not far from the city of Chester; it was also an important fording point across the Dee to the Wirral. The site of Baschurch in Shropshire is referred to in Welsh poetry as 'Eglwyssau Bassa', but there is no river of any note nearby.[23]

The Wood of Celidon (Coed Celyddon)

Coed Celyddon (the wood of Celidon or, in Latin, Silvia Celidonis) has for a long time been identified with the wood of Caledonia (Silva Caledonia or Caledonius Saltus) of the classical historians Tacitus and Pliny, which is thought to have run between Loch Lomond and Dunkeld in Scotland. The similarity in names is beyond doubt, but this alone is insufficient evidence for such a seemingly definite identification. Indeed, scholars have not always accepted this identification, and it has been suggested that there were other forests known as Coed Celyddon. E. K. Chambers thought that 'Celidon might be any forest; perhaps Chiltern',[24] and the Revd A. W. Wade-Evans thought that the name applied to a large tract of woodland that at one time ran 'between the Severn and the Cotswold Hills',[25] with the name 'Celidon' surviving in 'Cheltenham'.

A person named Celyddon Wledig appears in *Culhwch and Olwen* as the grandfather of Culhwch. Could it be that the Coed Celyddon of the Welsh tradition is simply named after the only Celyddon known to that tradition? If so, can an area be found in the earliest Arthurian traditions to give us any clue as to the possible location of the Welsh wood of Celidon? A possible answer can be found in the opening section of *Culhwch and Olwen* concerning the story attached to Celyddon's son, Cilydd. After the death of Goleuddydd, his first wife and the mother of Culhwch, Cilydd decides to seek out another wife and is told by one of his councillors to marry the wife of King Doged. Following this advice, Cilydd kills King Doged and takes possession of both his kingdom and his wife. The only place with any attachment to Doged is a church dedicated to him in the village of Llanddoged (the Church of Doged) near Llanrwst in the Conwy valley. This led P. C. Bartrum to suggest that 'If Doged, the king slain by Cilydd, ruled over territory in the neighbourhood of Llanddoged, a place on the River Conway ... it may be supposed that Cilydd's territory was regarded as being not far from this region.'[26] This possibility finds confirmation in a line from *Y Gododdin* in *The Book of Aneirin* where a warrior named Gorthyn ap Urfai 'of the blood of Cilydd', whose war horses and blood-stained armour were seen around the banks of the River Aled, is referred to as the 'defender of Rhufoniog'. The River Aled runs down from the Denbigh Moors to join the River Elwy to the east of Llanfair Talhaiarn, and the region of Rhufoniog encompasses the high ground on either side of this river and the upper reaches of the River Conwy.

The original name, 'Celyddon', is obviously Welsh, and it also appears within the Welsh *Ystoria Trystan*, concerning the elopement of Trystan ap Tallwch with Essyllt, the wife of King Mark.[27] As we saw earlier, King Mark is known to Welsh tradition as March ap Meirchion, who ruled over part of Gwynedd and is traditionally associated with the Lleyn Peninsula. According to the tale, March goes to see his cousin Arthur to ask for help in finding his wife, who has eloped to Coed Celyddon with Trystan. This suggests that the area covered by the wood of Celidon is again in North Wales. Traditions in the area of the Flintshire/Denbighshire border record in several place names that Mark's father, Meirchion, had strong attachments to the area. As well as Tremeichion (Town of Meirchion) – the earlier version in the Domesday Book being Din Meirchion (the Fortress of Meirchion) – there are also Afon Meirchion (the River of Meirchion), Llys Meirchion (the Court of Meirchion) and Castell Meirchion (the Castle of Meirchion). Trystan's name is remembered in the river called Afon Tryston that runs into the River Dee near Cynwyd, and Carnedd Trystan – no doubt representing Trystan's grave – is said to have been located on Carnedd Llywelyn in Snowdonia.[28]

When the place names and textual evidence are combined, the most likely site for the Coed Celyddon of Welsh tradition is in the area of North Wales bounded by the rivers Clwyd and Conway. In the case of the *Ystoria Trystan*, P. C. Bartrum states that 'it is unlikely that the Caledonian forest is intended in this particular case',[29] and this is a view that has to be taken seriously and extended to other occurrences of this name in Welsh tradition.

Castello Guinnion

This has proved to be the most obscure of the battle sites, and no location has ever been satisfactorily identified. The problem has been the meaning of the word 'Guinnion', but identification becomes much easier when we understand that 'Guinnion' is simply a Latinised form of the Welsh word 'Gwynion'. There are several fortifications in Wales that contain the name 'Gwynion', such as the castle mound of unknown origin at Caeaugwynion Mawr to the south of Denbigh.[30] There is also a hill fort named Carreg Gwynion situated above the village of Llanarmon Dyfryn Ceiriog in the Berwyn mountains,[31] and a farm called Caeugwynion on Offa's

Dyke, the large earthwork that has long been a boundary between the Welsh and the Saxons, near the town of Chirk in north-east Wales.

Urbes Legiones

The name of this site translates as 'City of Legions' or, in Welsh, 'Caerlleon'. It is generally accepted that this reference is to the city of Chester, and other evidence from the later bardic tradition to Arthur fighting in this vicinity makes this particular reference more interesting. Chester was one of the most important cities in Ynys Prydein and was the scene of a later battle between the Britons and the Saxons *c.* AD 600 – some scholars have suggested that the reference in the *Historia Brittonum* is actually to this later battle of Chester. However, there is no firm evidence either way, and it is just possible that, despite all the uncertainty about which particular battles can be attributed to Arthur, he actually did fight a battle in the locality of Chester, though whether it would have been against Saxons, Picts or Scots is open to debate.

The River Tribruit

This entry in the battle list is by far the most interesting, as the Tribuit of the *Historia Brittonum* appears in independent Arthurian material from the earliest traditions. 'Tribruit' is a Latinisation of 'Tryfrwyd', a name found in the poem *Pa Gur?* from *The Black Book of Carmarthen* on two occasions:

Neus tuc manauid	Manawyd brought
Eis tull o trywuid	Shattered timbers back from Tryfrwyd.[32]
Ar traethev Tryvruid	on the shores of Tryfrwyd[33]

The exact meaning of the name is uncertain, but 'Many-Coloured' is a suggestion that is often put forward.[34] No river of this name survives in Wales, a fact made all the more frustrating as this is the only battle that can be independently verified as associated with Arthur from Welsh tradition. The site remains unidentified.

The Mountain Called Agned

This is another location that remains unidentified. The only other reference to this site can be found in *Brut y Brenhinedd*, where the building of a castle there is attributed to the pre-Christian king Efrog: 'And then the king built Caer Efrog, Caer Alclut and Castell Mynydd Agned, which is now called Castell Morwynyon [Maidens] on Mynydd Dolurus.'[35]

Mons Breguion

This battle site occurs only in the Vatican manuscript of *Historia Brittonum*, in place of the mountain called Agned noted above. The name might be a Latinised form of 'Brewyn', which is the name of a battle site of Urien Rheged in a poem from *The Book of Taliesin* – '*Kat gellawr brewyn*' – 'A battle in the huts of Brewyn'[36] – and it has been suggested that this battle found its way into the list of Arthur's battles by mistake.[37]

The Roman settlement of Bravonium at Leintwardine on the Welsh borders was suggested as a possible site as far back as 1905.[38] The name 'Brewyn' was considered by T. Gwynn Jones to be a mutated form of 'Berwyn', which raises the possibility that the battle may have happened at a site on the Berwyn mountains of North Wales.[39] Although many historians have tried to link the names in the battle list with Roman forts, it is more likely that the original sites existed in more minor locations, and a study of field and stream names is more likely to bring results.

Mons Badonis

The battle of Badon is the most widely discussed battle of the Dark Age period, owing to its being named in the earliest source for the period, the *De Excidio* of Gildas. Gildas wrote his work *c.* 540, and states that the Britons were under the rule of the Saxons *'usque ad annum obsessionis Badonici montis'* – 'up to the year of the siege of the Badonic hill'.[40] He also states that Mons Badonis was 'pretty well the last defeat of the villains, and certainly not the least',[41] but he does not name the leader of the British armies.

Although several locations have been suggested for this battle, the true site still remains obscure. There is no context for the site of the battle in the *De Excidio*, but in Welsh tradition the battle of Badon is first mentioned in an Arthurian context in the *Annales Cambriae* under the entry for the year 516: *'Bellum Badonis in quo Arthur portauit crucem Domini nostri Iesu Christi tribus diebus & tribus noctibus in humeros suos & Brittones uictores fuerunt'* – 'The Battle of Badon, in which Arthur carried the cross of our Lord Jesus Christ for three days and three nights on his shoulders, and the Britons were victorious'.[42]

There are no clues as to the geographical location of the battle from this chronicle, whereas the next source is quite specific. *The Dream of Rhonabwy* describes the route taken by Arthur and his warriors on the way to Caer Faddon, the Welsh name for Badon. 'And then they traversed the great plain of Agryngroeg as far as Rhyd-y-Groes on the Severn. And a mile from the ford, on either side of the roads, they could see the tents and pavilions and the mustering of a great host. And they came to the bank of the ford. They could see Arthur seated on a flat island below the ford.'[43]

The plain of Agryngroeg has been identified with the two places called Gungrog fawr and Gungrog fach just to the north of Welshpool. Rhyd-y-Groes is mentioned in the *Brut y Tywysogion* under the year 1039 and has been identified with the ford over the River Severn in the vicinity of the village of Buttington to the east of Welshpool.[44]

Later in the story one of the riders exclaims 'that it was to him a greater marvel how there should be here at this very hour those who promised to be in the battle of Badon by mid-day'.[45] This implies that the site of Badon is not far away. The next section of the story enables us to be more specific, as the soldiers set out 'in the direction of Cefyn Digoll'.[46] Cefyn Digoll is recorded as being the old name for Long Mountain, the hill above Buttington to the east.[47] Soon after setting out, 'Arthur and his host of the Mighty had descended below Caer Faddon'.[48] This material suggests that the site of Caer Faddon is very close to Long Mountain, and one possible site is the conspicuous hill known today as Breidden – a suggestion we put forward in our previous work.[49] On the summit of Breidden are the remains of several fortifications that have been excavated in recent years and show evidence of occupation at this period.

In their translation of *The Mabinogion*, T. P. Ellis and John Edward Lloyd (the latter of whom later wrote *A History of Wales*, one of the standard works on the subject) include the following note: 'The peculiar character of the story indicates, we think, the locality, or traditional locality, in which the site of Badon might be sought, that is, somewhere within half a day's march of Rhyd-y-

Map 4 ARTHUR'S BATTLE SITES

Groes on the Severn.'[50] We agree with this opinion. Despite the other oddities included within its text, *The Dream of Rhonabwy* does appear to contain geographical elements that are far too detailed and precise to not be derived from some pre-existing knowledge. The site of Badon as far as the Welsh were concerned in the twelfth century was near Welshpool, whether or not this battle was originally attached to Arthur.

Caer Faddon is also mentioned by the *Gogynfeirdd* poet Cynddelw Brydydd Mawr, but no geographical clues other than that the battle seems to have taken place in Wales can be gleaned from this.[51] It should be pointed out that Arthur is never actually associated with this battle by the *Gogynfeirdd* poets, and Badon or Caer Faddon is never mentioned in the Triads – unlike the battle of Camlan, which is always associated with Arthur from the *Annales Cambriae* onwards, but is suspiciously absent from the *Historia Brittonum*. In the earliest reference to the battle of Badon in the work of Gildas the British leader remains anonymous, yet by the time of its appearance in the *Historia* it has found its way into the list of Arthur's battles. Whether or not it actually belongs there will always be a matter of opinion.

ARTHUR'S BATTLES FROM THE WELSH POETIC TRADITION

As we have seen, the battle list associated with Arthur in the *Historia Brittonum* is probably a compendium of battle names from earlier traditions, very few of which are likely to have much to do with him. We must now turn to the Welsh poetic traditions regarding his battles.

The most striking point raised by the Welsh poems is that, unlike the Latin texts (and some later Welsh prose texts), they *never* refer to Arthur as fighting Saxons or Picts, and where the enemies of Arthur are identified they all appear to be of British origin. This leads us to wonder whether the reference to Saxon enemies in the *Historia Brittonum* is an addition to the battle list at a later date (perhaps reflecting the situation then current), or whether the battle list should even be associated with Arthur at all. The only battle named that has a direct link to Arthur in Welsh tradition is that of Tryfrwyd (the Tribruit of the battle list in the *Historia Brittonum*), although the other battles mentioned the *Historia Brittonum* may well have belonged to other British heroes either before or after the time of Arthur. Early references to battles with an Arthurian context can be found in *Culhwch and Olwen*, the poems entitled *Geraint ap Erbin* and *Pa Gur?*, and the corpus of later bardic poetry. These references were obviously to battle sites known by the audience of the day, even if modern readers are unsure of their exact locations.

Within *Culhwch and Olwen* there are obscure references to Arthur fighting people whom we now know nothing about – for example, 'I was there of old when thou didst slay the war-band of Gleis son of Merin, when thou didst slay Mil the Black, son of Dugum.'[52] The only faint clue we have in connection with this is that the name 'Merin' is found in Gwynedd at Bodferin near Clynnog-fawr.[53]

There is also the reference in *Culhwch and Olwen* to the remains of a saga concerning the death of Cai and the vengeance wrought by Arthur on the perpetrators – Cai was 'slain by

Gwyddog ap Menestyr, whom Arthur slew, as well as his brothers, in vengeance for Cai'.[54] This event is made even more interesting because in the same tale we are told that Arthur had offended Cai by composing a satirical song regarding Cai's victory over the giant Dillus Farfog, suggesting that Cai could not have slain him if the giant had not been asleep – a great insult. We are also told that the warriors of Prydein had trouble in making peace between Cai and Arthur, and that 'even when that was done Cai would have nothing to do with Arthur in his time of need from that time forward'.[55] This is very different from the story portrayed in the pages of Geoffrey of Monmouth's *Historia*, where Cai is killed at Chinon in France, while fighting fictitious battles on the Continent.

Glewlwyd, the gatekeeper at Arthur's court in *Culhwch and Olwen*, lists the places he has been with Arthur. The only place named in this list that is known elsewhere in an Arthurian context is 'Caer Oeth ac Anoeth', the references to which are obscure. The remainder of the list is of unknown places connected with stories from the original traditions that are now lost to us.

'Caer Oeth ac Anoeth' is generally taken to mean 'the Difficult and Extremely Difficult Fortress.' We are told in the Triads that Arthur 'was three nights in the prison of Caer Oeth ac Anoeth' and also 'was three nights imprisoned by Gwen Pendragon, and three nights in an enchanted prison under the Stone of Echymeint'; he was released from all three by his cousin Goreu.[56] The graves of the war-band of Caer Oeth ac Anoeth are stated in 'The Stanzas of the Graves' to be at Gwanas, a mountainous area to the south of Dolgellau near the mountain Cadair Idris, thereby associating them with North Wales:

Teulu oeth ac anoeth a dyuu ynoeth	The war-band of Oeth and Anoeth came thither
Y eu gur y eu guas	To their servant;
Ae ceisso vy clated guanas	Let him who would seek them, dig Gwanas.[57]

Llongborth

We know the battle of Llongborth only from the poem entitled *Geraint filius Erbin* (Geraint the son of Erbin) that survives in *The Black Book of Carmarthen*, *The Red Book of Hergest* and a fragment from *The White Book of Rhydderch*:

> In Llongborth I saw Arthur
> Brave men used to slay with steel
> Emperor(?), the leader in battle.
>
> In Llongborth were slain to Geraint
> Brave men from the region of Dyfnaint;
> And though they might be slain, they slew.[58]

Scholars trying to identify Geraint as a man named Geruntius of Dumnonia, mentioned in a letter from Bishop Aldhelm of Wessex in 705, have obscured the identification of this Welsh hero.[59] Their extremely unlikely identification has led to the general belief that the battle of Llongborth took place at Langport in Somerset. Geraint the son of Erbin dates from the sixth century, as does Arthur, and the reference to 'the region of Dyfnaint' has been presumed to mean Devon – part of the Latin Dumnonia – in order to link Geruntius and Geraint. 'Dyfnaint' or 'Dyfneint' is a name found at several different locations in Wales, and although it was used to denote a region of the south-west peninsula of England in later material, it is unlikely that this is the location intended in this poem.[60]

The name 'Llongborth' can also be read as 'Ship Port' or 'Harbour' – a meaning lent weight by the Triads, which refer to Geraint as one of the 'three sea-farers of Ynys Prydein'.[61] Welsh historians have long located the site of the battle of Llongborth near the village of Tresaith to the north of Cardigan, on the west coast of Wales. Theophilus Evans in 1740 stated that 'It is the judgement of some that the place which the bard calls Llongporth is Llamporth in the parish of Penbryn in Ceredigion. There is a place near there commonly called Maesglas, but the old name was Maes-y-llas (The Field of the Killing) or Maes Galanas (The Field of the Massacre). There is another site in the neighbourhood, in the parish of Penbryn, called Perth Geriant.'[62]

Until the end of the eleventh century the name Din Geraint (the Fortress of Geraint) was given to the site now occupied by Cardigan Castle, and in the vicinity of the castle are places called Bedd Geraint (the Grave of Geraint) and Betws Geraint (the Prayerhouse of Geraint). This shows that a genuine tradition placing Geraint in Cardiganshire existed at an early date, and any association of the Geraint in Welsh sources with Devon is due to a misidentification with another person named Geraint who lived 150 years later.

Caer Llwydcoed

The Latin text of Geoffrey's *Historia* contains a Welsh name for an Arthurian battle not found in the earlier *Historia Brittonum*. This battle site is called Kaerluideoit, which in modern Welsh would be Caer Llwydcoed (Fort of the Grey Wood). That Geoffrey adds the line 'now known as Lincoln'[63] may be because this was the diocese of his ecclesiastical superior, Bishop Alexander, to whom certain versions of his work were dedicated, and also the diocese within which Oxford, his place of writing, fell. This is another strong piece of evidence for manipulation of not only the events recorded, but also the geography portrayed. But where did Geoffrey find the name for this battle?

The only other source to mention this battle site in connection with Arthur is the *The History of Gruffudd ap Cynan*. This text dates from the mid twelfth century, and within its pages it notes the only defeat associated with Arthur. It states that he 'fought twelve notable battles against the Saxons and the Picts: in the first of them he was vanquished and a fugitive because of treachery in Caer Lwytgoed (this place was Dinas y Llwyn Llwyt): in other contests he was victorious, and deservedly paid in kind his oppressors'.[64]

The only thing that Geoffrey seems to have used is the actual name of the battle: everything else narrated about it in the pages of his *Historia* is for the glory of the town associated with his patrons, upon whom his future status and wealth depended. Whether Geoffrey ever had any more information apart from the name, from some written or oral Welsh source, we will probably never know.

Even with the help of this early source the exact site remains elusive, but the name 'Llwytgoed' appears on at least three occasions in Welsh manuscripts. It appears as the name of an estate near Mochdre in North Wales in a document from 1334 known as *The Survey of Denbigh*,[65] and also for a place near Aberdare in South Wales. The most interesting appearance of the name, however, is its being given to a piece of parkland in Hopedale, a region to the north-west of Wrexham, including the towns of Hope and Caergwrle. Documents exist for the enclosure of 'the wood of Loidcoid', and as there are several fortified hill tops in this area, which borders England, this is a very likely site for a battle in the sixth century.[66]

Completing the picture is a reference by the bard Bleddyn Fardd to his brother fighting 'like Arthur at Caer Fenlli',[67] which can be identified with the hill fort on the summit of Foel Fenlli in the Clwydian hills between Mold and Ruthin in north-east Wales, further enhancing the geographical framework outlined above.

Scholars have searched for the battles of Arthur all over Britain, and little consensus has been reached about their locations. The preceding chapters have narrowed down the area in which to look, and this chapter has shown that many of the names can be found in Wales in forms much closer to those in the original documents than some of the earlier identifications. The current state of place-name studies in Wales is far behind that in England: some areas have never had studies published. Until detailed place-name studies exist for every Welsh parish the geography of the Welsh sources will remain vague, and so will the sites of battles and graves associated with the heroes whom the sources record.

7

ARTHUR THE WARLORD

VEN if not fully aware of the details, everyone with an interest in western history or literature is familiar with some aspect of the Round Table of Arthurian romance and with the famous figures associated with it. The most celebrated names are those of Sir Galahad and Lancelot of the Lake – knights invented in the twelfth century by the authors of the French Grail romances and inseparable from the name of Arthur since the time of Malory. In the later Arthurian legends the Knights of the Round Table are Arthur's loyal servants and brothers in arms – embarking on quests and bringing peace and justice in his name. But, although this concept contains some residue of the close ties between lord and war-band in Arthur's day, the Knights of the Round Table have little in common with the Dark Age figures from which they originate.

As mentioned in Chapter 1, the Round Table first appears in Arthurian literature in 1155, in the *Roman de Brut* of Wace. Wace's description of the Round Table is based upon the courtly life and etiquette of his own day and represents a world far removed from that inhabited by a sixth-century Welsh warrior.

From the twelfth century on, the Round Table became a symbol of chivalry, loyalty and accomplishment throughout the medieval age – as the great table at Winchester testifies – and it has remained embedded for ever in the British psyche. The remains of the Roman amphitheatre at Caerleon in South Wales were long known as Arthur's Round Table, until excavation in the 1920s disproved this claim, and a garden feature in the grounds of Stirling Castle was referred to as Arthur's Table as far back as 1478. The Round Table itself, like many other famous Arthurian relics, can be disregarded in the search for the origins of Arthur, but what of the knights who sat around it? Can they be found in the earliest traditions?

Before considering the original warriors of Arthur it is first necessary to understand the background of the warrior societies in the period in question. In sixth-century Britain there were no knights in shining armour, no jousting and no great military organisation that enabled campaigns with huge armies such as are portrayed in the pages of Geoffrey of Monmouth. Arthur belonged to a time when a war-band of 300 was considered impressive, a time when the war cries of Briton, Pict, Scot and Saxon echoed across the west, and when the drumming of horse's hooves and the chink of chain mail heralded death and destruction. This was not a time of all-conquering Continental campaigns as described in the *Historia Regum Britanniae*, but one of civil war, invasion and constant raiding.

The central theme of later Arthurian legends is the adventures of Arthur and his Knights of the Round Table; Arthur's court provides little more than a background to these exploits. As previously shown, Geoffrey had access to early Welsh material, and it is within this that the names of many of Arthur's famous companions originate. A clue to the origins of Arthur's war-band can be found in *Brut y Brenhinedd*, the Welsh version of Geoffrey's *Historia*. Within this source the companions and warriors surrounding Arthur are referred to as his *teulu*, a term which in modern Welsh means 'family', but which in medieval Welsh was also used to mean a 'retinue' or 'war-band'. The Welsh sources for the medieval period abound with references to the actions of the *teulu* of various leaders, lords and kings – laying waste to kingdoms; raiding towns, villages, churches and courts; burning, pillaging and marauding through the chronicles, annals and heroic poetry of the age – attesting to the continuous nature of warfare and its primary place in the society of this time.

Living in our comfortable modern civilisation, it is hard to imagine the scene of a Dark Age battle – the horrendous sound of shattering spears, cleaved shields and steel on steel as two opposing shield walls clashed, man after man stepping forward to fill the gaping holes left by his fallen brothers in the to and fro of battle; the immense crush as hundreds of men pressed rank against rank into the mêlée, each side exerting all its strength to try to break the opposing wall, to hack a path through the enemy, knowing that the first side to break was virtually doomed. When the centre of the shield wall collapsed or the line became overstretched and outflanked by the enemy, the real slaughter began and the battle was over very quickly. The broken enemy forces were run down, and few, if any, survivors were left.

The weapons used for this type of warfare were brutal, designed to split a man in half or to run him through, leaving him to die in agony. To protect against these, many of the warriors would have had only the most rudimentary leather armour or none at all. Most warriors would have been armed with little more than a shield and a spear: the swords and the small amounts of armour, helmets and mail available at the time would have been reserved for the high-born and professional warrior class. Shields were used as a weapon as well as for defence, the boss being used to smash the enemy to the ground and to clear the way for the blade or spear. Cavalry were of limited use in this type of warfare, coming into their own only once the shield wall was broken and the routed enemy could be cut down with ease.

Thus the type of warfare that took place in the sixth century was not the romances' ritualised tournaments with flying heraldic pennants, but bloody carnage in which acts of extreme bravery were not only expected but demanded. This was the context in which, come defeat, the last few heroes of the war-band would assemble around their lord and sell their lives dearly in his defence. Even after his death they would fight on, refusing the option of retreat and the eternal shame of outliving their lord. What was the driving force behind this warrior culture and the heroic acts recorded in song by the bards?

The military structure of Dark Age Britain was very similar regardless of ethnic group. Every king had his war-band or retinue of highly trained professional warriors, which was the mainstay of his prestige and power. (On the Continent a similar system was in force: in France the Merovingian kings had their *leudes*, the Saxons had their *heorogeneatas* or 'hearth companions', and the term applied to this personal retinue in Latin sources is *comitatus*.) The role and entitlements of every person in Welsh society are outlined in great detail in the Welsh laws, and the *teulu* was an integral part of that society. The most important of the twenty-four officers at the Welsh royal court was the *penteulu* (chief of the *teulu*), whose worth was considered to be one-third of that of the king. He was responsible for the bodyguard of the king and the organisation of warriors to go on raids, and he would occupy the hall in the king's absence.[1]

The *teulu* consisted of young men from the local area who at the age of majority (fourteen) were pledged to the local lord or king. Their future status and advancement depended entirely upon their relationship with that lord and their total loyalty to him. There are allusions to rulers making use of renowned warriors from outside their locality, and as a chieftain or king grew in stature and renown he would be able to draw on warriors from a wider area. Once accepted into the service of their lord, the young men lived a good life, with rights and privileges well above those of an ordinary man – including entitlement to a part of the plunder from raiding expeditions and other bounty of warfare. However, their place at the lord's table and their enjoyment of his gifts and generosity came at a price: the frequent fighting and raiding of the *teulu* meant that many men died young and few lived to old age.[2]

One of the best-known war-bands in Welsh literature is that of Mynyddog Mwynfawr, as immortalised in the poem *Y Gododdin*. After feasting at their lord's table for a year, the warriors ride to death and glory against the men of Deifyr and Bryneich at a battle site known as Catraeth. Only three of them return to tell the tale.[3] *Y Gododdin* extols the spirit and behaviour expected from these professional warriors as one by one, stanza by stanza, it celebrates in song the heroes of the battle of Catraeth, their reputations, deeds and bravery, and ultimately their deaths on the battlefield.

The average size of a war-band was 120 men, but *Y Gododdin* tells us on many occasions that over 300 men went to Catraeth, and near the end of the poem it states that the exact number was 363 – three *teulu* and the three survivors.[4]

The Triads record the *teulu* of other Welsh rulers and emphasise the lengths to which they would go for their lord:

> Three Faithful Teulu of the Island of Britain:
> The teulu of Cadwallawn son of Cadfan, who were with him
> seven years in Ireland; and in all that time they did not ask him for
> anything, lest they should be compelled to leave him;
> and the second, the teulu of Gafran son of Aeddan, who went to
> sea for their lord;
> and the third, the teulu of Gwenddolau son of Ceidiaw at
> Arderydd, who continued the battle for a fortnight and a month
> after their lord was slain.[5]

The purpose, function and strict honour code of the *teulu* created a bond of honour – a bond stronger than blood ties, fear and even life itself; a bond that, if broken, would lead to total disgrace and dishonour, not just within the offender's own lifetime but also down through the ages:

> Three Faithless Teulu of the Realm:
> The teulu of Goronwy the Radiant of (Penllyn), who refused to
> receive the poisoned spear from Lleu Skilful-Hand on behalf of
> their lord, at the Stone of Goronwy at the head of Cynfal;
> and the teulu of Gwrgi and Peredur, who abandoned their lord at
> Caer Greu, when they had an appointment to fight the next day
> with Eda Great-Knee; and there they were both slain;
> and the teulu of Alan Fyrgan, who turned away from him by
> night, and let him go with his servants to Camlan. And there he
> was slain.[6]

In Welsh tradition the *teulu* of other leaders are just as important as Arthur's war-band – in many cases more so.

The concept of a group of warriors who were loyal to their lord and undertook raids against the enemy was adapted by the writers of the twelfth century to become that of a band of knights in armour who embarked on quests to prove their purity and adherence to the code of chivalry. Another example of the development of an idea from its humble and rather brutal origins in the sixth century is the way in which Arthur evolved to become a king. A quick look at the different titles attached to Arthur in the earliest Welsh traditions shows that his people considered him to be a military commander, not a monarch.

Y Gododdin

The poem names Arthur in a comparative sense, in the line 'though he was no Arthur',[7] indicating that Arthur was considered to be a great warrior. No actual title is attached to him.

Annales Cambriae

Arthur is named twice in these annals – by name only; no title is attached to him. As both entries refer to his fighting battles, we can assume that he was renowned for his prowess in combat.

Historia Brittonum

In the various versions of this text Arthur is portrayed as '*dux bellorum*' (literally 'leader of battles'), indicating that he was a military chief of some repute. A version of the manuscript in Cambridge describes Arthur as follows: 'though there were many more noble than himself, yet he was twelve times chosen their commander and was often a conqueror'.[8] This indicates that Arthur was not considered to be descended from the most noble bloodlines and was therefore not a king but a great leader in battle – a job he was chosen to do, not one that he had a right to by birth.

Culhwch and Olwen

The oldest Arthurian tale portrays Arthur as '*Penn Teyrned yr Ynys honn*' – 'Chief Lord of the Realm (or Island)'. The Welsh word for king is '*Brenin*', a word never found associated with Arthur in the earliest Welsh sources.

Geraint filius Erbin

This poem from *The Black Book of Carmarthen* gives Arthur the title '*ameraudur*', a Welsh version of the Latin term '*imperator*' ('military commander'). Some translations use the term 'emperor', but this is a rather grandiose title for the context of the poem and a bit misleading.

Not one of these sources calls Arthur a king. The first instance of this title being attached to him occurs in *The Life of St Cadog*, written by the Cambro-Norman cleric Llifris of Llancarfan *c.* 1080. In this Arthur is called 'the most illustrious king of Britannia',[9] which in this text means Wales, not Britain.

The evidence above indicates that in Welsh tradition Arthur was widely considered to be a warlord of some renown. A warlord of sixth-century Wales would have had a role very similar to that of the *penteulu,* as described in the Welsh laws – commanding the armies and being second only to the king, but not a king himself. That Arthur had such a role conforms to the customs of the day, provides a vital clue as to his true identity, and answers one of the most persistent questions to dog the study of a historical Arthur: If Arthur is the historical figure attested to by the *Annales Cambriae* and the *Historia Brittonum*, why is he not named in the only historical record we have for sixth-century Britain, the *De Excidio* of Gildas?

Gildas was a monk renowned for his wisdom, and references to him in Irish chronicles and ecclesiastical works show that his reputation was widespread.[10] The *De Excidio*, written *c.* 540, was primarily concerned with the state of affairs in western Britain at the time and focuses upon five kings whom the author berates for their tyrannical ways. Before launching into his attack, Gildas gives a short potted history of Britain up to his day, from the arrival of Christianity, through the Roman occupation, to the period of chaos that followed with invasions by Picts and Saxons. Gildas's text is very important to historians, as it is the only native source of any note that provides any information about the state of British affairs in the period after the withdrawal of the Roman legions, and in the eighth century it was the major source for Bede's *Historia Ecclesiastica Gentis Anglorum*, in itself one of the main sources for the *Anglo-Saxon Chronicle*, which was put together in the tenth century and details the history of England from Roman times. These works were then used by the Norman historians Henry of Huntingdon and William of Malmesbury, upon which much of our knowledge of pre-Norman Britain is based. What it is important to remember, however, is that Gildas was not a historian but a man of the church, and the purpose of *De Excidio* was not to write a history of Britain but to attack the leaders of his day: the history he wrote was intended merely as an introduction to the main section of his work. We rely upon it so heavily because it is the only native source of any note we have for this period.

During his tirade, Gildas relates that the kings of Britannia are tyrants.[11] The major reason for his hatred towards them is their belligerence: these kings 'wage wars – civil and unjust'.[12] The men who lead these armies into battle, says Gildas, 'despise the harmless and humble, but exalt to the stars, so far as they can, their military companions [*commanipulares*], bloody, proud and murderous men, adulterers and enemies of God'.[13] The Latin term '*commanipulares*', used to denote the warlords of these kings' war-bands, could be viewed as an equivalent to the Welsh term '*penteulu*'. The five kings are clearly named, and the geographical regions over which they ruled are either mentioned or can be identified from other sources:

Constantinus, the ruler of Dumnonia, the south-west peninsula of England.

Aurelius Caninus. His kingdom is not named, but is thought to have been in Powys, along the border between what are now England and Wales.

Vortiper, tyrant of the kingdom of Demetia in South Wales. His gravestone was uncovered in the churchyard of Castelldwyran near Carmarthen in 1895.

Cuneglasus, of the Bear's Stronghold, has been identified with Cynlas Goch, the ruler of Rhos in North Wales, the Bear's Stronghold being the hill fort of Dinarth (Fortress of the Bear) on the North Wales coast.

Maglocunus, better known as Maelgwn Gwynedd, the king of Gwynedd, which covered most of North Wales.

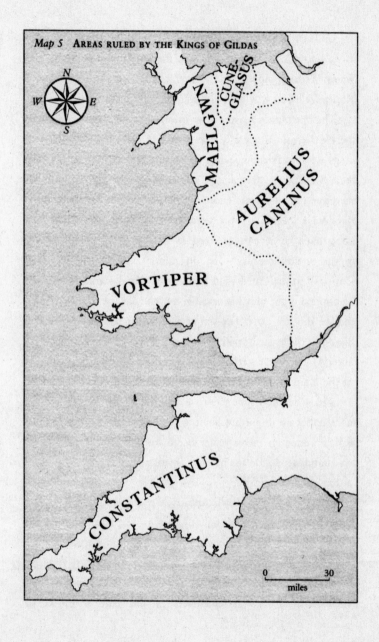

Map 5 AREAS RULED BY THE KINGS OF GILDAS

N
W E
S

MAELGWN

CUNE-GLASUS

AURELIUS CANINUS

VORTIPER

CONSTANTINUS

0   30
miles

Gildas was primarily concerned not with the whole of Britain as we know it today, but only with the south-west peninsula and Wales. We have shown that the family of Arthur was focused upon North Wales, so why does Gildas neglect to mention him?

The most likely reason why Arthur does not rate a mention in the *De Excidio* is actually very simple. Gildas names only those kings who were ruling when he wrote, and Arthur, as we have seen, was not a king but a *penteulu* or war leader and was therefore not significant enough to be mentioned. For years historians have looked in vain for a powerful king who could have undertaken the events ascribed to Arthur in the Latin sources of the twelfth century – fighting battles against Saxons, from Cornwall to the Caledonian Forest in Scotland – and as he is not mentioned in the only historical text of the day they have assumed that he did not exist. The simple fact is that before the Norman hijacking of the Arthurian tradition Arthur was merely a warlord, and if Gildas was aware of him it was in all likelihood only as one of the many *commanipulares* mentioned in *De Excidio*. Such an awareness is impossible to prove, as none of the military men is named, but the important point to be made is that in origin Arthur was a minor character remembered for successfully leading his war-band into battle against other British enemies, not for keeping at bay the Saxon invaders.

Nowhere in the Welsh Arthurian poetic tradition is there a direct reference to Arthur fighting Saxons. The battles ascribed to him in the *Historia Brittonum* were dealt with in the last chapter; the only other references to the conflicts of Arthur are found in Welsh sources, where he fights only British (and possibly Irish) enemies. If Arthur was remembered as the leader of the British resistance against the Germanic invaders, why are there no references to this fact in Welsh material? Even in the Lives of the Welsh saints (the first sources to crown him king) he is only ever represented in conflict with British opposition. This lack of evidence from Welsh sources also explains why Arthur is never mentioned by Bede or by the authors of the *Anglo-Saxon Chronicle*, the chroniclers of the very people he was supposedly fighting against. They never mention him for the very simple reason that the Saxons, whose history they record, never fought against him. The evidence shows that the conflicts involving Arthur took place during the civil wars of the rulers of Wales, in the first half of the sixth century.

. Gildas states that following the battle of Badon, where the Britons inflicted a huge defeat on the Saxons, there was a period of peace from Saxon incursions. But, with no external enemy to fight, the rulers turned against themselves, and it is this period that is traditionally assigned to the emergence of Arthur.[14] Is it possible that Arthur could have been a *penteulu* under one of the kings named by Gildas? If so, which one? Gildas tells us that one king was particularly renowned above all others for battles against his neighbours; the ruler concerned is Maelgwn Gwynedd.

Gildas singles out Maelgwn Gwynedd as 'higher than almost all the generals of Britannia, in your kingdom as in your physique',[15] and goes on to say that Maelgwn has 'removed many . . . tyrants from their country and even their life'.[16] Apart from the details given in *De Excidio* we know very little about the exploits of the other four kings named, but Maelgwn appears both in Welsh poetry and in the Lives of the Welsh saints as fighting in the southern half of Wales, outside his kingdom of Gwynedd, on many occasions.[17] The locations associated with his family in Chapter 4 suggest that Arthur originated from Gwynedd. As the most powerful ruler of the day ruled the same kingdom, could not Arthur have led the war-bands under the king of Gwynedd? The *Annales Cambriae* state that Maelgwn died in 547 and Arthur in 539, placing them in the same era.[18] The Lives of the Welsh saints are primarily concerned with saints from South Wales, and the two people who most often come into conflict with them are Maelgwn Gwynedd and Arthur. Maelgwn was invading the south from North Wales. Could Arthur have been doing the same, perhaps on Maelgwn's behalf?

Gildas associates each of the five kings he berates with an animal. Four of them are called lioness, lion, leopard and bear, but Maelgwn is referred to as '*insularis draco*' – 'the dragon of the island'.[19] Could this title have been the origin of the Welsh term 'Pendragon'? The other references to the title in Welsh tradition ascribe it to rulers of Gwynedd, and the poem *Pa Gur?*, in which it first appears, is also concerned primarily with Gwynedd. Although we have no evidence that the term was ever actually ascribed to Arthur himself, we must wonder whether the *penteulu* of the army of the 'dragon of the island' might have been referred to as the 'pendragon'. Unfortunately this possibility must remain in the realms of speculation, as we have no sources available to take this reasoning any further, but it would seem to make sense of what evidence we do have and to correspond with the geography of the earliest Arthurian traditions.

8

THE LOST SAGA OF CAMLAN AND THE DEATH OF ARTHUR

Then the king looked about him, and then was he ware, of all his host and of all his good knights, were left no more alive but two knights; that one was Sir Lucan the Butler, and his brother Sir Bedivere, and they were full sore wounded. Jesu mercy, said the king, where are all my noble knights become? Alas that ever I should see this doleful day, for now, said Arthur, I am come to mine end. But would to God that I wist where were that traitor Sir Mordred, that hath caused all this mischief. Then was King Arthur ware where Sir Mordred leaned upon his sword among a great heap of dead men. Now give me my spear, said Arthur unto Sir Lucan, for yonder I have espied the traitor that all this woe hath wrought. Sir, let him be, said Sir Lucan, for he is unhappy; and if ye pass this unhappy day ye shall be right well revenged upon him. Good lord, remember ye of your night's dream, and what the spirit of Sir Gawaine told you this night, yet God of his great goodness hath preserved you hitherto. Therefore, for God's sake, my lord, leave off by this, for blessed be God ye have won the field, for here we be three alive, and with Sir Mordred is none alive; and if you leave off now this wicked day of destiny is past.[1]

O it is that Malory records the closing moments of Arthur's final battle, with Arthur lying mortally wounded among the heaped and broken bodies, the only members of his great retinue to survive him being Bedivere and his brother Lucan. Of the opposing force only Medrod remains standing, leaning exhausted on his sword among a mound of the dead and dying. Seeing Medrod, Arthur, despite his wounds, demands his spear from Lucan and, taking it in both hands, makes one final attack, delivering retribution on his nemesis. Thrusting beneath his opponent's shield, Arthur impales Medrod, who, knowing his death blow has been delivered, thrusts himself further on Arthur's spear and in a final act of vengeance delivers Arthur a crushing blow to the side of the head, cleaving his helmet and opening his skull before sinking corpselike to the ground.

Lying injured on the battlefield, Arthur commands Bedivere to take his sword, Excalibur, and throw it into the nearby lake. Bedivere pleads with Arthur not to return Excalibur to the waters, but twice leaves and returns saying that he has done as bid. Arthur asks what he saw when he threw the sword into the lake, and Bedivere replies that he saw nothing. Knowing that Bedivere has not done as he was asked, Arthur orders him one final time to throw the sword in the lake. This time Bedivere obeys, and sees an arm emerge from the waters to grasp the sword and carry it to the depths, bringing to an end the reign of the mighty King Arthur. Malory's text goes on to relate the arrival of a mystical ship occupied by three queens: Morgana la Fay (the sister of Arthur), the Queen of the Wastelands and the Queen of North Wales. As Arthur sails into the western sunset, his final words to Bedivere make his destination clear: 'for I will into the vale of Avilion to heal me of my grievous wound'.[2]

These are the events of Arthur's last battle as portrayed in numerous, novels, films and plays over the centuries, and alongside the sword-in-the-stone episode they form the best-known series of events in romantic Arthurian literature. But it should be stressed that Malory wrote a work of literature, not history, deftly weaving together all the romance material available to him to create one of the classics of the English language.

Malory's account of Arthur's last battle sets it upon an unspecified area of Salisbury Plain in southern England and is fundamentally different from the version related by Geoffrey of Monmouth in the *Historia Regum Britannia*. Geoffrey tells us that, while Arthur is campaigning in Gaul, Medrod seizes the crown and marries Gwenhwyfar. Arthur returns to Britain and, after a number of engagements, drives Medrod to the River Camblanus in Cornwall. Next Arthur divides his force into nine companies and, following a hard-fought battle, eventually breaks through the enemy lines to slay Medrod.[3] Arthur himself is mortally wounded and hands the crown of Britain to his cousin Constantine, the son of Cador, Duke of Cornwall. The final reference to Arthur has him carried off 'to the Isle of Avalon, so that his wounds might be attended to'.[4] Further variations concerning the battle and its location can be found among the mass of later Arthurian romances, but what concerns us is the material on which Geoffrey was basing his version of the story, as this was the basis for all the later romantic fiction.

Before his account of Camlan, Geoffrey gives us the following clue as to this source:

About this particular matter, most noble Duke, Geoffrey of Monmouth prefers to say nothing. He will, however, in his own poor style and without wasting words, describe the battle which our most famous King fought against his nephew, once he had returned to Britain after his victory; for that he found in the British treatise already referred to. He heard it, too, from Walter of Oxford, a man most learned in all branches of history.[5]

As we have already seen, 'the British treatise already referred to' is a Welsh source, and the only place that had written and oral traditions regarding Camlan in the early twelfth century was Wales. By the time Malory wrote his version of the Arthurian legends, Camlan – along with many other pieces of the original Arthurian tradition – had long been obscured, submerged under layers of Continental romance and propaganda. But Camlan survives as Arthur's most famous battle in Welsh literature, and it is from the fragments of this surviving tradition, preserved within the history and literature of Arthur's own people, that the facts must be sought.

The Lost Saga of Camlan

Traditional Welsh sources contain references to Camlan that enable us to piece together an outline of why and where the battle took place. The evidence of the Triads and other Welsh sources indicates that there was an extremely strong tradition concerning Arthur's last battle, completely independent of Geoffrey's *Historia*, until as late as the sixteenth century, and the numerous differences between this tradition and Geoffrey's narrative are of great interest.

The Welsh claim that the battle was started because of an argument between two sisters, and Medrod – the villain in Malory

– is portrayed as a hero. It is details such as this, in conjunction with other Welsh traditions, that have led some scholars to believe in the one-time existence of a Welsh saga, now lost, concerning Arthur's last battle: 'There may well have been a chwedl [saga] of Camlan, alluded to, not always seriously, in another triadic grouping in *Culhwch ac Olwen*, but which was, nevertheless, an integral part of the Welsh legend of Arthur.'[6]

The earliest surviving reference to Camlan is found in the *Annales Cambriae* under the year 539. This does not state that Arthur killed Medrod: just that both of them died at the battle – 'The battle of Camlan in which Arthur & Medraut fell'.[7] The sources that contain the most detailed information regarding Camlan, however, are the Triads, five of which provide the majority of our knowledge for the traditions surrounding the battle. These allusions help establish at least an outline of the tradition that was obviously well known when the Triads took their written form (in the thirteenth century), and point to the existence of a series of tales that may have made up the now lost saga of Camlan.

According to *Culhwch and Olwen*, the true cause of the battle seems to have been an argument between Gwenhwyfar, the wife of Arthur, and Gwenhwyfach, her sister.[8] The two triads that relate to this incident are given below:

> The second [Harmful Blow of Ynys Prydein] Gwenhwyfach struck upon Gwenhwyfar: and for that cause there took place afterwards the Action of the Battle of Camlan.[9]
> And the third and the worst [Futile Battle of Ynys Prydein]: that was Camlan, which was brought about because of a quarrel between Gwenhwyfar and Gwenhwy(f)ach.[10]

The reasons for the battle of Camlan as related by Geoffrey and the romances are far more grandiose than a quarrel between two sisters!

A triad concerning the 'Three Unrestrained Ravagings of Ynys Prydein' elaborates upon the reasons for the battle and helps us to understand how Arthur and Medrod became involved:

> The first of them (occurred) when Medrawd came to Arthur's Court at Celliwig in Kerniw; he left neither food nor drink in the court that he did not consume. And he dragged Gwenhwyfar from her royal chair, and then he struck a blow upon her;
>
> The second Unrestrained Ravaging (occurred) when Arthur came to Medrawd's court. He left neither food nor drink in the court;[11]

These triads obviously preserve information regarding the cause of the battle of Camlan that did not make it into the later romances; they show a tradition of enmity between Arthur and Medrod and a slowly escalating inter-family feud, started by a disagreement between the two sisters. Arthur and Gwenhwyfar need no introduction, but what of Medrod, the famous traitor of later legend, and of Arthur's sister-in-law, Gwenhwyfach?

Culhwch and Olwen states that Gwenhwyfach is the sister of Arthur's wife, Gwenhwyfar, but apart from the triads already mentioned and a brief reference in Bonedd y Saint she plays no further part in Welsh tradition. The note in Bonedd y Saint, however, may explain why she was so central to the causes of the battle which saw the deaths of both Arthur and Medrod. The text says that she was the mother (by somebody called Medrod ap Cawrdaf) of St Dyfnog, the saint of Llanddyfnog in the Vale of Clwyd, also known as Llanrhaeadr yng Nghymeirch (the Sacred Enclosure by the Waterfall in the Commote of Cymeirch).

Although the actual manuscript of Bonedd y Saint in which this particular information appears is late (mid sixteenth century), earlier texts also mention Medrod ap Cawrdaf. The sources that mention Medrod in association with Arthur never give any indication of his parentage, and the genealogy ascribed to him in Brut y Brenhinedd is based solely upon the one created by Geoffrey of Monmouth. Strangely, however, no other person from Welsh tradition bears the name 'Medrod', so could the obscure Medrod ap Cawrdaf be the Medrod of the later Arthurian material, as was suggested by the Revd A. W. Wade-Evans in 1934?[12] When this suggestion is viewed alongside the traditional geography that we have presented within this book the identification becomes even more compelling.

The *Gogynfeirdd* of the twelfth century refer to Medrod not as the villain of later romantic traditions, but as the epitome of courage and courtesy. It is also clear from these bardic references that Medrod played a part in the independent pre-Geoffrey Arthurian tradition, with no reference to the genealogical fictions portrayed in the Historia, suggesting that a different tradition regarding the supposed killer of Arthur existed at one time.[13]

Medrod ap Cawrdaf was a grandson of Caradog Freichfras, a first cousin to Arthur previously mentioned in Chapter 4, and the evidence concerning Caradog's children, including Medrod's father, suggests that he was from North Wales. The name 'Medrod' may also be preserved in a river named Afon Medrad, which flows into the River Dee near the village of Llangwm twelve miles south-west of the dedication to his son, St Dyfnog, in the Vale of Clwyd.

From information recorded in the two Arthurian tales from

The Mabinogion it would seem that third parties deliberately encouraged the enmity between Arthur and Medrod. In *Culhwch and Olwen* someone called Gwyn Hyfar is referred to 'as one of the nine that plotted the battle of Camlan',[14] and in *The Dream of Rhonabwy* a person named Iddawg the Embroiler of Prydein tells Rhonabwy that he kindled strife between Arthur and Medrod at Camlan by acting as a messenger between the two men and changing the messages in order to provoke them to battle. Perhaps the fact that it was due to a quarrel between two sisters and then purposefully inflamed by Iddawg and others led to Camlan being called one of the 'futile battles of Ynys Prydein'. One final reference to the cause of the battle of Camlan is found in a poem by the bard Tudur Aled, who claims that the battle 'happened over two nuts'.[15] Answers on a postcard, please.

The well-known story of Medrod's treachery while Arthur was fighting on the Continent, used by Geoffrey of Monmouth, has no historical or traditional basis whatsoever and was simply a literary device to enable Geoffrey's patron's family to establish their divine right to rule the lands to which they laid claim, both in Britain and on the Continent. In Wales, Camlan was remembered as a brutal battle for centuries – so much so, in fact, that it became used as a means of comparison by which the bards gauged the devastation of many later engagements. For example, the bard Cynddelw (*fl. c.* 1155–95) praises Hywel ap Owain Gwynedd for his victory in battle in the lines

Gnawd gosgo gosgordd yn ddiflan	The host is sure to be bowed, fading away,
Fal ymosgryn mawr Gawr Gamlan.	As in the great contention of the Battle of Camlan.[16]

With its Armageddon-like overtones, Camlan also became used as a term for a 'rabble' or 'confused mob' – a development which according to Dr Rachel Bromwich 'is in itself eloquent testimony to the widespread knowledge of traditions [in Wales] about Arthur's last battle'.[17]

IN SEARCH OF ARTHUR'S LAST BATTLE

The evidence above gives us an outline of the events that led up to the battle of Camlan, but provides very little detail of the battle itself and even less regarding the perennial question of where it took place.

The actual location of the battle has been discussed for centuries, and numerous scholars have attempted to place it. Geoffrey identifies the site of Arthur's last battle as *'fluuium Camblani'* in Cornwall,[18] the modern-day River Camel that runs from the hills above Camelford to the sea at Wadebridge, and several local 'traditions' have been created to back this up.[19] The later romances place the battle on Salisbury Plain, though the Scottish chronicler Boece would have us believe it took place on the River Humber. A view often quoted in modern works is that the battle took place on Hadrian's Wall at the Roman fort of Cambloganna – an identification first proposed by O. G. S. Crawford in an article in 1935.[20] This argument rests insecurely upon the similarity of the names 'Cambloganna' and 'Camlan' and some rather weak linguistics, and it is surprising that this identification has become widespread, considering that there is absolutely no evidence to support it in any of the sources.

The surprising thing is that Camlan still exists on the map, as has been pointed out on many occasions in the last 130 years. It was first pointed out in 1872 in the pages of the periodical *Archaeologia Cambrensis* that there are three sites all bearing the name 'Camlan' within a few miles of Dolgellau in North Wales.[21] A river known as Afon Gamlan runs downs from the Rhinog mountains and flows into the River Eden near the village of Llanelltyd; a mountain pass from Dolgellau over to Mallwyd appears on the earliest Ordnance Survey maps as Camlan; and a stretch of the Dyfi river to the south of Mallwyd is known as Camlan and a farm in the area is still called Maes-y-Camlan (Field of Camlan), which is suggestive in itself. Several authors have noted these sites over the decades, but the age-old Cornish view popular in medieval times and the modern academic view are still better known.

Two more pieces of evidence remain to confirm this area of Wales as the site of Arthur's final battle. The earliest and most important is found in 'The Stanzas of the Graves' from *The Black Book of Carmarthen*; the second, of lesser authority, is a collection of references to people who survived the battle of Camlan.

Bet mab ossvran yg camlan	The grave of Osfran's son is at Camlan;
Gvydi llauer kywlavan	after many a slaughter,
Bet bedwir in alld tryvan.	the grave of Bedwyr is on Tryfan's height.[22]

The importance of this reference in 'The Stanzas of the Graves' is not immediately apparent, as the lines appear to tell us nothing regarding the location, but once the geography attached to Osfran and the survivors of Camlan is established the location becomes self-evident. The name 'Osfran' is not common in Welsh tradition, and apart from the reference above it appears on only two other occasions, both in reference to the church of St Cadfan at

Tywyn.[23] The interesting geographic point raised by these poetic references is that the church of St Cadfan is only eighteen miles from Camlan near Mallwyd. The line of the stanza referring to the grave of Bedwyr refers to the mountain of Tryfan in Snowdonia, making it very unlikely that a site in Cornwall or on Hadrian's Wall is meant.

THE SURVIVORS OF CAMLAN

Accounts of the survivors of Camlan in later romantic literature usually focus upon Bedivere and Arthur's butler, Lucan, either one of whom consigns Arthur's sword, Excalibur, into a nearby lake. Welsh tradition, however, is at variance with the later romances, and within it there exist two lists of the warriors who survived this great battle, although the lists differ from each other in the names and numbers of survivors. The earliest reference can be found in *Culhwch and Olwen*:

> Morfran ap Tegid (no man placed a weapon in him at Camlan, so exceedingly ugly was he; all thought he was a devil helping. There was hair on him like the hair of a stag), and Sandde Angel-face (no one placed his spear in him at Camlan, so exceedingly fair was he; all thought he was an angel helping), and Cynwyl the Saint (one of the three men that escaped from Camlan. He was the last to part from Arthur, on Hengroen (Old Skin) his horse).[24]

The second list is unfortunately found only in a manuscript of the seventeenth century, but it does introduce some names also mentioned by the bards in relation to Camlan:

> Here are the names of the seven men that escaped from the Battle of Camlan: Sandde Bryd Angel because of his beauty was thought to

191

be an Angel; Morfran ap Tegid because of his ugliness was thought to be a devil; St Cynfelyn who escaped by the speed of his horse; St Cedwyn by the world's blessing; St Pedrog by the strength of his spear; Derfel Gadarn by his strength; Geneid Hir by his speed. The year of Christ when the Battle of Camlan took place: 542.[25]

When we look at what little information has been preserved regarding these survivors and the locations associated with them, it can be shown that without a doubt the battle took place in North Wales.

Cedwyn

According to Section 74 of *Bonedd y Saint*, Cedwyn was the son of Gwgon Gwron ap Peredur. His grandfather Peredur, if the entry in *Annales Cambriae* is to be believed, died in 580, making it very unlikely that Cedwyn was able to fight in a battle *c.* 540. He is commemorated at two places called Llangedwyn – one in Ystrad Yw and another near Llanrhaeadr y Mochnant, eighteen miles from Camlan.

Cynwyl the Saint

Cynfelyn in the second list appears to be a mistake for the earlier reference to Cynwyl in *Culhwch and Olwen*. Very little is known about him, and only three churches in Wales preserve his name – two in Aberporth in Ceredigion and one at Penrhos on the Lleyn Peninsula. The fact that he escaped on Arthur's horse Hengroen is perhaps of more interest, as the horse's name is remembered in the township of Dinhengroen (Fort of Hengroen) at the hill fort known today as Castell y Gawr near Abergele on the North Wales coast.

Derfel Gadarn

Derfel Gadarn was the patron saint of Llandderfel, north-east of Bala in North Wales, and later poets such as Tudur Aled and Lewis Glyn Gothi also record his presence at Camlan.[26] A wooden image of him was revered in the church at Llandderfel until 1538, when it was removed and burnt at Smithfield in London.[27]

Geneid Hir

Apart from the reference in the second list, nothing is known about him.

Morfran ap Tegid

Morfran ap Tegid is also mentioned in one of the Triads, where he is referred to as one of the 'Three Slaughter Blocks of Ynys Prydein'.[28] He also appears in a later text regarding Taliesin known as *Ystoria Taliesin*, which states that his father was called Tegid Foel of Penllyn.[29] Bala Lake in the region of Penllyn is known in Welsh as Llyn Tegid, after the name of Morfran's father, indicating that Morfran had close associations with this area.[30]

Pedrog

A tradition of Pedrog fighting with Arthur at Camlan is first mentioned by the bard Dafydd Nantmor in the fifteenth century: 'One of them is a saint because of his spear: precious Petroc was renowned with his weapon at the death of Arthur.'[31] A relic known as Pedrog's spear was kept at the church of Llanbedrog on the Lleyn Peninsula and is last mentioned in a document from 1535.[32] A Latin *Life of St Pedrog* dating from the twelfth century places him in Cornwall, where over twenty dedications to him exist, although Camlan is not mentioned. It appears that his name became associated with the survivors of Camlan only at some point between the late twelfth century and 1450.

Sandde Angel-face

There is evidence from the Welsh genealogies that Sandde Angel-face has been confused with Sandde son of Llywach Hen, about whom we know very little except that he died in Wales.[33]

The concept of a set number of survivors from a battle can also be found in *Y Gododdin* and the poem *Preiddeu Annwn* from *The*

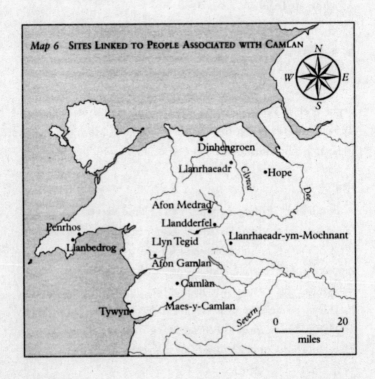

Map 6   SITES LINKED TO PEOPLE ASSOCIATED WITH CAMLAN

Dinhengroen

Llanrhaeadr

Hope

Afon Medrad

Penrhos

Llandderfel

Llyn Tegid

Llanrhaeadr-ym-Mochnant

Llanbedrog

Afon Gamlan

Camlan

Tywyn

Maes-y-Camlan

0   20
miles

Book of Taliesin, and one has to wonder whether the author of *Culhwch and Olwen* didn't just introduce the three people who survived as a parallel to these earlier examples. The names of seven survivors in the second list appear to be based upon a previous tradition, but it is impossible to tell how old this might be – apart from *Culhwch and Olwen,* the earliest reference to the survivors is found in the poem by Dafydd Nantmor quoted above. The most important aspect of the traditions attached to the survivors is that they can all be associated with sites in North Wales, reinforcing the evidence for this area being the site of Arthur's final battle.

THE TRUE HISTORY OF THE DEATH OF ARTHUR

Next we turn to a Latin manuscript that, although providing a missing section of the life of Arthur, was not printed in full until as late as 1981. The tract is known as *Vera Historia De Morte Arthuri* (The True History of the Death of Arthur) and fills the gap left by Geoffrey of Monmouth between the end of the battle of Camlan and Arthur's sojourn in Avalon. The text is of immense interest to Arthurian scholarship, not only because of its contents, but also because of where and when it was written. The earliest surviving manuscript, dated to *c.* 1300, is now housed at the Grays Inn Library in London and was previously owned by the Franciscan friars of Chester.[34] Internal evidence within the manuscript points to a Gwynedd origin, and it is likely to have been written at the Cistercian abbey of Aberconwy at some point between 1199 and 1203, during the reign of Llywelyn ap Iorwerth, Prince of Gwynedd.[35] The *Vera Historia* appears to pick up the story from where Geoffrey of Monmouth ends his narrative of Arthur, and gives an account of the final stages of the battle of Camlan.

After the battle Arthur leans on his shield suffering from exhaustion and, knowing himself to be mortally wounded, drops to the ground and orders his followers to disarm him in case his armaments should cause him pain and worsen his injury. As this is done, a handsome youth on horseback appears carrying an elm shaft in his right hand. The text elaborates on the qualities of this shaft by stating that it was 'stiff, not twisted or knotted' and sharper than any lance because it had been tempered by fire, water and finally dipped in adder's venom.[36] The unnamed youth makes straight for Arthur, hurls the elm shaft at him, and then flees; as he does so, Arthur takes the spear and launches it, striking his assailant in the back and piercing his heart such that the youth 'breathed out his last breath'.[37] The injury caused by the youth's spear has only added to Arthur's already serious wounds and, aware that he is not long for this world, Arthur tells his followers that he is soon to die. The text then details in a rather melodramatic way the despair and anguish among those gathered around him and the lamentation for the safety of the Britons.

This text is important for two reasons: first, it is the earliest detailed account of the aftermath of the battle and, second, it preserves traditions that help us to confirm the geography associated with Camlan. The text itself includes several motifs and references that establish a Gwynedd origin for the text, in particular the choice of weapon. The elm spear used by both Arthur and the youth that wounds him is the traditional weapon of the men of Gwynedd, as recorded by Giraldus Cambrensis, who in 1188 tells us that 'Just as the bow is the chief weapon in South

Wales, so here in Gwynedd they prefer the spear. A cuirass of chain-mail offers no resistance to one of these lances, when it is thrown a short distance as a javelin.'[38]

The *Vera Historia* then continues with what is possibly the most important information contained in any Arthurian text concerning the last days of Arthur: 'At length the king slightly restored by an improvement in his condition, gives orders to be taken to Venedocia [Gwynedd] since he had decided to sojourn in the delightful Isle of Avalon because of the beauty of the place (and for the sake of peace as well as for the easing the pain of his wounds).'[39] The importance of this statement is obvious. The *Vera Historia* is the only text that definitively locates the mysterious Avalon in an identifiable geographic region: the kingdom of Gwynedd, which, as we have already seen, consisted of most of North Wales and was home to many of Arthur's family members.

The most incredible aspect of this text is that it remained unknown to the world until 1905, and the first complete printed edition was not published until 1981.[40] Why did this version of the death of Arthur remain ignored and unknown, while the false tale of Arthur's exhumation at Glastonbury in 1191 became known all over Europe and is today famous across the world? Following the 'discovery' of Arthur's body, the monks of Glastonbury managed to 'find' the remains of dozens of saints on the site, and had many more transferred there from other abbeys. Glastonbury went on to become one of the richest abbeys in England – no doubt aided by the large number of pilgrims who came to see its relics. Arthurian material continued to be drawn to Somerset over the following centuries, and many of the tales that are attached to the site today can be shown to originate elsewhere.[41]

The *Vera Historia* was written during the time of a great Welsh renaissance, as evidenced by the poetry of the *Gogynfeirdd*, and its dating means that it was written at the same time as Giraldus Cambrensis wrote about the discovery of Arthur's grave in Glastonbury. It is still not certain which account came first. Did the Welsh write the *Vera Historia* to counter the claims of Glastonbury, or did Giraldus write his work to deny the claims of the Welsh?

The next section of the *Vera Historia* describes the funeral of Arthur as taking place at a chapel dedicated to the Virgin, the entrance to which was so narrow that the mourners had to enter by first forcing their shoulder into the gap and then dragging the rest of their body through the opening. While the funeral took place inside the chapel, a large storm blew up and a mist descended, so thick that it was impossible to see the body of Arthur – which had been left outside, as it would not fit into the chapel. Following the storm the mourners came out to find that the body had gone and the tomb prepared for Arthur was sealed shut, 'such that it rather seemed to be one single stone'.[42] The *Vera Historia* provides more detail than any other text regarding the fate of Arthur's body, but is still tantalisingly unclear about the exact location.

The internal evidence of the text tells us that Arthur wanted to be taken to Gwynedd, indicating that the battlefield of Camlan on which he was lying was not in that kingdom. If Maes-y-Camlan near Mallwyd was the original site of Camlan then this would fit with this, as it is located in the Welsh kingdom of Powys, not Gwynedd. From Camlan there are two routes to Gwynedd – one over the pass, also called Camlan, towards the town of Dolgellau, the other along the banks of the River Dyfi to Pennal near Machynlleth.

The only other piece of evidence that can be gleaned from the

Vera Historia is that the funeral of Arthur took place at a small remote chapel dedicated to the Virgin Mary. This is important, for this information is as old, if not older, than the claims that Arthur was buried in Glastonbury. But which chapel dedicated to the Virgin in Gwynedd *c.* 1200 did the author have in mind? Before looking at possible locations for this chapel we must look at the earliest reference to the grave of Arthur in Welsh literature.

THE MYSTERY OF ARTHUR'S GRAVE

'*Anoeth bid bet y arthur*',[43] the passage regarding Arthur's burial from 'The Stanzas of the Graves', is usually translated as 'The world's wonder a grave for Arthur', which appears rather ambiguous. It is often understood to mean that Arthur's grave is a mystery, a wonder of the world, leading many to believe that even the bards did not know of its location. It has also been interpreted to mean that Arthur's grave would remain undiscovered 'until doomsday' or 'the end of the world'. If this second meaning is the correct interpretation, the penchant of the Welsh bards for word play and place-name lore should lead us to consider whether the site of Arthur's grave has been hidden for centuries within this oblique reference. Could *anoeth bid* be a place? '*Bid*' is the Welsh word for 'world', but the exact meaning of the word '*anoeth*' is more problematic. As we have seen, '*anoeth*' is also found in the place name 'Caer Oeth ac Anoeth' and is usually thought to mean 'something difficult to obtain' or a 'wonder'. But, although this is the usual sense ascribed to this word, '*anoeth*' also has another meaning not usually put forward in the interpretation of this passage: in the context of something precious it can also mean a 'jewel'. This would give us the translation 'The world's jewel, a grave for Arthur'.

Although this does not provide any more evidence about the location of the grave, this interpretation reverses the idea that the Welsh themselves were unaware of a tradition regarding Arthur's grave and suggests that knowledge of its whereabouts was preserved for the privileged few. By the time 'The Stanzas of the Graves' had taken written form, Arthur had already developed from being a benchmark against which a warrior's valour could be compared, and heroic accretions to his legend had begun in earnest. As can be seen, even the earliest reference to Arthur's grave is enigmatic, providing several possibilities as to its meaning.

Despite the claims of William of Malmesbury and other Norman historians of the twelfth century, nowhere in early Welsh literature is there any reference to Arthur as being thought of as still alive and waiting to return and help his country in its time of need. All earlier poetic references to Arthur refer to him in the past tense, and the twelfth-century bard Pryddyd y Moch clearly states that Arthur is dead in the lines

Maredut marw yw heuyd Maredudd also is dead
Mal modur Arthur arth gryd as is sovereign Arthur.[44]

The earliest version recorded in Gwynedd tells us that Arthur's final battle against Medrod took place not at one of the several places called Camlan near Dolgellau, but in a valley named Cwmllan. This valley comes down from the summit of Snowdon to Nant Gwynant, the valley in which Dinas Emrys is situated. Arthur chased Medrod up the valley until reaching the pass between the summits of Snowdon and Lliwedd, where he was ambushed in a hail of arrows. Two different endings of the tale exist: one says that he was buried beneath a cairn on the pass, which became known as Carnedd Arthur, and the other that he was taken down the steep cliffs of Lliwedd and hidden in a cave that became known as Ogof Llanciau Eryri (Cave of the Youths of Snowdonia).[45] (The motif of Arthur being buried in a cave is widespread across Europe and even as far afield as the island of Sicily.) In the 1920s the cliffs of Lliwedd were home to the best mountaineers in the world, and the earliest Everest expeditions trained among their slabs and gullies; today they are home to ravens and the occasional climber looking to get away from it all. Any cave attached to Arthur has long since been forgotten. The exact location of the cairn known as Carnedd Arthur is uncertain, but many cairns exist on the pass, any one of which might be the grave of Arthur as recorded in the tradition above.

THE CHAPEL OF ST MARY AND ARTHUR'S GRAVE

As the *Vera Historia* appears to have been written at the Cistercian abbey of Aberconwy, could the monks have set the story at a site known to them? In the charters concerning lands owned by the abbey of Aberconwy itself, one place stands out as a possible setting for the scene of Arthur's funeral as described in the *Vera Historia*. The register of Aberconwy dating from 1251 states that the monks held a chapel at Rhyd Llanfair in the grange of Hiraethog. 'Rhyd' simply means 'ford' and 'Llanfair' denotes a sacred enclosure dedicated to the Virgin Mary.[46] The actual chapel of Llanfair mentioned in the register no longer exists and all trace of it has unfortunately disappeared, but the place name survives on modern maps. To the west of Pentrefoelas on the A5 London-to-Holyhead road is the name 'Rhyd Llanfair' attached to a bridge over the River Conwy, but of more interest is the very important archaeological site that was uncovered during the construction of this road.[47]

In the summer of 1820 the workmen building Thomas Telford's new highway through the heart of Gwynedd uncovered one of the few Dark Age cemeteries known to exist in Wales. In a field known as Dol y Tre Beddau (the Meadow of the Town of the Graves) they found forty stone-lined graves, in an area twenty yards by ten yards. Among the stones was one bearing the inscription 'BROHOMAGLI IATTI (H)IC IACIT ET UXOR EIUS CAUNE' – '[The stone] of Brohomaglus Iattus. He lies here, and his wife Caune'.[48] This inscription has been dated to the mid sixth century – the very period in which Arthur is portrayed as having fought at Camlan and died.[49] The fact that there are so many stone-lined graves in one place suggests that it was a graveyard for people of some importance. The Dark Age cemetery of Tre Beddau is located upon the lands owned by the monks of Aberconwy and is situated less than two miles upstream from the original site of a chapel of St Mary at Rhyd Llanfair. Did the monks of Aberconwy base the *Vera Historia* upon some local tradition attached to this cemetery of Dark Age nobility on the lands they owned in this remote part of Gwynedd?

No other inscriptions are known from this site, probably because it was uncovered not during an archaeological dig, but in the destruction of a hillside to build a road, at a time when such finds were fortunate to be recorded at all. The true origins of the cemetery at Tre Beddau may never be known, but what we do know is that *c.* 1200 the monks of Aberconwy abbey wrote a text

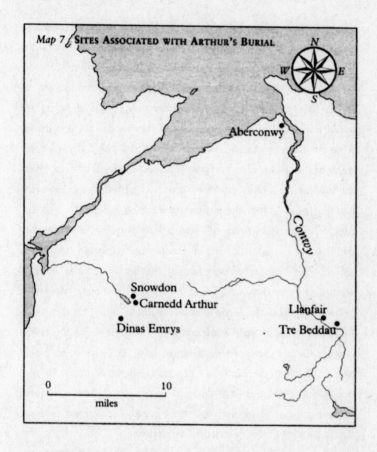

Map 7 **SITES ASSOCIATED WITH ARTHUR'S BURIAL**

detailing the final days of Arthur, his funeral and the site of his tomb. We have identified a site that fits what little evidence can be gleaned from the text, and located nearby is a cemetery that is known to have been used as a burial ground for important people of the sixth century. The site is now quiet unimposing, with no indication of the importance of this burial place, and since the graves were discovered in 1820 there has been no archaeological research there. What lies beneath the ground in the surrounding area – are there more graves, a Dark Age chapel or a long-lost village? – only time and the archaeologist's trowel will tell.

We stood next to the very road whose construction had led to the discovery of the graves we had come in search of, trying to avoid the traffic of the modern world passing by. We wondered what Arthur – an obscure warrior from the hills of Wales – would think of the books, films and poems he had inspired. Looking over the myriad hills before us, we realised that, although our research had narrowed down the search for Arthur's origins to a small region of this island, we still had a long way to go before the problem of the whereabouts of Arthur's grave could finally be solved. The chances of ever finding the bodily remains of this sixth-century warlord who lies at the very heart of one of the best-known legends in the world are infinitesimally small, for the grave of Arthur was of little consequence to the Welsh of the sixth century. Before the Normans adopted him, Arthur was no more important than the hundreds of other people recorded in the poetry and chronicles of Wales. The burial site of Arthur was no more significant than that of Urien Rheged, the warrior sons of Llywarch Hen or the heroes of Y Gododdin.

If we have been able to prove in this book that a cohesive Arthurian tradition did exist in Wales before the arrival of the Normans, and that fragments of it still remain, then we have achieved our aim. The traditions and place names of this region have still to undergo the same depth of research as has been undertaken elsewhere. We hope that as much energy can be focused on this task as is focused on other parts of the country, for it is surely among the hills of Wales that the true origins of the Arthurian legend lie.

Epilogue

·

THE UNTOLD
STORY OF ARTHUR

URING the course of this book we have looked at the earliest material that exists regarding Arthur and have shown that his legend is rooted in the part of Great Britain known today as Wales. Over the years there have been many attempts to explain the origins of Arthur, using the same handful of early sources, but almost all the various theories have agreed on one point: that Arthur was leader of the British resistance to the Saxon invaders. Until recently this was an opinion we also held, but while re-evaluating the early Welsh material for the publication of an Arthurian sourcebook it became clear that in this material Arthur never fights the Saxons – in fact they are never even mentioned.

Aside from the dubious reference to Arthur fighting Saxons in the opening section of the battle list of the *Historia Brittonum*, there is little to support the idea of Arthur fighting such enemies, and the battle list itself seems to contain a mishmash of conflicts from differing periods, belonging to other heroes, both known and unknown. This, of course, does not mean that Arthur never came into conflict with the Saxons, but it does show that, if he did, this is not what he was remembered for by his own people. According to the Welsh sources, Arthur fights enemies with British names like Gleis ap Merin, Mil Du ap Dugum, Gwyddog ap Menestyr and Medrod. These battles against his own people would seem to confirm Gildas's description of the political situation in Wales during the first part of the sixth century, and the locations of Arthur's battles in the original traditions are at such sites as Tryfrwyd, Caer Oeth ac Anoeth, Caer Fenlli and Camlan.

The Welsh sources make no mention of the fictions of Camelot and the Knights of the Round Table; instead they locate Arthur's courts at Gelliwig and Penrhyn Rhianedd. Arthur's *teulu* consisted of figures such as Cai ap Cynyr, Bedwyr, Trystan ap Tallwch and March ap Meirchion, who accompanied him into the later romances only to find themselves jousting and seated at an enormous Round Table. What of Arthur's other warriors, such as Derfel Gadarn, Morfran ap Tegid, the sons of Caw, and the sons of Iaen of Caer Dathal? What were their stories, and where did they come from?

In the search for Arthur, all we have left to work with are the traditions found in the early Welsh poetry, annals and tales – traditions that continued to be represented in the poetry of the *Gogynfeirdd* at the same time as the Anglo-Normans elaborated upon the figure of Arthur in their romances and poetry. It should be remembered that it was not, as is commonly thought, Geoffrey of Monmouth who first exploited Arthur in this way, but the Cambro-Norman school of hagiographers working in South Wales at the start of the twelfth century. It was they who first crowned Arthur king and introduced him to the world outside Wales – as a pawn in the game of attributing land and rights to the abbeys and monasteries of the Norman-controlled areas of Britain. A generation later, the traditions used by these hagiographers were elaborated upon by Geoffrey, who created a new Arthur and placed his battles in landscape unknown to the earliest sources. This revised geography played no small part in the process by which the new Norman dynasty attempted to unite and lay claim to a country over which it had no right to rule. The lands detailed in Geoffrey's work were the lands owned by his patrons and political allies – the very people on whom his future advancement depended – and it is against this background that Arthur became a figurehead of Norman Britain.

Instead of attempting to discover Camelot, or some other such fantasy, anyone in search of the authentic Arthurian tradition should turn to interpreting the hints and allusions in the sources detailed in this book concerning events such as the death of Llacheu son of Arthur, the battle of Tryfrwyd, the events in the hall of Awarnach, and the battles of Dinas Eidyn, Ystawingun and Llongborth. What can be discovered of the lost sagas concerning the battle of Camlan, the feud between Arthur and Huail the son of Caw, and the tradition that Arthur's body was buried in Gwynedd? What are the original meanings of certain obscure geographical terms in Welsh literature, and how safe is the evidence gleaned from the hagiographical works, written with ecclesiastical claims in mind? These and many other questions remain to be answered.

From the earliest Welsh references Arthur had already been drawn into a semi-legendary word, and from there he developed into a king, emperor and even a conqueror over the Roman Empire. This has led many to look for this important figure in places he simply cannot be. Arthur will not be found gloriously buried in an English monastery, but somewhere on a remote hillside in the ancient Welsh kingdom of Gwynedd. The fate of the Arthur portrayed in early Welsh texts was to be buried and perhaps forgotten in a corner of his native land, his only concerns before death being to live the life of a warrior, earn his mead and, if possible, die in battle. It was thus that Arthur was remembered by his own people – sometimes as a tyrant, sometimes as a touchstone for valour and ability on the battlefield – only to be adopted and transformed into an unrecognisable figure by new invaders. And these invaders not only destroyed the hierarchy of Arthur's old enemies, but raised this Welsh warlord to the status of a king. They used him as their figurehead in laying claim to an empire of their own making – an empire conceived by medieval politicians and spin doctors, and realised with a sword in one hand and Geoffrey's good book in the other.

If we cannot find some remnant of the real Arthur in the earliest histories and legends of his own people then he is lost to us, drowned in a morass of fairy tale and romance, his modest origins engulfed by his later literary success. The chances of new manuscript evidence ever coming to light from a contemporary or near contemporary source are very remote, and no spectacular archaeological finds are likely, for we are looking for an individual person, not a cultural movement that can be uncovered by the discipline of the trowel. Nor is it likely that a stone will be discovered with the name 'Arthur' emblazoned across it for the entire world to see – like the manufactured lead cross at one time displayed in Glastonbury. Unfortunately, names found on stones are seldom also recorded in the written sources.

The final word on any of the material contained in this early tradition is far from written, and the names we have noted are but a very small part of the real Arthurian tradition hidden in the landscape and manuscripts of Wales. We hope that we have explained enough of this early tradition for the reader to be in no doubt as to where the land of Pendragon and the origins of Arthur really belong. We firmly believe that Arthur is there, hidden in the shadows of the manuscripts, lurking in the background of the original legends, waiting to be reborn to the world not as the once and future king of later fable, but as the Dark Age warlord he was, riding to fame under the banner of one of the greater rulers of the period.

Appendix 1

---·---

THE WARRIORS OF ARTHUR

and Other Characters Associated with him in the Earliest Welsh Sources

THE aim of this appendix is to show that many characters' names are associated with Arthur in several different Welsh sources, demonstrating that a cohesive tradition was known to the authors of these sources. The fact that many of the names appear in three or four of the texts, or in the case of Cai in all but one of the six sources named here, show that the Arthurian tradition in Wales was not as fragmented as the surviving sources would suggest. The criterion for inclusion of a name in the list below is that it appears in association with Arthur in *at least two* of the early Welsh sources discussed in this book. Some of the names noted below and the place names associated with them can be found in Chapter 4, and Map 8 shows the distribution of sites linked to the people named. Together, the map and the table show the geographical area from which the earliest names associated with Arthur were drawn.

The notes given below the table are intentionally brief, being intended only to show the locations associated with each person. For a full discussion of each person see the relevant entries in P. C. Bartrum, *A Welsh Classical Dictionary: People in History and Legend up to about A.D. 1000* (National Library of Wales, 1993). The initials along the top of the table correspond to the texts as follows:

CO   *Culhwch and Olwen.* The list of Arthur's warriors can be found on pp. 84–90 of Gwyn Jones & Thomas Jones, *The Mabinogion* (Everyman, rev. edn, 1993).

BBC   *Black Book of Carmarthen.* This text can be found in A. O. H. Jarman, *Llyfr Du Caerfyrddin* (University of Wales Press, 1982).

BT   *Book of Taliesin.* This text can be found in J. Gwenogvryn Evans, *The Book of Taliesin* (Llanbedrog, 1910).

TYP   Triads. These can be found in Rachel Bromwich, *Trioedd Ynys Prydein* (University of Wales Press, 2nd edn, 1978).

DR   Dream of Rhonabwy. The list of Arthur's forty-two counsellors can be found on pp. 125–6 of Gwyn Jones & Thomas Jones, *The Mabinogion* (Everyman, rev. edn, 1993).

LWS   Lives of the Welsh Saints. This material can be found in A. W. Wade-Evans, *Vitae Sanctorum Britanniae et Genealogiae* (University of Wales Press, 1944).

Name	CO	BBC	BT	TYP	DR	LWS
Annwas Adeiniog	•	•				
Bedwini the Bishop	•			•		•
Bedwyr	•	•		•		•
Cadyrieth ap Saidi				•	•	
Cadwy ap Geraint	•			•	•	•
Cai	•	•		•	•	•
Caradog Freichfras				•	•	•
Cysceint ap Banon	•	•				
Dyfyr ap Alun Dyfed	•				•	
Edern ap Nudd	•				•	
Ffleudur Fflam	•			•	•	
Garwen ferch Henin Hen	•	•				
Glewlwyd Great Gasp	•	•				
Gobrwy ap Echel Big Hip	•			•	•	
Goreu ap Custennin	•			•	•	
Greidiol Gallddofydd	•				•	
Gwair ap Gwystyl			•	•		
Gwalchmai ap Gwyar	•	•		•	•	
Gwarthegydd ap Caw	•				•	
Gwenhwyfar	•			•		
Gwenwynwyn ap Naf	•				•	
Gwyn Godyfrion	•	•				
Gwythyr ap Greidiol	•	•		•		
Gyrthmwl Wledig		•		•	•	
Hyfeidd One-Cloak	•				•	
Indeg ferch Garwy Hir	•			•		
Llacheu		•		•		
Llary ap Casnar Wledig	•			•		
Llawfrodedd Farfog	•			•	•	
Llenlleog Wyddel	•		•			
Llwch Llaw-Wynniog	•	•				
Mabon ap Mellt	•	•				
Mabon ap Modron	•	•			•	
Maelgwn Gwynedd	•			•		•

Name	CO	BBC	BT	TYP	DR	LWS
Manawydan ap Llyr		•	•	•		
March ap Meirchion		•		•	•	
Menw ap Teirgwaedd	•			•	•	
Morfran ap Tegid	•			•	•	
Morien Mynog	•				•	
Nerth ap Cadarn	•				•	
Peredur Paladr Hir	•			•	•	
Rhufon Befr	•	•		•	•	
Rhahawd ail Morgan				•	•	
Trystan ap Tallwch				•	•	

Annwas Adeiniog

Annwas Adeiniog is one of Arthur's warriors in *Culhwch and Olwen* and in the poem *Pa Gur?* from *The Black Book of Carmarthen*.

Bedwini the Bishop

Culhwch and Olwen refers to Bedwini as one of the members of Arthur's court 'who blessed meat and drink.'[1] *The Dream of Rhonabwy* lists him among the forty-two counsellors of Arthur, and the Triad concerning Arthur's courts makes him chief bishop of Gelliwig (see Chapter 5).

Bedwyr

Along with Cai, Bedwyr is one of the oldest and most consistent companions of Arthur. The earliest mention of him can be found in *The Life of St Cadog*, when he aids Arthur and Cai in defeating the armies of Brychan so that Gwynllyw can escape with Gwladus, Brychan's daughter, whom he has snatched. This event is located on the border of the old Welsh kingdoms of Brycheiniog and Gwynllyw,

Map 8 SITES LINKED TO PEOPLE ASSOCIATED WITH ARTHUR IN TWO OR MORE SOURCES

Cornwy

Ynys Seiriol

Penrhyn Rhianedd
Morfa Rhianedd

Deganwy

Dinorben

Walwen

Tryfan

Celyddon?

Nantlle

Glyndyfrdwy

Ruabon Mountain

Caer Gai

Old Oswestry

Conwy

Clwyd

Dee

Severn

Knucklas

Teme

Wye

Teifi

Cwm Cerwyn

Usk

Towy

Taff

Border of Brycheiniog and Gwynlltyw

Tawe

Loughor

N
W E
S

0   20
miles

near Abergavenny, and local traditions of the area record that a well named after Bedwyr once existed there.² The warrior list from *Culhwch and Olwen* makes him only second to Cai and adds that 'No one in the land was as handsome as he except Arthur and Drych ai Cibdhar, and although he was one-handed, no three warriors drew blood in the same field faster than he.'³ The poem *Pa Gur?* from *The Black Book of Carmarthen* places Bedwyr in the battle of Tryfrwyd associated with Arthur in the *Historia Brittonum* (see Chapter 6). 'The Stanzas of the Graves' from *The Black Book of Carmarthen* place his grave on Alld Tryvan, 'the Hill of Tryfan' – probably the prominent peak of Tryfan in Snowdonia in North Wales.⁴

Cadyrieth ap Saidi

Cadyrieth was one of the forty-two counsellors of Arthur according to *The Dream of Rhonabwy*, which adds that 'there was not a man in Prydein more mighty in counsel than he'.⁵ It has been suggested that he is the same person as Cadyrieith ap Porthawr Gandwy, one of the 'Three Chieftains of Arthur's Court' according to the Triads.⁶ No locations can be associated with either of them.

Cadwy ap Geraint

See Chapter 4.

Cai

See Chapter 4.

Caradog Freichfras

See Chapter 4.

Cysceint ap Banon

Cysceint ap Banon is one of Arthur's men named in the poem *Pa*

Gur? and probably the same as the person named Iscawyn ap Panon in *Culhwch and Olwen*. Cysceint is one of Arthur's warriors slain at Cwm Cerwyn in Dyfed by the great boar Trwyth.

Dyfyr ap Alun Dyfed

Dyfyr is another of Arthur's forty-two counsellors from *The Dream of Rhonabwy*. This also leads to the possibility that he might be the same as the unnamed warrior of Arthur's court who is the son of Alun Dyfed in *Culhwch and Olwen*.

Edern ap Nudd

Edern ap Nudd is one of Arthur's warriors in *Culhwch and Olwen*, along with his brother Gwyn ap Nudd (who is often associated with the otherworld in Welsh mythology). Edern is among the forty-two counsellors of Arthur in *The Dream of Rhonabwy*, which also makes him the King of Denmark. He is also the subject of an early piece of Arthurian folklore hijacked by Glastonbury in the thirteenth century. First found in the interpolations to William of Malmesbury's *De Antiquitate Glastoniensis Ecclesiae* (The Antiquities of the Church of Glastonbury) is a story concerning Edern (there called Ider) being decorated by Arthur as a knight. In order to prove his worth he has to go and fight three giants on a hill, which he duly does and then collapses from exhaustion. When Arthur arrives he thinks that Edern has been killed, and returns to Glastonbury and lavishes lands upon the monastery so that the monks will pray for his soul. Another version of this tale, found in the Chronicle of John of Glastonbury, places this hill in North Wales and is thought to preserve some earlier tradition about this episode. For a more detailed discussion of this point see our *The Keys to Avalon*, pp. 183–6.

Ffleudur Fflam

As with many of the other people in this appendix, Ffleudur Fflam is both a member of the list of Arthur's warriors in *Culhwch and Olwen* and of one of his forty-two counsellors in *The Dream of Rhonabwy*. In addition to this he is also mentioned in one of the earliest triads as one of the 'Three Chieftains of Arthur's Court'.[7] No locations are associated with him.

Garwen ferch Henin Hen

See Chapter 4.

Glewlwyd Great Gasp

Glewlwyd Great Gasp is Arthur's chief porter and gatekeeper in *Culhwch and Olwen*, where he also gives a speech in which he recounts the far-off places he has visited with Arthur – including India and Greece. He is also mentioned in *Pa Gur?* as the gatekeeper to whom Arthur is talking when he recounts the deeds of the men who accompany him. No locations are associated with him.

Gobrwy ap Echel Big Hip

Gobrwy is both one of Arthur's warriors in *Culhwch and Olwen* and among his forty-two counsellors in *The Dream of Rhonabwy*. He also appears in one of the earliest triads as one of the 'Chieftains of Arthur's Court'.[8] No locations are associated with him.

Goreu ap Custennin

See Chapter 4.

Greidiol Gallddofydd

Greidiol Gallddofydd appears in the list of Arthur's warriors in *Culhwch and Olwen* and as one of his forty-two counsellors in

The Dream of Rhonabwy. No places are known to be associated with him.

Gwair ap Gwystyl

See Chapter 4.

Gwalchmai ap Gwyar

See Chapter 4.

Gwarthegydd ap Caw

Gwarthegydd accompanies Arthur on his hunt for the great boar Trwyth in *Culhwch and Olwen* and is slain at Cwm Cerwyn in Dyfed. In *The Dream of Rhonabwy* he is said along with Bedwini the Bishop to have sat at the side of Arthur and to have been one of his forty-two counsellors.

Gwenhwyfar

See Chapter 4.

Gwenwynwyn ap Naf

Gwenwynwyn is referred to in *Culhwch and Olwen* as Arthur's 'first fighter' and in *The Dream of Rhonabwy* as one of his forty-two counsellors. The Triads name him as one of the 'Three Seafarers of Ynys Prydein' along with two other people associated with Arthur: March ap Meirchion and Geraint ap Erbin.[9] No place names are associated with him.

Gwyn Godyfrion

Nothing is known about Gwyn Godyfrion apart from the appearance of his name in the warrior list in *Culhwch and Olwen* and the poem *Pa Gur?* from *The Black Book of Carmarthen*.

Gwythyr ap Greidiol

Gwythyr is one of Arthur's warriors in *Culhwch and Olwen*, and in a strange triad concerning the three queens of Arthur all named Gwenhwyfar he is said to be the father of one of them.[10] The only location associated with him comes from *Culhwch and Olwen*, which places him 'in the north'.[11]

Gyrthmwl Wledig

Gyrthmwl Wledig is one of the forty-two counsellors of Arthur according to *The Dream of Rhonabwy*. The Triads call him the 'Chief Prince' of Arthur's court at Penrhyn Rhianydd (see Chapter 5). 'The Stanzas of the Graves' place his burial at a site called Celli Friafael, 'where the Lliw flows into the Llychwr', which scholars have identified with a site near the village of Loughor on the Gower Peninsula in South Wales.[12]

Hyfeidd One-Cloak

Hyfeidd One-Cloak is named as one of Arthur's warriors in *Culhwch and Olwen* and as one of his counsellors in *The Dream of Rhonabwy*. No locations are associated with him.

Indeg ferch Garwy Hir

See Chapter 4.

Llacheu

See Chapter 4.

Llary ap Casnar Wledig

Llary is one of the warriors of Arthur in *Culhwch and Olwen* and one of his counsellors in *The Dream of Rhonabwy*. No locations are associated with him.

Llawfrodedd Farfog

Llawfrodedd Farfog is one of Arthur's warriors according to *Culhwch and Olwen* and one of his counsellors according to *The Dream of Rhonabwy*. No locations are associated with him.

Llenlleog Wyddel

Llenlleog Wyddel is one of Arthur's warriors in *Culhwch and Olwen*. It was Llenlleog who killed Diwrnach with the sword Caledfwlch (later to become Excalibur) so that Arthur and his men could steal his magical cauldron. This event is paralleled in the Arthurian poem *Preiddeu Annwn* from *The Book of Taliesin*. According to *Culhwch and Olwen*, Llenlleog Wyddel was from 'Pentir Garmon', which has been identified as Loch Garman in County Wexford on the south-eastern tip of Ireland.[13]

Llwch Llaw-Wynniog

Llwch Llaw-Wynniog is named as one of Arthur's warriors in *Culhwch and Olwen*, where he is said to be the father of sons 'from beyond Mor Terwyn', which has been identified as the Tyrrhenian Sea, a region of the Mediterranean between Sicily and Sardinia.[14] In the poem *Pa Gur?* From *The Black Book of Carmarthen*, Llwch is said to have been 'defending Eidyn on the border': the possible location of Eidyn was discussed in Chapter 5.

Mabon ap Mellt

According to *Culhwch and Olwen*, Mabon ap Mellt accompanied Arthur to a region called Llydaw; the exact location of this region, however, is far from certain – see p.88. Mabon is also one of Arthur's companions in the poem *Pa Gur?* from *The Black Book of Carmarthen*.

Mabon ap Modron

Mabon ap Modron is rescued by Cai from his prison in Caerloyw. Caerloyw is usually identified with Gloucester, but for an alternative suggestion and a detailed discussion of this episode in *Culhwch and Olwen* see our *The Keys to Avalon*, pp.147–54. Later on in the same tale Mabon follows the boar Trwyth into the River Severn and takes a razor from between its ears. He is one of the forty-two counsellors of Arthur in *The Dream of Rhonabwy*. Mabon is also mentioned in the poem *Pa Gur?* from *The Black Book of Carmarthen*, as the 'servant of Uthyr Pendragon',[15] and in 'The Stanzas of the Graves' his grave is described as being 'on Nantlle's height'.[16] 'Nantlle' is the name of a village in Snowdonia in North Wales. His name is also preserved on the moorland tract known today as Ruabon mountain, but originally called Rhiwabon (the Hillside of Mabon).

Maelgwn Gwynedd

Maelgwn is named in most of the earliest historical and poetical sources concerning Wales. He was a king of Gwynedd, and his main residence was his castle at Deganwy. The *Annales Cambriae* state that he died in 547,[17] and later Welsh tradition says that he died at the church in nearby Rhos and his body is interred on Ynys Seiriol, better known today as Puffin Island.[18] He is associated with Arthur in the tale of *Culhwch and Olwen*, where he appears as one of his warriors, and also in the Triads, where is called the 'chief elder of Mynyw (St David's)' (see Chapter 5).

Manawydan ap Llyr

Manawydan is one of Arthur's warriors in *Culhwch and Olwen* and also in the poem *Pa Gur?* from *The Black Book of Carmarthen.* The tale *Manawydan fab Llyr* found in *The Mabinogion* associates him primarily with Dyfed in south-west Wales.[19]

March ap Meirchion

See Chapter 4.

Menw ap Teirgwaedd

Menw is one of Arthur's warriors in *Culhwch and Olwen* (which depicts him as having the ability to change his shape) and one of his counsellors in *The Dream of Rhonabwy*. According to the Triads, he learned his magic ability from Uthyr Pendragon.[20] No locations are associated with him.

Morfran ap Tegid

See the discussion of the survivors of the battle of Camlan in Chapter 8 for places associated with Morfran.

Morien Mynog

Morien Mynog is yet another person found both in the list of Arthur's warriors in *Culhwch and Olwen* and in the list of his counsellors in *The Dream of Rhonabwy*. No locations are associated with him.

Nerth ap Cadarn

Nothing is known about Nerth ap Cadarn except that he is found as one of Arthur's men in both *Culhwch and Olwen* and *The Dream of Rhonabwy*.

Peredur Paladr Hir

Peredur Paladr Hir is associated with Arthur in the earliest Welsh traditions as one of his warriors in *Culhwch and Olwen* and one of his counsellors in *The Dream of Rhonabwy*.

Rhufon Befr

Rhufon Befr is one of the warriors of Arthur in *Culhwch and Olwen* and one of his counsellors in *The Dream of Rhonabwy*. Later tradition associates him with Gwynedd, and a poem by Gwilym Ddu (*c.* 1320) places him 'near Cawrnwy', which has been identified as Cornwy on the isle of Anglesey.[21]

Rhahawd ail Morgan

Rhahawd ail Morgan is one of Arthur's forty-two counsellors in *The Dream of Rhonabwy* and, according to one of the Triads, one of the 'three Peers of Arthur's Court'.[22] No location is associated with him.

Trystan ap Tallwch

See notes to the battle of Coed Celyddon in Chapter 6 for locations associated with Trystan.

Appendix 2

THE HEARTLAND OF ARTHUR'S WARRIORS

ESPITE the fragmentary nature of the material that has survived, the warriors associated with Arthur in the earliest Welsh Arthurian tradition – in such sources as *Pa Gur?* and *Culhwch and Olwen* – establish that the Arthurian legend in medieval Wales had a cohesive geography. The evidence available establishes not only the consistency of this tradition across the different sources, but also the independent nature of the Welsh material in comparison to the later romantic literature. The aim of this appendix is briefly to show that two different parts of the Welsh Arthurian material co-exist in a specific area of North Wales.

GILDAS, HUAIL AND ARTHUR

The only chronicle to detail the situation in Britain during the time of Arthur is Gildas's *De Excidio*, and this text describes the British nobility as fighting not against the Saxons, but among themselves.

Within Welsh sources there are numerous references to Arthur fighting British opposition, as pointed out in Chapter 6, but in this appendix we will take a look at one of these references recorded in the *Life of Gildas* written by Caradog of Llancarvan. This work was written in the early part of the twelfth century at the same time as Geoffrey's *Historia*, or possibly even earlier, making it a text of great importance in the search for the origins of the Arthurian legend. The work makes use of even earlier traditions concerning Arthur, and it is these that we will look at here.

The early section of Caradog of Llancarvan's *Life of Gildas* is actually based upon an earlier text written by a monk of Rhuys in Brittany at the end of the eleventh century, but, like much of the hagiographical material from this period, this earlier text conflates the lives of two different saints. The first section deals with Gildas, but midway through the text the author writes about a saint known as Gueltas, a native of Brittany and the real object of his work. This text from Brittany does not mention Arthur, because the section of it dealing with Gildas concerns only his early life; material on Gueltas is in the place where the Arthurian section would be expected to appear.

What little is known about Caradog of Llancarvan strongly suggests that he was one of the professional hagiographers employed by many of the religious houses in England to record the history, land grants and pre-eminence of each establishment. Unfortunately, from the historian's point of view, when proper evidence was lacking these professional hagiographers thought nothing of counterfeiting documents or appropriating traditions from elsewhere. For instance, the abbey of Glastonbury claimed to own the relics of St Dunstan, even though they were known to be housed at Canterbury, and in a letter rebuking the monks of Glastonbury concerning this the monk Eadmer commented that the professional hagiographers would tell any lie if paid enough.[1] A large amount of the material recorded in the works of these ecclesiastical spin doctors is simply propaganda designed to set the house of their employers above the houses of their neighbours, for political and economic gain. This activity became more widespread after the Norman Conquest, as the new monarchy demanded that each religious house provide evidence for its claim to own lands – evidence that, for the right price, Caradog of Llancarvan and his ilk would create.

Caradog of Llancarvan's *Life of Gildas* is important to Arthurian studies because it was the first source to associate Arthur with Glastonbury, although the main reason for its composition was to associate Gildas with the abbey, not Arthur. With Caradog's Cambro-Norman ecclesiastical background, it is not surprising to find that he freely utilised Welsh traditions in his manufacturing of stories, and one of the lesser-known stories he used concerns Arthur and his conflict with Huail, the son of Caw and brother of Gildas. It is obvious that Caradog simply relocated Welsh traditions concerning Gildas and Arthur to Glastonbury, and by using obscure traditions from areas outside of direct Anglo-Norman influence he avoided the mistake made with the relics of St Dunstan.

The Arthurian story of a conflict between Arthur and Huail recorded by Caradog of Llancarfan differs markedly from the version of the story recorded by the bards of Wales. By using these Welsh sources we can identify the geographical origin of the tale and find evidence for Arthur fighting British opposition, rather than Saxon.

The traditions available to the monk of Rhuys in Brittany at the end of the eleventh century inform us that Gildas was 'born in the very fertile district of Arecluta, and descended from his father Caunus . . . the district of Arecluta, as it forms a part of Britannia, took its name from a certain river called the Clut, by which the district is, for the most part, watered'.[2] In Welsh sources the father of Gildas is named as Caw or Caw of Prydein, and the earliest and most substantial story concerning him can be found in *The Life of St Cadog*, written by Llifris of Llancarvan *c.* 1080. We know for certain that this text was well known to Caradog, as he later rewrote it. The narrative can be summarised as follows.

St Cadog went on a pilgrimage to 'Albaniam' (Scotland), and on his return he stopped at a place 'on this side of mons Bannauc'. He stayed at this place for seven years, converting the people, and while building a monastery on the site he found the bones of a giant. Thinking that the giant would be useful in helping him to build the monastery, Cadog resurrected him. The giant was very grateful to the saint for saving him from hell, and dedicated his life to him. He told Cadog that his name was Caw of Prydyn, and that he had 'reigned formerly for many years beyond mons Bannauc'. The giant also told Cadog that when he lived he had plundered the coasts with his troops of robbers, until he and his army were pursued and destroyed by a local king.[3]

Because of the reference in this text to 'Albaniam', Caw is usually associated with Scotland, and the region of 'Arecluta' in which he lived is identified with the River Clyde. The monastery he helped build is identified as the church of Cambuslang, near Glasgow,[4] and 'mons Bannauc' with Bannockburn, near Stirling. The reason that Llifris located this episode in Scotland was to show that the cult of St Cadog stretched so far north and that his church owned lands in this region (though there is no evidence that it ever did): 'As the fame of this miracle spread throughout Scotland, the kings of the Scottish folk presented him with twenty-four homesteads.'[5] If, however, Caradog was using earlier traditions about the family of Caw it should be possible to show that both 'Arecluta' and 'mons Bannauc' were originally place names from the areas of Wales connected to Caw and his family and therefore representative of an older tradition.

'Arecluta' means 'land by the river Clut', and scholars currently associate this with the River Clyde that flows through Glasgow. But another possibility exists in Wales. The River Clwyd, which flows into the Irish Sea near Rhyl in North Wales, is recorded in the Domesday Book as the 'Cloit' and variously throughout the twelfth century as 'Cluyt', 'Cluit' and 'Clwyth'.[6] The name is also applied to the whole of the very fertile valley through which the river runs and 'is, for the most part, watered'. Confusion between the Clwyd and the Clyde has caused problems for scholars for many years; for example, the Saxon fort of Cledemutha was for a long time considered to be on the Clyde, but is now firmly identified with Rhuddlan, near the mouth of the River Clwyd.[7] Our research also suggests that many of the events associated with the River Clut should in fact be located on the Clwyd, not the Clyde.

The relocation of 'Arecluta' from the Clyde to the Clwyd is further strengthened when we find that the 'mons Bannauc' of the Latin text can also be located in the vicinity of the Clwyd. The name translates into Welsh as 'Mynydd Bannog' – the word '*bannog*' meaning 'horn shaped' or something conspicuous – and this is a place referred to by the Welsh bards on several occasions. The mountain was obviously a major landmark, as events are said to have taken place *'tra Bannog'* ('beyond Bannog').[8]

One poem attributed to Llywarch Hen clearly states that Bannog is 'Where the Clwyd goes into the Clywedog'.[9] Overlooking the Vale of Clwyd is a mountain called Bron Bannog, culminating in a double-peaked summit 1,500 feet above sea level, and from its slopes the two rivers of the Clwyd and the Clywedog begin their journeys to the Irish Sea. The existence of the place names Cefn Bannog and Waen Bannog on the high ground surrounding the peak shows that the term 'Bannog' was applied across this considerable upland area.[10]

The place names 'Arecluta' and 'mons Bannauc' can therefore both be identified with sites in North Wales, and if we accept that the association of Caw with Scotland is spurious we then have no reason to place him or his children, including Gildas, in Scotland as many historians currently do. Having, we hope, proved this point we can now look at the Welsh evidence available for Caw and his children – especially Huail and his conflict with Arthur.

ARTHUR AND THE SONS OF CAW

The figure of Caw was addressed in Chapter 5, when discussing the tasks undertaken by Arthur in *Culhwch and Olwen*. In Welsh tradition he is renowned for being the father of many children, the most important being Gildas, the author of *De Excidio*, and Huail, whom we will discuss below, though twenty of his sons were also members of Arthur's court according to *Culhwch and Olwen*.[11] Within Welsh genealogical material the family of Caw is

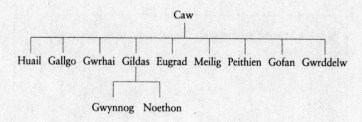

Chart 7 DESCENDANTS OF CAW

frequently associated with Gwynedd and, although the information available is sparse, the most prominent names and the locations associated with them are detailed in the chart and in the paragraphs below.[12]

Eugrad, Gallgo and Peithien

These three children of Caw are mentioned in the Breton *Life of St Gildas*: 'Egreas (Eugrad), with his brother Alleccus (Gallgo) and their sister Peteova (Peithien), a virgin consecrated to God, having also themselves similarly given up their patrimony and renounced worldly pomp, retired to the remotest part of the country, and at no distance from each other, built, each one for himself, an oratory, placing their sister in the middle one.'[13] The oratories they built were in Twrcelyn, an area of Anglesey.

Gofan ap Caw

Gofan is the saint of a now extinct chapel at St Govan near Bosherton in Pembrokeshire.[14]

Gwrddelw ap Caw

Gwrddelw is the saint of Llangwyllog on the isle of Anglesey.[15]

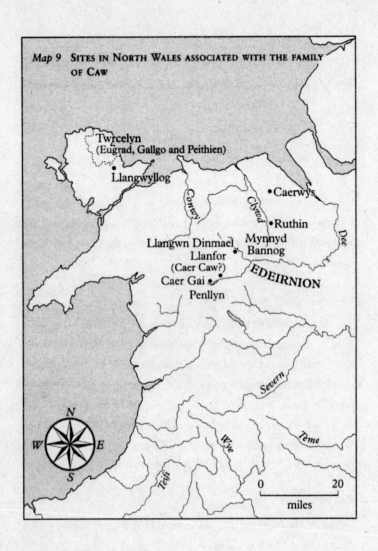

Map 9 SITES IN NORTH WALES ASSOCIATED WITH THE FAMILY OF CAW

Twrcelyn
(Eugrad, Gallgo and Peithien)

Llangwyllog

Conwy

Clwyd

Dee

Caerwys

Ruthin

Llangwn Dinmael
Llanfor
(Caer Caw?)

Mynnyd
Bannog

Caer Gai

EDEIRNION

Penllyn

Severn

Wye

Teme

Teifi

N
W   E
S

0   20
miles

Gwrhai ap Caw

Gwrhai is the saint of Penystrywaid near Llandinam in Montgomeryshire.[16]

Gwynnog

Gwynnog is the saint of Llanwnog and Aberhafesb near Newtown in Montgomeryshire, of two now extinct chapels at Llanwynnog near Clodock in Herefordshire, and of Capel Gwynog in the parish of Caerleon on Usk.[17]

Meilig ap Caw

Meilig is mentioned in *The Book of Llandaf* as the saint of Llowes in Elfael;[18] the site of his foundation is known today as Croes Feilig, and is near Llowes.[19] He also has a dedication at Llanfaelog in Anglesey.

ST NOETHON

Noethon is commemorated with his brother at Llangwm, as mentioned in Chapter 5.

Other Welsh sources associate Caw with three different regions of North Wales: Twrcelyn in Anglesey,[20] Cwm Cawlwyd near Capel Curig in Snowdonia[21] and, most importantly in the context of this appendix, the Edeirnion valley, centred on Corwen.[22]

THE LOST SAGA OF HUAIL AND ARTHUR

The story of Arthur's feud with Huail ap Caw is very important, for it was never included in later Arthurian material and therefore remains a rare example of an Arthurian story surviving in a form unaffected by Geoffrey of Monmouth and the later romances.

The earliest reference to this episode is found in *Culhwch and Olwen*, which states, 'Huail ap Caw, he never submitted to a lord's hand.'[23] Later on in the tale we are told that a feud existed between Arthur and Huail concerning Gwydre, 'because Huail his uncle stabbed him, and thereby there was feud between Huail and Arthur because of that wound.'[24] Caradog later expands upon these few details in his *Life of Gildas*:

> St Gildas was the contemporary of Arthur, the king of the whole of Britannia, whom he loved exceedingly, and whom he always desired to obey. Nevertheless his twenty-three brothers constantly rose up against the afore-mentioned rebellious king, refusing to own him as their lord; but they often routed and drove him out from forest and battlefield. Huail, the elder brother, an active warrior and most distinguished soldier, submitted to no king, not even Arthur. He used to harass the latter, and to provoke the greatest anger between them both.[25]

The story of the feud between Huail and Arthur is next found in Giraldus Cambrensis's *Description of Wales*, written in 1188. Giraldus was a product of the Anglo-Norman society of South Wales and, like Caradog of Llancarfan, also found employment writing propaganda for Glastonbury. Born into the same society that first crowned Arthur and began his long transformation from Welsh warlord into the all-conquering English sovereign of the later romances, Giraldus was one of the few who voiced strong reservations about Geoffrey's *Historia*, dismissing it as a fabrication – which is rather ironic coming from the man who first recorded the fabricated discovery of Arthur's body at Glastonbury.

He mentions the antagonism between Arthur and Huail in the section of his work where he explains why there is no reference to Arthur in the works of the famous Gildas:

> The Britons maintain that, when Gildas criticised his own people so bitterly, he wrote as he did because he was so infuriated by the fact that King Arthur had killed his own brother, who was a prince of Albaniae. When he heard of his brother's death, or so the Britons say, he threw into the sea a number of outstanding books which he had written in their praise and about Arthur's achievements. As a result you will find no book which gives an authentic account of that great prince.[26]

The earlier *Life of Gildas* by the monk of Rhuys tells us that Huail was 'a very active man in war, who, after his father's death succeeded him to the kingdom'.[27] According to the evidence above, this places him in the region of the Edeirnion ruled by his father. However, the most complete version of the tale concerning the enmity between Arthur and Huail can be found in a chronicle of *c.* 1530 written by Elis Gruffudd and is summarised below.

Huail was spotted cavorting with one of the mistresses of Arthur, and a fierce fight broke out between the two men, during which Huail wounded Arthur on the knee. A peace was made between them on the condition that Huail would never reproach Arthur in regard to the injury he had inflicted. Arthur returned to his court at Caerwys, but was for ever after slightly lame. On a subsequent occasion Arthur was dressed in women's clothing in order to visit a girl in the town of Ruthin. As Arthur was dancing with the girl, Huail passed by and, recognising Arthur because of his lameness, shouted out, 'The dancing were all right if it were not for the knee.' Arthur heard this and knew that it was Huail who had spoken. He returned to his court and ordered Huail to be brought before him and reproached for his faithlessness. Huail was taken to Ruthin and his head was cut off on a large stone which to this day is known as Maen Huail (the Stone of Huail).[28]

The setting of this tale complements the geography of Caw and his sons as oulined above, and Caerwys, Ruthin, and Maen Huail are all located in a relatively small area of North Wales. In fact the ancient stone of Maen Huail can still be seen in the corner of the town square in Ruthin with a small plaque that reads

MAEN HUAIL
On which tradition states King Arthur beheaded Huail,
brother of Gildas the Historian.

Thomas Jones in his article 'Chwedl Huail ap Caw ac Arthur' commented that 'As far as I can tell, the story of Huail, brother of Gildas, and his connection with king Arthur has not survived to this day apart from the brief summary of it on the stone, but observe that there is here an appeal to tradition that supports the period'.[29] Jones was of the opinion that 'there is no doubt that the anecdote about Huail ap Caw and Arthur and Huail's execution on the stone in Ruthin was a story he [Elis] heard by word of mouth' and that there are 'other references in Elis's story which show that this part of the country already had some Arthurian connections'.[30]

It would seem that Elis recorded one of the episodes that made up the, now lost, saga of the feud between Arthur and Huail. However, there is evidence that traditions about Huail existed at an earlier date, as the bards of the fifteenth century refer to him in a comparative way when praising their patrons. The bard Lewis

Glyn Cothi refers to Huail on several occasions: in one instance he states that his patron had '*corff Huail ap Caw*', 'Huail ap Caw's body',[31] and in another he compares the grave of Master Watkin, lord of Herast (modern Hergest), to the grave of '*Huail e hun*', 'Huail himself'.[32] Thomas Jones was of the opinion that this was 'a clear suggestion that Lewis knew of some peculiarity which characterised the hero's grave; and one cannot help but wonder whether he knew about the large stone in Ruthin'.[33]

Huail is also associated with other Arthurian heroes in one of the triads:

> Three Battle-Diademed (Taleithyawc) Men of Ynys Prydein:
> Trystan son of Tallwch,
> And Hueil son of Caw,
> And Cai the son of Cynyr Ceinfarfog.
> And one that was diademed above the three of them:
> That was Bedwyr the son of Bedrawc.[34]

As we showed in Chapter 4, Trystan, Cei and Bedwyr are heroes linked to Arthur in the earliest sources. The original meaning of '*taleithyawc*' raises an interesting possibility. The Welsh word '*taleithyawc*' translates as 'one who wears a *talaith*', which is a coronet or chaplet and according to Rachel Bromwich 'was evidently a mark of distinction worn on the head by the foremost champions in battle, perhaps as an incentive to draw the enemy's attention to them'.[35] As we pointed out in *The Keys to Avalon*, this might explain one of the most intriguing events in Welsh history. Following his conquest of North Wales, Edward I took possession of the relics of Gwynedd at Aberconwy Abbey in June 1283. The most important of these relics was a circlet known as the Crown of Arthur. Edward placed great importance upon this relic, and had it regilded and paraded through the streets of London to Westminster Abbey, where it was presented to the shrine of Edward the Confessor as a symbol of his successor's superiority over the Welsh. Could this simple gold band have been not the crown of Arthur the non-existent king, but the *taleith*, as worn by many warriors of the period, of Arthur the warlord?[36]

As can be seen by the evidence above, the story of Huail and Arthur was well known in Wales at an early date – and probably much earlier than any of the written sources suggest. Thomas Jones best sums up the situation regarding the various references to this episode. 'Based on the whole, one must come to the conclusion that a heroic story about Huail was being told at least as early as the eleventh century.'[37]

So what can we piece together from the fragments that have survived? We can surmise that the saga of Arthur and Huail started with the tale of the wounding of Huail's nephew Gwydre. Following on from this, Huail and twenty-two of his brothers waged war on Arthur and often beat him in battle. This point is very important, as it contradicts the image of Arthur as an all-conquering hero as portrayed in virtually all later sources and also shows that he spent a great deal of time fighting fellow Welshmen. Huail used every opportunity to harass and to provoke Arthur, looking for the opportunity for confrontation, and probably in the original tale there were several episodes woven around the theme of how Huail outwitted and defeated Arthur, just like the episode in Ruthin. At every chance Huail and his brothers would raid Arthur's lands, looting and pillaging, enhancing Huail's fame as a feared and renowned warrior (as he was remembered in Welsh poetry centuries later). One final reference from the *Life of*

Gildas by Caradog of Llancarvan shows that the local populace considered Huail, not Arthur, to be their rightful ruler, in the line concerning Huail, who 'as the inhabitants used to assert and hope, was destined to become king'.[38] Huail was finally killed by Arthur in Ruthin, and his resistance was then over.[39]

THE LLANFOR STONE

In the wall of the church of Llanfor, a small village just north of Bala and at one time a very important ecclesiastical site, can be found a very interesting inscribed stone. It was first mentioned by the great Welsh scholar Robert Vaughan of Hengwrt near Dolgellau in the first half of the seventeenth century,[40] and the most recent reading of the inscription gives the following:

Cavo(s) (son) of (Seniargios) (lies here?).[41]

V. E. Nash-Williams dated the inscription to between AD 500 and 533, and during our research it struck us that the name recorded on the stone could well be that of Caw, as Llanfor is only a few miles south of the Edeirnion valley in which he is said to have ruled and he also lived in the right period.[42] The earliest form of the name 'Caw' in written Latin sources is in the *Life of Gildas* by the monk of Rhuys in Brittany, where the name appears as 'Cauno' – very similar to the form in the inscription.[43] This possibility has not been previously considered because Caw has always been supposed to come from Scotland, which as we have shown is not acceptable. The father of Caw is unnamed in any source, but does the fact that Caw's name is associated with the very area in which the stone exists mean that the inscribed stone of Llanfor records the name of one of Arthur's warriors? In fact some scholars, such as Sir John Rhys, have tried to identify the name with that of another of Arthur's warriors, Cai, owing to the proximity of the Roman fort known as Caer Gai, and it is to this Arthurian connection with the area that we will turn our attention now.

CAER CAI AND 'THE WELSH VERSION OF THE BIRTH OF ARTHUR'

In the preceding chapters we have mentioned how the story portrayed in the widely circulated *Historia Regum Britanniae* and later romantic literature eventually overtook and obscured the original Welsh Arthurian tradition, even to the point where the Welsh themselves found it politically necessary to adapt their independent stories in an attempt to incorporate them within the new foreign Arthurian legends. In spite of this, it is possible to find the remnants of a more archaic Arthurian corpus among the Welsh adaptations of the later romances. One of the best examples of this kind of survival is within the fifteenth-century Welsh adaptation of part of the Vulgate Merlin, contained in the National Library of Wales manuscript Llanstephan MS 201, known as 'A Welsh Version of the Birth of Arthur'. At the end of this appendix the English translation of this text is reprinted in full for the first time since 1913. J. H. Davies, who first edited and translated the text, pointed out that, although the tale is undoubtedly drawn from the

Merlin section of the Vulgate Cycle, the 'Welsh redactor was acquainted with the traditional form of the tale in Wales'.[44] One of the most interesting additions in the Welsh text is the identity ascribed to the foster-father of Arthur.

The Vulgate Merlin names Arthur's foster-father as Antor (or sometimes Auctor), and the later *Morte D'Arthur* of Malory calls him Sir Ector; however, the 'Welsh Version of the Birth of Arthur' names him Cynyr Ceinfarfog of Penllyn. Cynyr Ceinfarfog is referred to as the father of Cai in both *Culhwch and Olwen* and the Triads, showing that this relationship was common knowledge in Wales, as mentioned in Chapter 4. Davies also believed that the author of the Welsh redaction 'must have obtained the name Cynyr Varvawc [Ceinfarfog] from local tradition or from some earlier text'.[45]

The region of Penllyn is centred on Llyn Tegid (better known as Bala Lake), the source of the River Dee, and within the region, in the parish of Llanuwchllyn at the southern end of Bala Lake, stands the Roman fort of Caer Gai (Fort of Cai). The historian Sir J. E. Lloyd believed that 'Caer Cai may have been the Royal residence at the head of the lake from which the district took its name of Penllyn [i.e. "Head of the Lake"]'.[46] This association was known in the early seventeenth century to Robert Vaughan, who states in his notes regarding Merionethshire, 'In the parish of Llanuwchllyn . . . over against [Carn Dochan Castle] is Caer Gai built in the time of the Romans. This place was called Caer Gai, of Cai Hir ap Cynyr, that was King Arthur's foster brother, who dwelt there.'[47]

The tradition is also remembered in the works of the Welsh bard William Lleyn (d. 1587), but he refers to Caer Gai as Caer

Gynyr (Fort of Cynyr), Cai's father.[48] However, the tradition goes back still further than this, and in a short article in 1944 the scholar Thomas Roberts gathered together many of the references to the tradition of Arthur being fostered at Caer Gai, from Welsh bardic poetry. After citing many of the bardic references, he came to the conclusion that the tradition of Arthur and Cai at Caer Gai 'was very well-known, definitely, among the poets and story-tellers of the Middle Ages, as the people of Wales had linked Caergai with the name of Cai ap Cynyr since an early age'.[49]

The fame of the tradition was not limited to Wales, and the poet Edmund Spenser refers to it in his epic allegorical poem *The Faerie Queene*, published in 1590. While speaking of Arthur's birth and upbringing, he says of Arthur's foster-father (who for some reason he calls Timon):

> Old Timon, who in youthly yeares hath beene
> In warlike feates th'expertest man alive
> His dwelling is low in a valley greene,
> Under the foot or Rauran [Aran] mossy hore,
> From whence the river Dee, as silver cleene,
> His tombling billowes rolls with gentle rore;
> There all my daies he traind mee up in vertuous lore.[50]

When this tradition is understood in the context of the evidence regarding Cai in the earliest sources, it becomes even more relevant. In these sources Cai is Arthur's chief warrior and constant companion, and he is the central figure in the Arthurian poem *Pa Gur?* from *The Black Book of Carmarthen*, where he is portrayed as leading the men of Gwynedd into battle:

Rac riev emreis	Before the lord of Emrys [Gwynedd].
Gueleis e Kei ar uris.	I saw Cai hastening.[51]

Within the same poem he is also referred to as leading a host into battle in the lines

Oet hyneiw guastad   He was a constant chief
Ar lleg ar lles gulad.   Over a host for the sake of a land.[52]

As suggested in Chapter 7, Arthur himself appears to be firmly attached to Gwynedd in the early poetry, and probably held the position equivalent to the *penteulu* of the house of Gwynedd. Cai, the foremost warrior of Arthur's war-band, leading the men of Gwynedd reinforces this suggestion. Within *Pa Gur?* the only firmly identifiable places mentioned in connection with Cai are Emrys (a pseudonym for Gwynedd) and Mon (Anglesey), also a part of the kingdom of Gwynedd, though place names such as Gwryd Cai (Cai's Fathom) near Pen y Gwyrd, west of Capel Curig in Snowdonia, show that other traditions concerning him must once have existed in this region.

In the early tradition the references to Cai are always heroic and mainly complementary in nature, and from the references in the early poetry and prose tales there can be little doubt that there was once an independent cycle of tales concerning Arthur's relationship with Cai. Evidence for this can be discerned within *Pa Gur?* and *Culhwch and Olwen*, where there are allusions to stories concerning Cai and Arthur which the audience, in the period before the tale achieved written form, would have had some knowledge of – in, for example, the episode concerning the giant Dillus Farfog in *Culhwch and Olwen*, when Arthur suggests that Cai could not have slain Dillus if the giant had been awake at the time. From this point on Cai would have nothing to do with Arthur, but later on in the tale there is reference to Arthur slaying Gwyddog ap Menestyr and his brothers in revenge for their slaying of Cai.[53]

One final point concerning the story of Arthur's early life in the 'Welsh Version of the Birth of Arthur' is the reference to Arthur being fostered – a common practice in Wales in the medieval period. Fosterage was an important part of the social system in the age of Arthur, and involved the delivery of one's son, at about the age of seven or eight, to the court of an allied lord or one's kinsman to be raised with others of his own age and taught the skills needed for a military career. The child would remain in this foster family until he reached the age of majority at fourteen, when he would enter the *teulu* of that lord. The bonds that fosterage engendered within a *teulu* cannot be overestimated, and probably provided the cohesion necessary for the *teulu* to adhere to the code of honour expected from the society of that time. What better than the bond of childhood and shared experience to form the foundation of the Dark Age war-band that had to live, eat, sleep, fight and possibly die together?[54] The close ties implied by the tradition of Arthur being a foster-brother to Cai might well explain why Cai is his constant companion in nearly all of the earliest sources – see Appendix 1.

The two little-known parts of the Arthurian legend looked at in this appendix are probably the most substantial survivals of what was once a far larger corpus of stories known to the Welsh bards. Many obscure place names and traditions from the Welsh sources can only begin to be understood when we view them in a narrowed-down geographical area and within the context of the society of Dark Age Wales, not the medieval age of shining armour and huge stone castles.

A WELSH VERSION
OF THE BIRTH OF ARTHUR

The following English translation was originally published in 1913 in the article 'A Welsh Version of the Birth of Arthur' in the journal *Y Cymmrodor*, Vol. XXIV, pp. 247–64. It is reprinted here with the kind permission of The Honourable Society of Cymmrodorion. The translation was made by J. H. Davies, who also edited the Welsh text based upon the earliest and most complete manuscript of the text found in Llanstephan MS 201 from the National Library of Wales and dating from the fifteenth century. An earlier fragment of the text dating from the fourteenth century is found in folio 505 of Llanstephan MS 4 and, according to J. Gwenogfryn Evans, is written in a very similar hand to that of the famous *Red Book of Hergest*.[55] A later copy of Llanstephan MS 201 was made by the Welsh scholar John Jones of Gellilyfdy, Flintshire, in 1611 and is preserved in Peniarth MS 215, and Davies used this manuscript to fill in the gaps left by Llanstephan MS 201 where the text is now illegible. These sections are printed in italics in the text below. The manuscript itself actually begins in the middle of a line, but Davies felt that it was quite complete in this form as there are 'no missing pages traceable'.[56]

The Text

. . . to her a portion of his kingdom *whilst* he lived. And a short time *afterwards* he caused a feast to be prepared for the nobles of the island, and at the feast he married *Eigyr* and made peace with the *kinsmen of Gwrleis* and all his allies. *Gwrleis* had two daughters by Eigyr, *Gwyar* and *Dioneta*. Gwyar was a widow, and after *the death of* her husband *Ymer Llydaw* (she dwelt) *at her father's court with her son, Hywel.* Now Uther *caused Lleu, the son of Cynvarch,* to marry her, and they had children, two sons, *Gwalchmai* and *Medrawd, and three* daughters, Gracia, *Graeria* and *Dioneta.* The Duke's *other daughter,* Uther *caused (to be sent) to Ynys Avallach,* and of all in her age she was most skilled in the seven arts. *Now when the feast was over* and all had taken their *leave,* Merlin drew near Uther and *spoke to him thus,* 'Lord,' said he, 'in sooth *it was by my aid* that thou didst obtain thy *will* in all places up to the present, now therefore *pay me for* my pains as thou didst promise.' 'Gladly will I pay thee,' said Uther. 'Sir,' said Merlin, 'Eigyr is now with child since the night thou didst sleep with her in Dindagol Castle, and whatever heir thou dost have, he will not be recognised in the island as thine, since he was conceived before marriage. Therefore conceal this matter well until the child be born, and then let (the child) be *given* unto me, and I will cause him to be nurtured *with care in secret* so that neither *thou nor thy lady* shall be put to shame, and possibly this heir *may rule the kingdom* after thy day.' And at night *in bed* Uther *spoke to* Eigyr in the manner Merlin *had taught him.* '*It seemeth* to me,' said he, 'that *thou art with child.*' 'Sir,' said Eigyr, '*thy protection I crave,* and I will speak the truth. *When I was in the castle of Dindagol,* and thy army *lay around the castle* where Gwrleis was, *there came in unto me* three men in form *like unto Gwrleis,*[57] and he slept with me that *night, and when he went* away the following day he *left me* with child.' 'The best counsel *that I wot* is to *be silent,*' said Uther, 'until the birth (of the child) and *then will I* send it to a place where it will be lovingly nurtured.' And this they agreed upon until such time as a handsome son was born, and a messenger took (the child) to the court of Cynyr Farfog, Lord of Penllyn, and with him letters from Uther and Merlin. And when he came to the court, he placed the lad before Cynyr and he gave him the letters, and Cynyr opened them and read the following words: 'Uther Pendragon, chief of the Britons, sendeth greetings and true lordship to Cynyr Farfog, may thy presence know that I was commanded in my sleep to go outside the door of my chamber and whatever living being I saw there, was I to cause to be nurtured lovingly, therefore command I thee to upbring the lad we found *there, whom we are* now sending to thee, and thy wife shall *suckle him* and provide *another nurse* for thine own son.' And when *Cynyr had read* the letters, he took the lad and caused *him to be baptized by* the name of Arthur, and *he nurtured him until* he was fourteen years old in all ways as *he had been commanded.* Uther *Pendragon ruled this* Island for ... *years altogether* and he had daughter born of *Eigyr* called Anna, and in the *fourteenth year* in the week of the feast of Martin came the end of Uther Pendragon as is related in the 'History of the Britons' [Geoffrey's *Historia*].

And after Uther's death the nobles of the isle met together at Caer Vuddai in the presence of the Archbishop Dyfric to take counsel with him as to whom they should make king to rule over the kingdom, and to see who in point of birth and morals and strength was worthy to be king, for they doubted not that Uther had died leaving no heir of his body except a daughter. And indeed necessity urged them to this, seeing that the Saxons whom Vortigern had settled in the island had no sooner heard of the death of Uther than they sent messengers to Germany to fetch their kinsmen, and they overcame the island from the mouth of the Humber to the sea of Caithness. And when Dyfric had heard of the peril and misery of the kingdom he felt compassion for the people, and he summoned the bishops of the kingdom and their chiefs and beseeched them in the name of God to choose a king. And thereupon they began to speak anew and straightway each one chose his own kinsman or his greatest friend, so that through their disagreement there was none who could receive the honour by common consent. Thereupon Dyfric reflected upon the tribulation of the people and thought of the words of Christ in the Gospel, 'every kingdom that is divided within itself shall be destroyed, and he perceived that the rich angered the poor, and the strong oppressed the weak, and the wicked despised the righteous from the want of justice and government.' And thereupon they agreed to ask Merlin whom they should elect as their king, for he had advised them on two previous occasions.

Thereupon Merlin said that it was not fitting that he should interfere in so important and wrath-provoking an affair as that, 'yet,' said he, 'I will give you counsel if you will abide by it.' Then they promised to abide by his counsel. 'Sirs,' then said Merlin, 'Uther Pendragon died after Martinmass, and it is now near Christmas corresponding to the day on which Christ the only son of God came to the world, born of our lady Mary the virgin, of the great love of the people, who is Lord of Lords and King of Kings, to whom the weak and strong pay obedience, from whom none that opposeth him can flee, who looketh not at the outward forms of men, but judgeth them by their hearts; now therefore gather ye all together and cleanse yourselves by that appointed time and come together to the church, and pray to God in all innocence that he may make clear who is worthy to reign over you, and if you truly trust in Him, your desire will be granted. For he said entreat, take, seek and ye shall find.' And when Merlin made this speech he asked the consent of the nobles to go to his own country. And thereupon they thanked him much for his advice and beseeched him to stay with them over the Christmas, but he tarried not and did not promise to return for that occasion because of appointment that he had with the bishop Blasius, his confessor and the scribe of all his prophecies. And so Merlin went to his own country. And on Christmas Eve the whole nation came together, weak and strong, rich and poor, and thither also Cynyr Farfog and Cai his son came, and Arthur knew not but that Cynyr was his father, and he honoured him in the way that a son should honour his father. And when the first cock crew they all did arise and go into the church, and the Archbishop began the service and requested everybody to pray to God as Merlin had advised. And after matins the Archbishop enrobed for the first mass, and said to the people: 'Sirs', said he 'three things are needful for us, salvation for our souls, success for our bodies, and a king to reign over us, and there is no way of obtaining any one of these by our own power, therefore pray to him in whose name everything is done and without who nothing can be done, and if he hearkeneth not let everyone repeat five times the prayer which Christ taught his disciples.' And when these words had been said mass was sung until after the gospel and then the dawn broke and those who had said mass first went outside the church to a level plot within the gates of the monastery: and they beheld in the midst of this plot a great four square stone of colour like unto marble, and in the stone there stuck a sword pointwise as firmly as if it grew out of the stone. And about the sword verses were written in golden letters, as follows:-

HOC GLADII SIGNUM MONSTRAT REGEM DEO DIGNUM.
NULLUS TOLLAT ILLUM SIC NISI SIT PER DOMINUM.

The meaning of the verses is this: 'This sword is a sign to point out a worthy king in the sight of God. None shall pull this sword out except one by the aid of God.' And when they had read this writing they sent messengers into the church to tell the Archbishop of this event. Thereupon the Archbishop thought that God had sent that sign and forthwith he went towards the place where the stone was, and the common people with him, and he sprinkled holy water over it, and they worshipped God, and ordered five of the best clerks and five of the laymen to take charge of the stone until mass was finished, and they returned to the church singing praises to God. And when mass was over they returned to the place where the stone was, and quarrelled amongst one another who first should pull the sword or who had the first right to attempt to pull the sword from the stone. Some demanded this because of their power, others on account of their comeliness and strength, others because of the numbers of their kinsmen. Thereupon Dyfric, seeing their envy, said to the people, 'O, my friends, we should rejoice together before God to-day for he, out of his infinite mercy from his high throne in heaven has hearkened to our prayer. Therefore do I beseech and command you with all the power God has given me, that none draw nigh to this holy sign to dishonour it. Let us pray God that he show us who shall be king to reign over us, and doubtless we could not, did we wish, prevent God from carrying out his will, let us therefore wait patiently for him whom God hath chosen for he cannot be deceived by gifts nor menaced by threats: he asks of man naught but his heart, for the service of man made he made the world and all that is in it, and man was made to serve him.' Then went they into the church for evening mass, and when the mass was done, they returned to the place where the stone lay, and Dyfric said to the nobles of the kingdom, 'Sirs, greatly ought ye to pay thanks to Christ in that he hath shown ye a sign like unto that which he shewed the disciples when he was going to his passion, and he said to them, "he that hath no sword let him sell his garment and buy one. One of the disciples said unto him, here are two swords. It is enough, said Christ."

'By the one sword is understood spiritual possession in the hands of the prelates of the church who should warn the people that they have sinned, and release them when repentant of their sins. By the other sword is to be understood the power of the lords of the earth who should succour the weak, punish the cruel, and maintain justice with the sword which God hath shown unto you this day.' And when he had said these words Dyfric chose fifty men and two hundred of the chief men of the kingdom and commanded them from the oldest to the (next) oldest to try and pull the sword from the stone, and none of them could withdraw it. And then Dyfric commanded all of them one after the other to withdraw the sword if they could, and there was none at that time that could do so. Then did Dyfric command ten of the men to take charge of the stone until . . . ,[58] and commanded everyone to come to that place on that day. And when they had come together at that time they told the Archbishop that they would not leave the city or its neighbourhood until they knew who should be king over them. And when they had heard the mass and everybody was in good spirits they went to joust and tourney,[59] and the people of the city went to watch the play even the tell men who had charge of the stone. Cai, the son of Cynyr, who had been knighted on the previous Allhallowmass had come there to win his spurs. And behold at the end of the play tumult and commotion arose amongst them and they smote each other lustily, and thereupon Cai broke his sword near the crosspiece and he sent Arthur to his lodging to fetch another sword. And when Arthur came near unto the lodging he could find no way to enter because of the people who were watching the play. And sad at heart he returned as far as the gate of the monastery, and there he spied the sword and the stone with nobody in charge, and he reflected that he had not attempted to withdraw the sword, and should he be able to draw the sword he would give it to his brother Cai instead of the one which he had broken in the play. And he dismounted and took hold of the handle of the sword and pulled it out without difficulty, and hid it under his armour and brought it to Cai. And when Cai saw the sword he recognized it and shewed it to his father, and said, 'I am the king! I am the king! I have pulled the sword from the stone!' But when Cynyr saw this he disbelieved Cai and the three of them went to the place where the stone was, and Cynyr asked Cai how he obtained the sword. Then he thought it wicked to anger his father, and said that Arthur had given him the sword. Thereupon Cynyr questioned Arthur and he told him the truth how he had withdrawn the sword. 'Put the sword in the place thou hadst it,' said Cynyr. And this Arthur did without difficulty. Then Cynyr asked Cai to withdraw the sword, and he could not. 'Withdraw the sword,' said Cynyr to Arthur, and Arthur did it immediately and then placed it back in the stone. And the three went into the church. And Cynyr took Arthur between his hands, and said to him in this wise, 'O thou my beloved son what honour wouldst thou grant to me were I to make thee king of this Kingdom.' 'Sire father,' said Arthur, 'what of wealth God giveth to me in this world, I will not share with thee but give it all into thy keeping.' 'Then,' said Cynyr, 'thy foster father am I, and thou takest me to be thy natural father. Yet know I not the father who sought thee nor the mother who bore thee into the world.' Then Arthur wept and said, 'O Lord God what wanted I in this world and I am without hope as one coming alone from the earth, why return not I now to the earth again.' Then said Cynyr to Arthur, 'I caused thee to be baptized and called Arthur, and nurtured thee, and if God gives thee honour thou oughtest to share it with me and remember me when thou comest into thy kingdom.' 'Take me as thy son,' said Arthur, 'and I will do what thou askest.' 'I request thee,' said Cynyr, 'to make Cai my son senesechal of thy kingdom and that he lose not his office on account of anything that he shall say or do. For should he be ill-bred it is not his fault but thine for thou wast suckled by his mother, and he, because of thee, was suckled by a mean alien woman.' And Arthur promised Cynyr all this, and then Cynyr told the Archbishop, 'I have a son who is not yet knighted, who begs that he be allowed to try to withdraw the sword.' Then the Archbishop commanded everybody to come to the place where the stone was, and when they had all come together Cynyr asked Arthur to place the sword in Dyfric's hand, and this he did without trouble. Then Dyfric took Arthur by the hand and led him towards the Church, singing praises to God. Thereupon the earls and barons were angered, and they said amongst one another, 'this man cometh of lowly blood, whereas we are of the blood of Uther Pendragon, how, therefore, can we suffer this man to reign over us.' Cynyr was standing with Arthur and the common people, and opposite him were all the earls and barons. Now, when Dyfric perceived their envy, he said to them, 'were we all opposed to the elect of God, that which God wills must needs be.' Then Arthur placed the sword in the stone again, and Dyfric ordered everybody to pull it out if they could, but none could. Then did they delay until Candlemass, and on that day did they all try to withdraw the sword, and none could do so. Then Dyfric commanded Arthur to bring the sword to him, and this Arthur did. Then did the mighty men of the kingdom ask that the matter might be delayed until Easter to see if it were possible to find a person of higher rank than Arthur. And on the eve of Easter, when they had come together, Dyfric asked them if they wished Arthur to be their king. Then straightway everybody said, let him be king over us, a deliverer and a protector. And the next morning the earls and the barons drew nigh unto Arthur and said unto him in this wise, 'Sir, as thou wilt be king over us, accept our homage, give us land, and at Whitsuntide we will crown thee. Give us a reply of thine own on this.' 'That will I,' said Arthur, 'I will neither accept homage, nor give land, nor take land from anyone until I am crowned, and joyfully will I wait for the crown, for I never thought of receiving any honour, except such as God should give me.' And when they could not deceive him in that way they sent many presents to him to see if he were greedy of riches and inclined to be miserly. But Arthur understood that, and he accustomed himself amongst them until Whitsuntide, so that some feared him and others loved him above all in the kingdom. And on Whit Saturday he was knighted and many others were knighted in his honour. And the next morning a royal robe was placed upon him, and he was brought to the place where lay the stone and sword. Then Dyfric said to him, 'Sir, here are the laws that thou must keep, valiantly must thou maintain the Catholic Faith, the church of God, and the weak and the poor, honour God and the saints as much as thou art able, hearken to thy counsellors patiently, make good laws, punish the wicked. And if thou promisest to do these things, take the sword that God hath sent thee as a token of love of thee and strength to us.' Then Arthur fell on his knees and raised his hands and said, 'God give me grace to direct my thoughts and deeds to his praise, and for the good of my own soul, and strength to govern you.' Then he took the sword in his hand and went into the church and sat in the royal chair, and the Archbishop placed the crown on his head, and the sceptre in his hand. And when mass was over they went out to seek the stone, and the stone was never seen from that time onwards, and then they feasted. And hence Arthur went to do battle and to govern the kingdom as is set forth in the history of the Britons. And Arthur kept the sword while lie lived, and it was called Caledfwlch. So endeth this story.

Appendix 3

·

THE SOURCE MATERIALS

HIS appendix is intended to give a brief overview of the publications that print and discuss the important source materials, both in their original language and in translation. Throughout our research it was surprising to find how difficult it was to obtain some of the most important works on the subject: even books published within the last twenty years are out of print and almost imposible to buy second-hand. Some books that are constantly referred to by scholars for this period were published over fifty years ago in print runs of only a few hundred, making it very difficult for people without access to one of the larger libraries to consult the text.

GILDAS (*c*. AD 540)

A Welsh monk who lived in the sixth century, Gildas is famous as the author of the earliest contemporary British document to have survived – *De Excidio Britanniae*, usually known as *De Excidio*. The standard edition of the text can be found in Theodore Mommsen (ed.), *Monumenta Germaniae Historica, Chronica Minora*, Vol. III (Berlin, 1894). This edition prints the Latin text based upon four different manuscripts, but is now very difficult to obtain. As all the introductory matter is also written in Latin, it is not easy to use either. The Latin text as printed by Mommsen was reprinted with a facing English translation and copious notes in two volumes by Hugh Williams as *Gildae De Excidio Britanniae* for the Cymmrodorion Record Series (Hugh Williams, 1899–1901). This edition also includes two Lives of Gildas: one by a monk of Rhuys in Brittany and the other by Caradog of Llancarvan. A third volume which was to include an index to the manuscript was unfortunately never published.

The edition most widely used today is Michael Winterbottom (ed.), *Gildas, The Ruin of Britain* (Phillimore, 1978), which prints the Latin text, an English translation and some basic notes (not as extensive as in the Williams edition). A new edition of the *De Excidio* is badly needed, based upon all the available manuscripts and accompanied by a detailed commentary. The best of recent scholarship on this text can be found in Michael Lapidge and David Dumville (eds.), *Gildas: New Approaches* (Boydell, 1984).

BEDE (AD 731)

Bede was an English monk from Jarrow in Northumbria and was one of the most influential writers of the Dark Ages. We are fortunate that the earliest manuscripts of this work date from the eighth century and are therefore contemporary with the author. He wrote many works, including chronicles, biographies of saints and commentaries on the Gospels, but the work that is of most interest is his *Historia Ecclesiastica Gentis Anglorum* (Ecclesiastical History of the English People). Written from an anti-British point of view, it is the major source of English history for the sixth and seventh centuries. A detailed academic edition was edited by C. Plummer in 1898 as *Baedae Opera Historica* (Clarendon Press) and was in turn translated by Leo Sherley Price as *A History of the English Church and People* (Penguin, 1968). The text was edited again in 1969, this time making use of the very early Leningrad manuscript, not known to Plummer in 1898, and B. Colgrave and R. A. B. Mynors (eds.), *Bede: Ecclesiastical History of the English People* (Oxford University Press), contains the Latin text with a facing English translation and a detailed introduction. The 1991 revised edition is now considered to be the standard version of this text. A detailed commentary on the text is J. M. Wallace-Hadrill, *Bede's Ecclesiastical History of the English People: A Historical Commentary* (Oxford University Press, 1988). Colgrave's translation was reprinted in the paperback Oxford Worlds Classics series as Bede, *The Ecclesiastical History*, ed. Judith McClure and Roger Collins (Oxford University Press, 1994). This also contains the first ever English translation of the section of Bede's *Greater Chronicle* that covers the period from the birth of Christ to the eighth century, making it the most useful edition of Bede's work.

HISTORIA BRITTONUM (EARLY NINTH CENTURY)

The most compete edition of the *Historia Brittonum* is still found in Theodore Mommsen (ed.), *Monumenta Germaniae Historica, Chronica Minora*, Vol. III (Berlin, 1894), based upon five groups of manuscripts, but, as mentioned above, this edition is not very user-friendly.

The work is often referred to under the name 'Nennius', as the Harleian MS version (the best text) claims him as the editor. The earliest actual manuscript is known as the Chartres MS and dates from *c.* 900. Unfortunately, however, this earliest manuscript is also the most incomplete, finishing as it does midway through the section regarding Vortigern, several chapters before reaching the Arthurian material. The Chartres MS begins with the line 'Here begin excerpts of the son of Urien found in the book of saint Germanus, and concerning the origin and genealogy of the Britons, and concerning the Ages of the World.' It has been suggested that 'the son of Urien' can be identified with the person named Rhun ap Urien mentioned in the text – which if correct would date the text's composition to the middle of the seventh century.

The Latin text was edited by L. Duchesne in the journal *Revue Celtique*, Vol. XV (1894), and an English translation with notes was published by A. W. Wade-Evans in the journal *Archaeologica Cambrensis*, 1937, pp. 64–85. Other editions of note are Ferdinand Lot's *Nennius et l'Historia Brittonum* (Paris, 1934), which contains both the Harleian and Chartres texts and copious notes (in French) and is probably the most accurate edition of these texts, with the exception of the edition of the Vatican group of manuscripts (see below). David Dumville is the leading expert on these texts and has published several important articles on the subject, the most important of which are 'The Historical Value of the Historia Brittonum', *Arthurian Literature*, Vol. VI (1986), pp. 1–26, and '"Nennius" and the Historia Brittonum', *Studia Celtica*, Vol. X–XI (1975–6), pp. 78–95.

The fruits of Dumville's research were due to be published in a ten-volume edition of the *Historia Brittonum* making all the different versions available to a high academic standard, but unfortunately publication of this series was halted after the appearance of only one volume: David Dumville (ed.), *The Historia Brittonum 3:*

The Vatican Recension (Boydell & Brewer, 1985). The appearance of the other volumes in this series would greatly aid research into this fascinating and important text, and one can only hope that the rest of the proposed volumes appear in the not too distant future.

An English translation of the Harleian MS version was published by A.W. Wade-Evans in *Nennius's History of the Britons* (SPCK, 1938), along with the genealogies and the *Annales Cambriae* (see below) from the same manuscript and some useful notes. The most commonly used edition is currently that of John Morris, published as *Nennius: British History and the Welsh Annals* (Phillimore, 1980), which contains the Latin text and a translation. This edition notes variants from different manuscripts, but does not denote which manuscripts they come from, thereby defeating the object of the exercise. So, although the easiest version to obtain and the most widely used, this edition is by far the least useful of the ones mentioned above.

THE *ANNALES CAMBRIAE* (TENTH CENTURY)

This important chronicle can be found in four manuscripts. Three of these (known as A, B and C) were edited together by John ab Ithel in *Annales Cambriae*, Rolls edition (HMSO, 1860), although the accuracy of the transcription leaves a lot to be desired. The earliest text (A) was edited by Egerton Phillimore in *Y Cymmrodor*, Vol. IX (1888), pp. 141–83, and this is still the best edition available. Another good English translation with notes can be found in Wade-Evans's 1938 edition of *Nennius* (see above). A basic edition of the Latin text of manuscript A with an English translation is also included in John Morris's edition of *Nennius* (see above). As with

Gildas's *De Excidio,* a new edition of this text is badly needed, as the inaccurate 1860 Rolls edition is the only source for texts B and C.

LIVES OF THE WELSH SAINTS

The Lives of a majority of the Welsh saints can be found edited and translated by A. W. Wade-Evans in *Vitae Sanctorum Britanniae et Genealogiae* (University of Wales Press, 1944); this work is due to be reprinted by the Welsh Academic Press in 2003. Sabine Baring-Gould and John Fisher (eds.), *The Lives of the British Saints* (Society of the Cymmrodorion, 4 vols., 1908–13), provides information on all saints connected to Wales, both famous and obscure. Although dated in places, this is still the standard starting point and collects together many Lives and other important documents in their original form and/or in translation. The four volumes have been recently been reprinted by Llanerch publishers in eight paperbacks (two per original volume, 2000–2002), making an important work available again.

The standard list of dedications for each parish in Wales was A. W. Wade-Evans, '*Parochialie Wallicanum*', *Y Cymmrodor*, Vol. XXII (1921). This has now been computerised and updated by Dr Graham Jones of the University of Leicester and can found at www.le.ac.uk/elh/grj1/database/dedwales.html (accessed 13 July 2002). This list details the dedications of every church, chapel, holy well and related site in Wales and the Marches – a very valuable resource.

Other works which are very useful for the study of Welsh saints and Christian life are:

A. W. Wade-Evans, *Welsh Christian Origins* (Alden, 1934);
E. G. Bowen, *Saints, Seaways and Settlements* (University of Wales Press, 1969);

Molly Miller, *The Saints of Gwynedd* (Boydell, 1979);

Elissa Henken, *Traditions of the Welsh Saints* (D. S. Brewer, 1987);

Elissa Henken, *The Welsh Saints: A Study in Patterned Lives* (D. S. Brewer, 1991).

THE *HISTORIA REGUM BRITANNIAE* AND *BRUT Y BRENHINEDD*

The Latin texts of Geoffrey's *Historia* have received a lot of attention from scholars in recent years, and this has resulted in the publication of four volumes that provide the most reliable editions and discussions of *Historia Regum Britanniae*:

Neil Wright (ed.), *The Historia Regum Britanniae of Geoffrey of Monmouth I: A Single-Manuscript Edition from Bern, Burgerbibliothek, MS. 568* (D. S. Brewer, 1985);

Neil Wright (ed.), *The Historia Regum Britanniae of Geoffrey of Monmouth II: The First Variant Version: A Critical Edition* (D. S. Brewer, 1988);

Julia Crick, *Historia Regum Britanniae of Geoffrey of Monmouth III: A Summary Catalogue of the Manuscripts* (D. S. Brewer, 1989);

Julia Crick, *Historia Regum Britanniae of Geoffrey of Monmouth IV: Dissemination and Reception in the Later Middle Ages* (D. S. Brewer, 1991).

The best English translation currently available is that by Lewis Thorpe, *The History of the Kings of Britain by Geoffrey of Monmouth* (Penguin, 1966), based upon the Latin text edited by Acton Griscom in *The Historia Regum Britanniae of Geoffrey of Monmouth* (Longmans, 1929). Griscom's edition also included an English translation of the Welsh text of *Brut y Brenhinedd* found in Jesus College

MS 61. The index to the Penguin edition includes place names from both the Latin and the Welsh texts, making it doubly useful.

The first publication of a text of *Brut y Brenhinedd* appeared in *The Myvyrian Archaiology* (3 vols., 1801–1806, reprinted as one volume in 1870) under the title *Brut Tysilio*. This version was translated by Peter Roberts in *The Chronicle of the Kings of Britain* (E. Williams, 1811). Although influential in its day, this was superceded by the translation of the same manuscript in Griscom's 1929 edition (see above). A version from *The Red Book of Hergest* was edited by John Rhys and John Gwenogfryn Evans as *The Text of the Bruts from The Red Book of Hergest* (Oxford University Press, 1890) and the version found in the manuscripts of Cotton Cleopatra B.V. and *The Black Book of Basingwerk* was edited with a facing translation by John J. Parry, *Brut y Brenhinedd, Cotton Cleopatra Version* (Medieval Academy of America, 1937), which had a print run of only 400. The earliest surviving Welsh MS (*c.* 1200) was edited by Henry Lewis in *Brut Dingestow* (University of Wales Press, 1942) with detailed notes (in Welsh). Extracts from Llanstephan MS 1 were edited by Brynley F. Roberts in *Brut Y Brenhinedd* (Dublin Institute of Advanced Celtic Studies, 1971), which also includes a very useful essay entitled 'The *Historia Regum Britanniae* in Wales'. The standard discussion of this work can be found in J. S. P. Tatlock's detailed *The Legendary History of Britain* (University of California Press, 1950).

THE MABINOGION

The collection of tales known as *The Mabinogion* survives primarily in two Welsh manuscripts: *The White Book of*

Rhydderch and *The Red Book of Hergest.* These have been published in diplomatic editions (where the text is reproduced in type exactly as it is on the manuscript) as *Llyfr Gwyn Rhydderch* (Llanbedrog, 1907), reprinted with a new introduction (in Welsh) by R. M. Jones by University of Wales Press in 1973, and as John Rhys and John Gwenogvryn Evans (eds.), *The Text of the Mabinogion and other Welsh Tales from the Red Book of Hergest* (Oxford University Press, 1887). The most widely used English translation of *The Mabinogion* is the Everyman edition by Gwyn Jones and Thomas Jones, and in 1993 a revised edition was published with a useful index of proper names. It contains an excellent introduction to the tales, and an appendix of variant readings from the different manuscripts makes it suitable for those who wish to make a closer study.

Another very worthwhile work is the little-used 1929 two-volume edition of *The Mabinogion* by T. P. Ellis and J. E. Lloyd (Clarendon Press). The translation is very literal, and hence not as easy to read as the Jones and Jones edition, though in many ways more useful. The translation is based upon the diplomatic editions mentioned above, and contains the corresponding folio numbers for easy comparison.

The two important Arthurian tales from *The Mabinogion* have also been edited individually. Rachel Bromwich and D. Simon Evans (eds.), *Culhwch and Olwen: An Edition and Study of the Oldest Arthurian Tale* (University of Wales Press, 1992), is an edition of the Welsh text with variant readings, an introduction and extensive detailed notes. Melville Richards (ed.), *Breudwyt Ronabwy* (University of Wales Press, 1948), is a detailed edition of *The Dream of Rhonabwy* with comprehensive notes (in Welsh).

THE TRIADS

The publication of *Trioedd Ynys Prydein* by Rachel Bromwich in 1961 made available the first reliable texts and translations of this important source. This work also included extensive notes on every person named in the ninety-six triads edited, which has made the book essential to any specialist in this field. A second edition was published by University of Wales Press in 1978 with forty-two pages of additional and updated notes. At the time of writing (summer 2002) a further revised edition of this valuable work is due for publication in the not too distant future.

During the nineteenth century many historians used a collection of triads known as the 'third series', upon which a lot of the dubious druidic material popular at the time, was based. The authenticity of these triads is in doubt, as much of the material contained within them does not appear in any other source and the manuscripts in which they are contained are very late. This situation is further complicated by the fact that the earliest texts are written in the hand of Iolo Morgannwg, an enthusiastic antiquarian from the early nineteenth century who is known to have forged material. Iolo's own English translation of these triads has been edited by Rachel Bromwich in 'Trioedd Ynys Prydain: The Myvyrian "Third Series"', *Transactions of the Honourable Society of Cymmrodorion*, 1968, Part II, pp. 299–338, and 1969, Part I, pp. 127–56.

WELSH BARDIC POETRY

One of the best discussions of the earliest Arthurian poetry can be found in Patrick Sims-Williams's 'The Early Welsh Arthurian Poems', in Rachel Bromwich, A. O. H. Jarman and Brynley F.

Roberts (eds.), *The Arthur of the Welsh: The Arthurian Legend in Medieval Welsh Literature* (University of Wales Press, 1991), pp. 33–71. The earliest Welsh poetry, including the sections relating to Arthur, can be found in the manuscripts detailed below.

The Book of Taliesin

The complete text of this manuscript has been published only once, in a print run of 800 by J. Gwenogfryn Evans (Llanbedrog, 1910). He reproduced a diplomatic edition of the text, and in 450 of the 800 printed he also published a complete facsimile of the manuscript as facing plates to the diplomatic text. The introduction and paleographical notes to the work, however, are a bit eccentric and of little use, although one or two of the points raised are still in need of discussion. The most important of the Arthurian poems in the manuscript is known as *Preiddeu Annwn* (The Spoils of Annwn), and has been translated and edited with detailed notes by Marged Haycock in '"Preiddeu Annwn" and the Figure of Taliesin', *Studia Celtica*, Vol. XVIII–XIX (1983–4), pp. 52–78. Translations of the other brief references to Arthur can be most easily accessed in Sims-Williams's article mentioned above.

The Book of Aneirin

A colour-facsimile edition of this manuscript was published by the National Library of Wales in conjunction with Glamorganshire Council in 1989 as *Llyfr Aneirin*, ed. Daniel Huws. This edition also contains the diplomatic text prepared by J. Gwenogfryn Evans in 1908, very detailed notes on the actual construction of the manuscript, and the marginal notes that were added to the manuscript over the years. The most comprehensive edition of the poem, with extensive notes (in Welsh), is by Ifor Williams as *Canu Aneirin* (University of

Wales Press, 1938). The poem has been translated by Kenneth Jackson in *The Gododdin: The Oldest Scottish Poem* (Edinburgh University Press, 1969) and by A. O. H. Jarman in *Y Gododdin* (Gomer Press, 1988), although Jarman omits over 150 lines from his edition. Most recently the hypothetical original text has been reconstructed by John T. Koch in *The Gododdin of Aneirin: Text and Context from Dark-Age North Britain* (University of Wales Press, 1997).

The Black Book of Carmarthen

A facsimile edition of this whole manuscript was published in 1888, and a diplomatic edition in 1906; both were published by J. Gwenogfryn Evans. The manuscript has most recently been edited by A. O. H. Jarman as *Llyfr Du Caerfyrddin* (University of Wales Press, 1982), with notes in Welsh. An accessible translation of *Pa Gur?* can be found in Sim-Williams's article noted above and one of the Llongborth poem in Jenny Rowland, *Early Welsh Saga Poetry* (D. S. Brewer, 1990). 'The Stanzas of the Graves' are discussed and translated in Thomas Jones, 'Stanzas of the Graves', The Sir John Rhys Memorial Lecture, *Proceedings of the British Academy*, Vol. LIII (1967), pp. 97–137.

An early poem from another MS that includes a reference to Arthur is entitled 'The Prophecy of the Eagle' and concerns Arthur's conversation with an eagle who turns out to be Eliwlod ap Madoc ap Uthyr and therefore his nephew. The conversation turns to matters of good and evil, and the eagle tells Arthur that his sins can be absolved by praying to Christ. For the text see Ifor Williams, 'Ymddiddan Arthur a'r Eryr', *Bulletin of the Board of Celtic Studies*, Vol. II (1925), pp. 269–86, and for a modern Welsh translation Marged Haycock, *Blodeugerdd Barddos o Ganu Crefyddol Cynnar* (University of Wales Press, 1994), pp. 297–312.

THE POETRY OF *THE GOGYNFEIRDD*
(1100–1282)

This important body of poetry first appeared amid a mass of other Welsh material in *The Myvyrian Archaiology* (3 vols, 1801–1806). A second edition appeared as a single volume (Gee & Son, 1870), and is the one usually referenced in older works; the poetry is found on pp. 140–356. The diplomatic edition of *The Poetry in the Red Book of Hergest* by J. Gwenogvryn Evans (Llanbedrog, 1911) also contains a large number of *Gogynfeirdd* poems, and those not in this work can be found in Evans's *Poetry by Medieval Welsh Bards* (Llanbedrog, 1926), which forms a companion volume with pagination following on and an index to the personal and place names of both volumes.

The oldest manuscript of *Gogynfeirdd* poetry (*c.* 1250) was rediscovered in the bottom of a wardrobe in 1910 at a house called Hendregadredd in Porthmadog, North Wales, and was bought by the National Library of Wales. It was edited by John Morris-Jones and T. H. Parry in *Llawysgrif Hendregadredd* (University of Wales Press, 1933), and is now considered to be the most important source for this poetry. The whole corpus of *Gogynfeirdd* poetry has been edited with notes (all in Welsh) and modern Welsh translations in the seven-volume series *Cyfres Beirdd y Tywysogion* (Series of the Poets of the Princes) under the editorship of R. G. Gruffydd (University of Wales Press, 1991–6). This is now the standard edition for the complete corpus of *Gogynfeirdd* poetry, and it is hoped that eventually this edition will appear with English notes and an English translation of the poems, as they contain material of immense interest to Arthurian and Welsh studies.

At present a handful of English translations can be found

spread across different works, and Patrick Sims-Williams's bibliography of these translations can be found in the journal *Ysgrifiau Beirniadol*, Vol. XIII (1985), pp. 39–47. See also

Joseph Clancy, *The Earliest Welsh Poetry* (Macmillan,1970);

Tony Conran (ed.), *Welsh Verse* (3rd edn, Seren, 1992; originally published as *The Penguin Book of Welsh Verse,* 1967);

Gwyn Jones (ed.), *The Oxford Book of Welsh Verse in English* (Oxford University Press, 1977).

The bards that lived after the *Gogynfeirdd* are known as the 'poets of the nobility', and the most important bards of this period have been edited in:

Iolo Goch – Dafydd Johnston (ed.), *Iolo Goch Poems* (Gomer Press, 1993);

Guto' Glyn – Ifor Williams and J. Lloyd Williams (eds.), *Gwaith Guto Glyn* (University of Wales Press, 1937);

Gutun Owain – E. Bachellery (ed.), *L'Œuvre poetique de Gutun Owain* (Librairie Ancienne Honoré Champion, 2 vols., 1950–1) (notes and translations in French);

Tudur Aled – T. Gwynn Jones (ed.), *Gwaith Tudur Aled* (University of Wales Press, 2 vols, 1926);

Lewys Glyn Gothi – Dafydd Johnston (ed.), *Gwaith Lewys Glyn Gothi* (University of Wales Press, 1995).

The remainder of the poetry from this period is being edited by the Centre for Advanced Celtic Studies in Aberystwyth, and each volume contains an index of proper names and an introduction for each poet; all notes are in Welsh. Translations of these poems can be found in the works noted above and also in Joseph Clancy, *Medieval Welsh Lyrics* (Macmillan, 1965).

GENEALOGICAL MATERIAL

P. C. Bartrum's *Early Welsh Genealogical Tracts* (University of Wales Press, 1966) edits together all the surviving early texts and is the standard work on the subject. Bartrum is also responsible for the eight-volume *Welsh Genealogies A.D. 300–1400* (University of Wales Press, 1974) and the eighteen-volume *Welsh Genealogies A.D. 1400–1500* (National Library of Wales, 1983). His latest work, *A Welsh Classical Dictionary: People in History and Legend up to about A.D. 1000* (National Library of Wales, 1993), is the product of a lifetime's research and the starting point for any serious study into early Welsh material and the origins of Arthur.

PLACE-NAME STUDIES

These studies are not as far advanced in Wales as they are in England, where The English Place-Name Society publishes excellent studies for each county – including seven volumes covering Cheshire and two volumes covering Shropshire. Place-name studies of many areas of Wales have yet to be published, but some of those that have are given below:

Hywel Wyn Owen, *The Place-Names of East Flintshire* (University of Wales Press, 1994). This is the best and most detailed work on place names in Wales, and sets the standard by which other studies should be judged. The parts of Flintshire not covered in this work can be found in Ellis Davies, *Flintshire Place-Names* (University of Wales Press, 1959), although not to the same standard of detail.

B. G. Charles, *The Place-Names of Pembrokeshire* (National Library of Wales, 2 vols., 1992);

John Lloyd-Jones, *Enwau Lleoedd Sir Garnarfon* (Cardiff, 1928); Gwynedd O. Pierce *The Place-Names of Dinas Powys Hundred* (University of Wales Press, 1968).

Melville Richards collected over 100,000 slips concerning place names in Wales. Known as the *Onomasticon*, this collection is now serving as the basis for the Welsh Place-Name Dictionary being compiled at Bangor. Richards's most important single work on the subject is *Welsh Administrative and Territorial Units* (University of Wales Press, 1968). Elwyn·Davies, *A Gazetteer of Welsh Place-Names* (University of Wales Press, 1968) is also very useful.

FOLKLORE

Folklore has been collected in Wales for over two hundred years, yet even today it is still possible to find oral traditions that have yet to be recorded. Two of the most important works concerning Arthurian folklore are John Rhys, *Celtic Folklore, Welsh and Manx* (Clarendon Press, 2 vols., 1901), and T. Gwynn Jones, *Welsh Folklore and Folk Custom* (Methuen, 1930). Chris Grooms, *The Giants of Wales* (Edwin Mellen, 1993), is an excellent work and contains some very important Arthurian material.

ARTHURIAN STUDIES

Many Arthurian titles can be found on the shelves, and here we give only a selection of what we consider to be the most useful studies. E. K. Chambers's *Arthur of Britain* (Sidgwick & Jackson, 1927; reprinted 1966) was the first serious study, and is still one of the best. It includes an appendix of the most important Latin and French manuscripts concerning Arthur, many of which have been translated and printed in Richard White's very useful *King Arthur in Legend and History* (Dent, 1997). This also includes extracts from some of the lesser-known Arthurian romances not found in *Arthur of Britain*. Richard Barber's *The Figure of Arthur* (Longman, 1972) provides a very good discussion of the available evidence and devotes much space to early Welsh sources. Rachel Bromwich, A. O. H. Jarman and Brynley F. Roberts (eds.), *The Arthur of the Welsh: The Arthurian Legend in Medieval Welsh Literature* (University of Wales Press, 1991), deals with the Welsh material in detail and is an essential work. All the works by Roger Sherman Loomis are a valuable aid to study, especially his *Wales and the Arthurian Legend* (University of Wales Press, 1956) and *Arthurian Literature in the Middle Ages* (Clarendon Press, 1959).

Articles published in academic journals which are very useful include:

Thomas Jones, 'The Early Evolution of the Legend of Arthur' (1958), trans. Gerald Morgan, *Nottingham Medieval Studies*, Vol. VIII (1964), pp. 3–21;

Rachel Bromwich, 'Concepts of Arthur', *Studia Celtica*, Vol. X–XI, (1975–6), pp. 163–81;

Brynley F. Roberts, 'Geoffrey of Monmouth and the Welsh Historical Tradition', *Nottingham Medieval Studies*, Vol. XX (1976), pp. 29–40.

Although a little dated, T. Gwynn Jones, 'Some Arthurian Material in Celtic', *Aberystwyth Studies,* Vol. VIII (1926), pp. 37–93, still provides a very good overall discussion of early Welsh and Irish texts regarding Arthur. Another valuable source of information is the annual *Arthurian Literature*, published by Boydell and Brewer and at present up to Volume XIX.

NOTES

Chapter 1

1. Lewis Thorpe, *The History of the Kings of Britain by Geoffrey of Monmouth* (Penguin, 1966), pp. 200–1.
2. Ibid.
3. Ibid., p. 201. This fact is never referred to again in the *Historia*.
4. Ibid., p. 202.
5. Rachel Bromwich, *Trioedd Ynys Prydein* (University of Wales Press, 2nd edn, 1978), p. 520.
6. Michael Winterbottom, *Gildas, The Ruin of Britain* (Phillimore, 1978), pp. 32–6, §§33–6. The island referred to in this case is Mon (Anglesey).
7. R. Geraint Gruffydd (ed.), *Cyfres Beirdd y Tywysogion* (University of Wales Press, 7 vols., 1991–6), Vol. I, p. 244.
8. T. D. Kendrick, *British Antiquity* (Methuen, 1950), pp. 10–11.
9. Judith Weiss, *Wace's Roman De Brut: A History of The British* (University of Exeter Press, 1999), p. 245.
10. Roger Sherman Loomis (ed.), *Arthurian Literature in the Middle Ages* (Clarendon Press, 1959), p. 88 and references therein.
11. Eugene Vinaver (ed.), *The Works of Sir Thomas Malory* (Clarendon Press, 3 vols., 1947), Vol. 1, p. cxiii.
12. For a detailed discussion on this relic see Martin Biddle, *King Arthur's Round Table* (Boydell, 2000).
13. Kendrick, *British Antiquity*, 1950, p. 42.
14. Richard Barber, *King Arthur: Hero and Legend* (Boydell, 1986), p. 142.
15. The information from the *Bibliographical Bulletin* of the International Arthurian Society has been brought together in four volumes of *The Arthurian Bibliography*, which covers all works relating to Arthur published up to 1998.
16. David Dumville, 'Sub-Roman Britain: History and Legend', *History*, Vol. LXII, (1977), pp. 173–92.
17. A slightly more generous overview of this material was put forward by Thomas Charles-Edwards in Rachel Bromwich, A. O. H. Jarman & Brynley F. Roberts (eds.), *The Arthur of the Welsh: The Arthurian Legend in Medieval Welsh Literature* (University of Wales Press, 1991), pp. 15–32.

18. Tacitus, *De Vita Agricolae*, ed. R. M. Ogilvie & Sir Ian Richmond (Clarendon Press, 1967), pp. 80–90.
19. As evidenced by the stories and tales recorded by folklorists at the end of the nineteenth century – e.g. John Rhys, *Celtic Folklore, Welsh and Manx* (Clarendon Press, 2 vols., 1901), and Rev. Elias Owen, *Welsh Folklore* (Woodall, Minshall & Co., 1896).

Chapter 2

1. In 1151 Geoffrey witnessed a grant of land as 'Episcopus Sancti Asaphi', and later in the same year he witnessed a charter of Robert de Chesney as 'Electus Sancti Asaphi'. J. S. P. Tatlock, *The Legendary History of Britain* (University of California Press, 1950), pp. 438–48.
2. A hypothesis put forward by some scholars is that Geoffrey was of Breton descent and connected to the priory at Monmouth founded by the Breton Wihenoc, Lord of Monmouth as of 1075. Tatlock, *The Legendary History of Britain*, p. 440.
3. Ibid., pp. 441–2. Walter the Archdeacon of Oxford has often been confused with Walter Map, deacon to Henry II some fifty years later. They are not the same person.
4. At that time Oxford was in the diocese of Lincoln.
5. Tatlock, *The Legendary History of Britain*, p. 442.
6. Ibid., pp. 68–9 and other references in the index.
7. A good discussion of these points and many other concerning Geoffrey can be found in Tatlock's excellent *The Legendary History of Britain*.
8. Geoffrey's reference to Gildas may also include the work known today as the *Historia Brittonum*. During the Middle Ages this work was often wrongly attributed to Gildas, the real author being unknown, although commonly referred to as Nennius.
9. These sections are discussed in detail in two articles by Neil Wright: 'Geoffrey of Monmouth and Gildas', *Arthurian Literature*, Vol. II (1982), pp. 1–40, and 'Geoffrey of Monmouth and Bede', *Arthurian Literature*, Vol. VI (1986), pp. 27–59.
10. Latin text from Neil Wright (ed.), *The Historia Regum Britanniae of Geoffrey of Monmouth I: A Single-Manuscript Edition from Bern, Burgerbibliothek, MS. 568* (D. S. Brewer, 1985), p. 1, §2; translation from Lewis Thorpe, *The History of the Kings of Britain by Geoffrey of Monmouth* (Penguin, 1966), p. 51.
11. Latin text from Wright, *The Historia Regum Britanniae of Geoffrey of Monmouth I*, p. 147, §208; translation from Thorpe, *The History of the Kings of Britain*, p. 284.
12. Latin text from Wright, *The Historia Regum Britanniae of Geoffrey of Monmouth I*, pp. 129–30, §177; translation from Thorpe, *The History of the Kings of Britain*, pp. 257–258.
13. Thorpe, *The History of the Kings of Britain*, p. 5.
14. For a detailed discussion on these Variant manuscripts see Neil Wright (ed.), *The Historia Regum Britanniae of Geoffrey of Monmouth II: The First*

Variant Version: A Critical Edition (D. S. Brewer, 1988), and for a complete catalogue of the surviving manuscripts of the Historia see Julia Crick, *The Historia Regum Britanniae of Geoffrey of Monmouth III: A Summary Catalogue of the Manuscripts* (D. S. Brewer, 1989).

15. Roger Sherman Loomis (ed.), *Arthurian Literature in the Middle Ages* (Clarendon Press, 1959), p. 87.

16. Tatlock, *The Legendary History of Britain*, pp. 422–5.

17. R. W. Southern, 'Aspects of the European Tradition of Historical Writing 1. The Classical Tradition from Einhard to Geoffrey of Monmouth', *Transactions of the Royal Historical Society,* Fifth Series, No. 20 (1970), pp. 173–96, p. 194.

18. Alexander Bell (ed.), *L'Estoire des Engleis By Geffrei Gaimar* (Anglo-Norman Text Society, 1960), p. 204, ll. 6448–53; translation from Sir Thomas Duffus Hardy & Charles Trice Martin (eds.), *Lestorie des Engles*, Vol. II, Rolls edition (HMSO, 1889), p. 203.

19. E. K. Chambers, *Arthur of Britain* (Sidgwick & Jackson, 1927), p. 55.

20. Loomis, *Arthurian Literature in the Middle Ages*, p. 81.

21. P. C. Bartrum, *A Welsh Classical Dictionary: People in History and Legend up to about A.D. 1000* (National Library of Wales, 1993), pp. 215–17.

22. J. Gwenogvryn Evans & John Rhys, *The Text of the Book of Llan Dav Reproduced from the Gwysaney Manuscript* (Oxford University Press, 1893), p. 225.

23. P. C. Bartrum, *Early Welsh Genealogical Tracts* (University of Wales Press, 1966), p. 4.

24. A detailed study of this material would require another book in itself, but, for example, the first four kings succeeding Arthur are names taken from Gildas's *De Excidio* and they all rule in Wales or the south-west peninsula, not in England or Scotland. Ceredig appears fictional, and the last three kings are the successive rulers of Gwynedd as mentioned in the *Historia Brittonum* and Bede's *Historia Ecclesiastica*.

25. The earliest manuscript is generally considered to be the one known as *Brut Dingestow*, printed in Henry Lewis, *Brut Dingestow* (University of Wales Press, 1942).

26. Charlotte Ward, 'Arthur in the Welsh Bruts', in Cyril J. Burne, Margaret Harry & Padraig O'Siadhail (eds.), *Celtic Languages and Celtic Peoples: Proceedings of the Second North American Congress of Celtic Studies* (St Mary's University, 1992), pp. 383–90, p. 383. This is an excellent article on the subject, and deserves a wider readership.

27. Thomas Jones, *Brut Y Tywysogyon or The Chronicle of the Princes, Peniarth MS. 20 Version* (University of Wales Press, 1952), p. 58.

Chapter 3

1. Thomas Jones, 'The Early Evolution of the Legend of Arthur' (1958), trans. Gerald Morgan, *Nottingham Medieval Studies*, Vol. VIII (1964), pp. 3–21, p. 3.

2. R. Geraint Gruffydd (ed.), *Cyfres Beirdd y Tywysogion* (University of Wales Press, 7 vols., 1991–6), Vol. III, p. 109.

3. For a more detailed discussion of this material see T. M. Charles-Edwards, Morfydd E. Owen & Paul Russell (eds.), *The Welsh King and his Court* (University of Wales Press, 2000), pp. 142–166, and A. O. H. Jarman & Gwilym Rees Hughes, *A Guide to Welsh Literature Volume 1* (Christopher Davies, 1976), pp. 123–188.

4. Patrick Sims-Williams, 'Clas Beuno and the Four Branches of the Mabinogi', in *150 Jahre Mabinogion Deutsch-Walisische Kulturbeziehungen* (Max Niemeyer Verlag, 2001), pp. 111–27, p. 113.

5. Rachel Bromwich, *Trioedd Ynys Prydein* (University of Wales Press, 2nd edn, 1978), p. lxv.

6. For an excellent and detailed discussion about Welsh manuscripts see David Huws, *Medieval Welsh Manuscripts* (University of Wales Press, 2000).

7. Bromwich, *Trioedd Ynys Prydein*, pp. lxiv–v.

8. Ibid., pp. lxvi–vii.

9. For good English language discussions of the bards see ibid., pp. lxx–lxxxiii, and the article by Ceri W. Lewis in Jarman & Hughes, *A Guide to Welsh Literature Volume 1*, pp. 11–50.

10. Lewis Thorpe, *The History of the Kings of Britain by Geoffrey of Monmouth* (Penguin, 1966), p. 284, n.1.

11. Hugh Williams, *Gildae De Excidio Britanniae*, Cymmrodorion Record Series No. 3 (Hugh Williams, 2 vols., 1899–1901), Vol. II, pp. 390–413.

12. For a discussion of some of the origins to the tales now associated with Glastonbury see Steve Blake & Scott Lloyd, *The Keys To Avalon* (Element, 2000), pp. 121–217.

13. These Lives can be found in A. W. Wade-Evans, *Vitae Sanctorum Britanniae et Genealogiae* (University of Wales Press, 1944).

14. Kathleen Hughes, 'British MS. Cotton Vespasian A. XIV ("Vitae Sanctorum Wallensium"): its purpose and provenance', *Studies in the Early British Church* (Cambridge University Press, 1958), pp. 183–200, p. 185.

15. Jeff Rider, 'Arthur and the Saints', in Valerie M. Lagorio and Mildred Leake Day (eds.), *King Arthur Through the Ages Volume I* (Garland, 1990), p. 8.

16. Ibid., p. 17.

17. These variants are noted in Theodore Mommsen's edition of the text in *Monumenta Germaniae Historica, Chronica Minora*, Vol. III (Berlin, 1894).

18. David Dumville, 'Nennius and the Historia Brittonum', *Studia Celtica*, Vol. X–XI1 (1975–6), pp. 78–95.

19. John Morris, *Nennius: British History and the Welsh Annals* (Phillimore, 1980), p. 9.

20. Ibid., p. 42.

21. Ibid., p. 37.

22. Michael Winterbottom, *Gildas, The Ruin of Britain* (Phillimore, 1978), p. 34, §34.

23. This point was briefly discussed in Blake & Lloyd, *The Keys To Avalon*, pp. 240–1. The earliest person to identify Catraeth with Catterick in Yorkshire would appear to be Edward Williams (Iolo Morgannwg) in *Poems, Lyrical and Pastoral* (E. Williams, 2 vols., 1794), Vol. II, p. 16.

24. These obscure poems have yet to be satisfactorily translated. For the Welsh text see Ifor Williams, *Canu Aneirin* (University of Wales Press, 1938), and for two partial translations see Kenneth Jackson, *The Gododdin: The Oldest Scottish Poem* (University of Edinburgh Press, 1969), and A. O. H. Jarman, *Aneirin: Y Gododdin* (Gomer Press, 1988).

25. The Welsh text can be found in D. Simon Evans, *Historia Grufudd ab Kynan* (University of Wales Press, 1977), and an English translation in D. Simon Evans, *A Mediaeval Welsh Prince of Wales – The Life of Grufydd ap Cynan* (Llanerch, 1996).

26. Huws, *Medieval Welsh Manuscripts*, p. 75.

27. Ibid., p. 79.

28. Marged Haycock, '"Preiddeu Annwn" and the Figure of Taliesin', *Studia Celtica*, Vol. XVIII–XIX (1983–4), pp. 52–78, pp. 62–3.

29. J. Gwenogvryn Evans, *The Book of Taliesin* (Llanbedrog, 1910), p. 27.

30. Ibid., p. 34.

31. Ibid., p. 71.

32. Ibid., p. 48.

33. Huws, *Medieval Welsh Manuscripts*, pp. 70–2.

34. A. O. H. Jarman, *Llyfr Du Caerfyrddin* (University of Wales Press, 1982), p. 66; translation from Rachel Bromwich, A. O. H. Jarman & Brynley F. Roberts (eds.), *The Arthur of the Welsh: The Arthurian Legend in Medieval Welsh Literature* (University of Wales Press, 1991), p. 40.

35. Jarman, *Llyfr Du Caerfyrddin*, p. 48; translation from Bromwich et al., *The Arthur of the Welsh*, p. 47.

36. Jarman, *Llyfr Du Caerfyrddin*, p. 73; translation from Bromwich et al., *The Arthur of the Welsh*, p. 44.

37. 'So Trioedd Ynys Prydein started off as being an oral index, for the mnemonic purposes, to the narrative traditional history of Britain. It became written, and degenerated into being matter regarded as valuable for its own sake with the vast background material lost.' E. I. Rowlands, 'Bardic Lore and Education', *Bulletin of the Board of Celtic Studies*, Vol. XXXII (1985), pp. 143–55, p. 152.

38. Bromwich, *Trioedd Ynys Prydein*, p. 16.

39. Ibid., p. lxix.

40. Sir John E. Lloyd, *A History of Wales* (Longmans, Green & Co., 3rd edn, 2 vols., 1939), Vol. II, p. 485.

41. T. Gwynn Jones, 'Some Arthurian Material in Celtic', *Aberystwyth Studies*, Vol. VIII (1926), pp. 37–93, p. 42.

42. Thomas Jones, 'A Sixteenth-Century Version of the Arthurian Cave Legend', in Mieczyslaw Brahmer (ed.), *Studies in Language and Literature in Honour of Margaret Schlauch* (Polish Scientific Publishers, 1966), p. 179.

43. R. G. Gruffydd, *Cyfres Beirdd y Tywysogion*, Vol. V, p. 124, ll. 7–8; translation from T. G. Jones, 'Some Arthurian Material in Celtic', p. 42.

44. T. G. Jones, 'Some Arthurian Material in Celtic', p. 42.

45. J. E. Caerwyn Williams, *The Poets of the Welsh Princes* (University of Wales Press, 1994), pp. 6–7. This work is an excellent overview of the work and background of these poets.

46. Rachel Bromwich & D. Simon Evans, *Culhwch and Olwen: An Edition and Study of the Oldest Arthurian Tale* (University of Wales Press, 1992), p. 98.

47. Bromwich et al., *The Arthur of the Welsh*, pp. 83–4.

48. Gwyn Jones & Thomas Jones, *The Mabinogion* (Everyman, rev. edn, 1993), p. 84.

49. Thorpe, *The History of the Kings of Britain*, p. 217.

50. Ibid., p. 120.

51. Bromwich, *Trioedd Ynys Prydein*, pp. 240–9.

52. Bromwich & Evans, *Culhwch and Olwen*, pp. 64–5.

53. Thorpe, *The History of the Kings of Britain*, p. 217.

54. In fact the *Historia Brittonum* and *Annales Cambriae* say that Arthur carried the image on his 'shoulders', but this is probably because of a confusion between the Welsh words '*scuit*', meaning 'shield', and '*scuid*', meaning 'shoulder'.

55. Bromwich & Evans, *Culhwch and Olwen*, p. 64 and references therein.

56. G. Jones & T. Jones, *The Mabinogion*, p. 114.

57. Bromwich, *Trioedd Ynys Prydein*, p. lxiv.

Chapter 4

1. Lewis Thorpe, *Gerald of Wales: The Journey Through Wales/The Description of Wales* (Penguin, 1978), p. 251.

2. A. O. H. Jarman, *Llyfr Du Caerfyrddin* (University of Wales Press, 1982), p. 66, ll. 13–14; translation from Rachel Bromwich, A. O. H. Jarman & Brynley F. Roberts (eds.), *The Arthur of the Welsh: The Arthurian Legend in Medieval Welsh Literature* (University of Wales Press, 1991), p. 40.

3. Jarman, *Llyfr Du Caerfyrddin*, p. 73, translation from Bromwich et al., *The Arthur of the Welsh*, p. 44.

4. Rachel Bromwich, *Trioedd Ynys Prydein* (University of Wales Press, 2nd edn, 1978), p. 521, n.1.

5. A new edition of this poem with a modern Welsh translation can be found in Marged Haycock, *Blodeugerdd Barddos o Ganu Crefyddol Cynnar* (University of Wales Press, 1994), pp. 297–312.

6. P. C. Bartrum, *A Welsh Classical Dictionary: People in History and Legend up to about A.D. 1000* (National Library of Wales, 1993), p. 13.

7. Ibid., p. 420 and references therein.

8. R. Geraint Gruffydd (ed.), *Cyfres Beirdd y Tywysogion* (University of Wales Press, 7 vols., 1991–6), Vol. V, p. 205, l. 23. This possibility is also discussed in Steve Blake & Scott Lloyd, *The Keys To Avalon* (Element, 2000), pp. 47–9.

9. Gwyn Jones & Thomas Jones, *The Mabinogion* (Everyman, rev. edn, 1993), p. 80

10. Ibid., p. 81

11. Ibid., p. 84.

12. Ibid.

13. Rupert H. Morris (ed.), *Parochialia: being a summary of answers to 'Parochial queries in order to a geographical dictionary, etc., of Wales' / issued by Edward Lhwyd* (1698) (Cambrian Archæological Association, 4 vols., 1909–1911), Vol. I, p. 70.

14. Bromwich, *Trioedd Ynys Prydein*, p. 140.

15. Chris Grooms, *The Giants of Wales* (Edwin Mellen, 1993), pp. 236–9.

16. G. Jones & T. Jones, *The Mabinogion*, p. 86.

17. P. C. Bartrum, 'Arthuriana from the Genealogical Manuscripts', *National Library of Wales Journal*, Vol. XIV (1965), p. 242.

18. Bartrum, *A Welsh Classical Dictionary*, p. 301 and references therein.

19. Ibid., p. 312.

20. RCAHM [Royal Commission on Ancient and Historic Monuments], *An Inventory of the Ancient Monuments in Wales and Monmouthshire, Volume IV – County of Denbigh* (Royal Stationery Office, 1914), p. 124.

21. G. Jones & T. Jones, *The Mabinogion*, pp. 86 & 110.

22. Bartrum, *A Welsh Classical Dictionary*, p. 332.

23. G. Jones & T. Jones, *The Mabinogion*, p. 85.

24. P. C. Bartrum, *Early Welsh Genealogical Tracts* (University of Wales Press, 1966), p. 85.

25. W. J. Gruffydd, *Math vab Mathonwy* (University of Wales Press, 1928), pp. 343–5.

26. A. W. Wade-Evans, *Vitae Sanctorum Britanniae et Genealogiae* (University of Wales Press, 1944), p. 194, §1. 'Audiens, interea, miles magnificus Arthurii regis sui consobrini magnificentiam, cupiuit uistare tanti uictoris curiam.'

27. Bartrum, 'Arthuriana from the Genealogical Manuscripts', pp. 242–5, p. 242.

28. Bromwich, *Trioedd Ynys Prydein*, pp. 1, 31.

29. G. Jones & T. Jones, *The Mabinogion*, p. 119.

30. Bartrum, *A Welsh Classical Dictionary*, p. 103.

31. G. Jones & T. Jones, *The Mabinogion*, p. 91.

32. Bromwich, *Trioedd Ynys Prydein*, p. 8.

33. Jarman, *Llyfr Du Caerfyrddin*, p. 37, ll. 24–5.

34. E. Bachellery (ed.), *L'Œuvre poetique de Gutun Owain* (Librairie Ancienne Honoré Champion, 2 vols., 1950–1), Vol. I, pp. 129, 191; Vol. II, p. 299. See also Bromwich et al., *The Arthur of the Welsh*, p. 50 and notes therein.

35. G. Jones & T. Jones, *The Mabinogion*, p. 119.

36. John Rhys, *Celtic Folklore, Welsh and Manx* (Clarendon Press, 2 vols., 1901), Vol. I, pp. 231–3.

37. Bartrum, *A Welsh Classical Dictionary*, p. 452.

38. Llanstephan MS. 100, p. 19, from Bartrum, *A Welsh Classical Dictionary*, p. 452.

39. Bartrum, *Early Welsh Genealogical Tracts*, p. 13, '[H]ic est terminus eorum: A flumine quod uocatur Dubr Duiu usque ad aliud flumen Tebi. Et tenuerunt plurimas regiones occidentali plaga Brittanniae.'

40. John Morris, *Nennius: British History and the Welsh Annals* (Phillimore, 1980), p. 42, §73.

41. Bartrum, *Early Welsh Genealogical Tracts*, p. 66.

42. G. Jones & T. Jones, *The Mabinogion*, p. 110.

43. Jarman, *Llyfr Du Caerfyrddin*, p. 68, ll. 76–7.

44. Ibid., p. 73, ll. 49–50.

45. R. G. Gruffydd, *Cyfres Beirdd y Tywysogion*, Vol. VII, p. 604, ll. 15–16.

46. Bromwich, *Trioedd Ynys Prydein*, p. 416.

47. For further references to him in later literature see Bartrum, *A Welsh Classical Dictionary*, p. 402.

48. Bromwich, *Trioedd Ynys Prydein*, p. 157.

49. Ibid., p. 354.

50. Jones, T. Gwynn, 1929, Vol. II, p. 357, a poem to Dafydd ap Hywel of Nanheudwy, a Welsh cantref centred on Llangollen.

51. Jarman, *Llyfr Du Caerfyrddin*, p. 43, ll. 213–8.

52. Patrick K. Ford, *Ystoria Taliesin* (University of Wales Press, 1992).

Chapter 5

1. Jurgen Spanuth, *Atlantis of the North* (Sidgwick & Jackson, 1979), p. 30.

2. This reference is based upon the proof entry for *ynys* kindly sent to us by Andrew Hawke and should be checked against the printed edition, due out late in 2002.

3. R. Geraint Gruffydd (ed.), *Cyfres Beirdd y Tywysogion* (University of Wales Press, 7 vols., 1991–6), Vol. I, p. 71, l. 10.

4. Ibid., Vol. IV, p. 118, l. 64.

5. Thomas Jones, 'Teir Ynys Prydein a'e Their Rac Ynys', *Bulletin of the Board of Celtic Studies*, Vol. XVII (1958), pp. 268–9 and references therein.

6. R. G. Gruffydd, *Cyfres Beirdd y Tywysogion*, Vol. I, p. 76, l. 22; translation from K. L. Maund, *Gruffydd ap Cynan: A Collaborative Biography* (Boydell, 1996), p. 183.

7. R. G. Gruffydd, *Cyfres Beirdd y Tywysogion*, Vol. IV, p. 58, l. 96.

8. Ibid., Vol. V, p. 72, l. 7.

9. Further examples can be found in Rhian Andrews, 'Rhai Agweddau ar Sofraniaeth yng Ngherddi'r Gogynfeirdd', *Bulletin of the Board of Celtic Studies*, Vol. XXVII (1976), pp. 23–30, pp. 25–6, J. Gwenogvryn Evans, *The Book of Taliesin* (Llanbedrog, 1910), p. ix, n. 6, and the same author's *Poetry by Medieval Welsh Bards* (Llanbedrog, 1926), p. 421. We hope to publish a thorough survey of these references at some point.

10. Andrews, 'Rhai Agweddau ar Sofraniaeth yng Ngherddi'r Gogynfeirdd', p. 26. We would like to thank Elin Llwyd Morgan for her help in translating this article.

11. R. G. Gruffydd, *Cyfres Beirdd y Tywysogion*, Vol. VII, p. 544, ll. 17, 23.

12. Gwyn Jones & Thomas Jones, *The Mabinogion* (Everyman, rev. edn, 1993), p. 27. The Welsh text reads, 'a dechrau o'r lle hwnnw peri anuin kennadeu y dygyuoryaw yr ynys honn y gyt. Ac yna y peris ef dyuot llwyr wys pedeir degwlat a seith-ugeint'. Notes to this section can be found in Ifor Williams, *Pedeir Keinc y Mabinogi* (University of Wales Press, 1930), pp. 190–1 (in Welsh).

13. Peniarth MS. 163, pp. 57–60; see J. Gwenogvryn Evans, *Report on Manuscripts in the Welsh Language* (Historical Manuscripts Commission, 2 vols., 1898–1910), Vol I, p. 954.

14. Simon Keynes & Michael Lapidge, *Alfred the Great: Asser's Life of King Alfred and Other Contemporary Sources* (Penguin, 1983), p. 71; the Latin text can be found in William Henry Stevenson, *Asser's Life of King Alfred* (Clarendon Press, 2nd edn, 1959), p. 12.

15. For an alternative view as to the origin of this earthwork see Steve Blake & Scott Lloyd, *The Keys To Avalon* (Element, 2000) pp. 60–7 & 302.

16. J. Gwenogvryn Evans & John Rhys, *The Text of the Book of Llan Dav Reproduced from the Gwysaney Manuscript* (Oxford University Press, 1893), p. 118, ll. 13–14.

17. Ibid., p. 120, ll. 5–6.

18. Neil Wright, 'Gildas's geographical perspective: some problems', in Michael Lapidge and David Dumville (eds.), *Gildas: New Approaches* (Boydell, 1984), pp. 85–106, p. 99: 'It could be objected that the author [Gildas], like other Welsh writers of the earlier Middle Ages, used Britannia to denote Wales rather than Britain and is thus speaking only of an irruption of the Picts into Wales.'

19. In Blake & Lloyd, *The Keys To Avalon*, pp. 55–60, we published our earliest findings on this matter and some of the possible implications. Research has continued apace since then, and it is hoped that our new findings, revisions and interpretations will be published at some point.

20. Blake & Lloyd, *The Keys To Avalon*, pp. 108–10.

21. Rachel Bromwich, *Trioedd Ynys Prydein* (University of Wales Press, 2nd edn, 1978), p. 1.

22. Ibid., p. 229.

23. For a more detailed discussion on the confusion between the two sites see Blake & Lloyd, *The Keys To Avalon*, pp. 31–3.

24. Rachel Bromwich, A. O. H. Jarman & Brynley F. Roberts (eds.), *The Arthur of the Welsh: The Arthurian Legend in Medieval Welsh Literature* (University of Wales Press, 1991), p. 234.

25. Ibid., pp. 234–8.

26. Blake & Lloyd, *The Keys To Avalon*, p. 229–30 and the first picture in the black-and-white-plates section.

27. G. Jones & T. Jones, *The Mabinogion*, p. 89.

28. Patrick Sims-Williams, 'The Irish Geography of *Culhwch and Olwen*', in

Donnchadh Ó Corráin, Liam Breatnach, Kim McCone (eds.), *Sages, Saints and Storytellers: Celtic Studies in Honour of Professor James Carney*, Maynooth Monographs No. 2 (An Sagart, 1989), pp. 412–26, pp. 413–17.

29. R. G. Gruffydd, *Cyfres Beirdd y Tywysogion*, Vol. IV, p. 52, l. 167.

30. T. Gwynn Jones, 'Some Arthurian Material in Celtic', *Aberystwyth Studies*, Vol. VIII (1926), pp. 37–93, p. 41.

31. Dafydd Johnston (ed.), *Iolo Goch Poems* (Gomer Press, 1993), pp. 24–5 and notes on pp. 161–2.

32. Ibid., pp. 12–3, and for notes that date the poem see p. 159.

33. E. Bachellery (ed.), *L'Œuvre poetique de Gutun Owain* (Librairie Ancienne Honoré Champion, 2 vols., 1950–1), Vol. II, p. 251, l. 18.

34. Colin A. Gresham, 'The Cymer Abbey Charter', *Bulletin of the Board of Celtic Studies*, Vol. XXXI (1984), pp. 141–57, p. 144.

35. G. Jones & T. Jones, *The Mabinogion*, p. 86.

36. Chris Grooms, *The Giants of Wales* (Edwin Mellen, 1993), pp. 214–18.

37. Bromwich, *Trioedd Ynys Prydein*, p. 239.

38. Ifor Williams, *Canu Aneirin* (University of Wales Press, 1938), p. 50, l. 1272, and Kenneth Jackson, *The Gododdin: The Oldest Scottish Poem* (University of Edinburgh Press, 1969), p. 153, for translation. This section is not in A. O. H. Jarman, *Aneirin: Y Gododdin* (Gomer Press, 1988).

39. Frances Lynch, *A Guide to Ancient and Historic Wales: Gwynedd* (Cadw, 1995), p. 80, suggests that the fort might be post-Roman in date, which lends more support to this idea.

40. A detailed discussion of these points is in preparation.

41. Michael Winterbottom, *Gildas, The Ruin of Britain* (Phillimore, 1978), p. 31, §32.

42. Lesser tasks are simply described as completed, with no additional details. Rachel Bromwich & D. Simon Evans, *Culhwch and Olwen: An Edition and Study of the Oldest Arthurian Tale* (University of Wales Press, 1992), pp. xlvii–liii.

43. G. Jones & T. Jones, *The Mabinogion*, p. 105.

44. Lewis Thorpe, *Gerald of Wales: The Journey Through Wales/The Description of Wales* (Penguin, 1978), p. 227, and Bromwich & Evans, *Culhwch and Olwen*, pp. 159–60.

45. Bromwich & Evans, *Culhwch and Olwen*, p. 156.

46. Ibid., pp. lxiv–lxx and notes therein.

47. G. Jones & T. Jones, *The Mabinogion*, p. 109.

48. Ibid., p. 112.

49. Ibid., pp. 112–13.

50. RCAHM [Royal Commission on Ancient and Historic Monuments], *An Inventory of the Ancient Monuments in Wales and Monmouthshire, Volume IV – County of Denbigh* (Royal Stationery Office, 1914), p. 129. Grid reference SH 964424.

51. A. W. Wade-Evans, *Welsh Christian Origins* (Alden Press, 1934), p. 239.

52. Peter Roberts, *The Chronicle of the Kings of Britain* (E. Williams, 1811), pp. 361–2. The lost manuscript also contained other Arthurian material. which would be of great interest if only it could be found. The few leads that exist are currently being followed up, and if we find it we will let you know!

53. G. Jones & T. Jones, *The Mabinogion*, p. 87.

54. Bromwich & Evans, *Culhwch and Olwen*, pp. lxxxii–iii.

55. Discussion of the few points that can be raised concerning the place names in the poem can be found in the notes to Marged Haycock, '"Preiddeu Annwn" and the Figure of Taliesin', *Studia Celtica*, Vol. XVIII–XIX (1983–4), pp. 52–78. While tracking down some traditions regarding a lake in Wales, we came across the following fact, which we have not seen referenced elsewhere, in Frank Ward's book *The Lakes of Wales* (Herbert Jenkins, 1931), p. 43: three small pools near the shore at Afon-Wen, not far from Criccieth were once known as 'Llynnoedd Annwn' (the lakes of Annwn). Any further information on this point would be gratefully received.

56. A. O. H. Jarman, *Llyfr Du Caerfyrddin* (University of Wales Press, 1982), p. 66; translation from Bromwich et al., *The Arthur of the Welsh*, p. 40.

57. *Caernarvonshire Historical Society Transactions*, Vol. 2 (1940), p. 30 and references therein.

58. Jarman, *Llyfr Du Caerfyrddin*, p. 67; translation from Bromwich et al., *The Arthur of the Welsh*, p. 41.

59. G. Jones & T. Jones, *The Mabinogion*, p. 102.

60. Jarman, *Llyfr Du Caerfyrddin*, p. 66, l. 28; translation from Bromwich et al., *The Arthur of the Welsh*, p. 40.

61. Jarman, *Llyfr Du Caerfyrddin*, p. 67, l. 43; translation from Bromwich et al., *The Arthur of the Welsh*, p. 41.

62. J. G. Evans, *The Book of Taliesin*, p. xxiii.

63. Jarman, *Llyfr Du Caerfyrddin*, p. 67, l. 64; translation from Bromwich et al., *The Arthur of the Welsh*, p. 43.

64. For references to these instances see J. Lloyd-Jones, *Geirfa Barddoniaeth Gynnar Gymraeg* (University of Wales Press, 8 vols., 1931–63), Vol. V, p. 475.

65. John Morris, *Nennius: British History and the Welsh Annals* (Phillimore, 1980), pp. 29–31, §§40–2.

66. Jarman, *Llyfr Du Caerfyrddin*, p. 68, l. 79; translation from Bromwich et al., *The Arthur of the Welsh*, p. 44. Page 45 of the latter work also contains some speculative discussion on this point.

67. Ibid.

68. Blake & Lloyd, *The Keys To Avalon*, pp. 225–6.

Chapter 6

1. See Chapter 3, n. 53.

2. John Morris, *Nennius: British History and the Welsh Annals* (Phillimore, 1980), p. 35, §56.

3. P. C. Bartrum, *A Welsh Classical Dictionary: People in History and Legend up to about A.D. 1000* (National Library of Wales, 1993), pp. 26–7.

4. Ibid., p. 27.

5. Thomas Jones, 'The Early Evolution of the Legend of Arthur' (1958), trans. Gerald Morgan, *Nottingham Medieval Studies*, Vol. VIII (1964), pp. 3–21, p. 3.

6. The term 'legendary' is often applied to figures who do not fit comfortably within the present understanding. Although some of these figures can be assigned a definitively legendary or mythological status, others already assigned legendary status should have this particular judgement reserved pending possible further evidence.

7. T. Jones, 'The Early Evolution of the Legend of Arthur', p. 4.

8. Rachel Bromwich, 'Concepts of Arthur', *Studia Celtica*, Vol. X–XI (1975–6), pp. 163–81, p. 168.

9. A good discussion can be found in Richard Barber, *The Figure of Arthur* (Longman, 1972).

10. H. M. Chadwick & N. K. Chadwick, *The Growth of Literature* (Cambridge University Press, 2 vols., 1932), Vol. I, p. 155.

11. This idea was first proposed at the start of the nineteenth century, but only found favour among the historians and antiquarians of South Wales. By the start of the twentieth century the idea was no longer being considered, and it wasn't until the late 1970s that two researchers, Alan Wilson and Baram Blackett, resurrected it. Their expansion upon the original theory confuses matters even further, as does their insistence that there is a huge conspiracy afoot to try to stop their research. Their views can be found in Adrian Gilbert, Alan Wilson and Baram Blackett, *The Holy Kingdom* (Bantam, 1998).

12. A. W. Wade-Evans, *The Emergence of England and Wales* (Heffer, 2nd edn, 1959), p. 73.

13. For a detailed discussion of this point see David Dumville, 'Nennius and the Historia Brittonum', *Studia Celtica*, Vol. X–XII (1975–6), pp. 78–95.

14. Morris, *Nennius: British History and the Welsh Annals*, p. 9.

15. Ibid., p. 47.

16. Ibid.

17. Bartrum, *A Welsh Classical Dictionary*, p. 239.

18. Chadwick & Chadwick, *The Growth of Literature*, Vol. I, pp. 154–5. It has also been accepted by Bromwich in 'Concepts of Arthur', pp. 169–72, and David Dumville in 'Sub-Roman Britain: History and Legend', *History*, Vol. LXII, (1977), p. 188.

19. T. Jones, 'The Early Evolution of the Legend of Arthur', p. 10.

20. Rachel Bromwich, *The Poems of Taliesin* (Dublin Institute for Advanced Studies, 1968), p. 1.

21. J. Gwenogvryn Evans, *The Poetry in the Red Book of Hergest* (Llanbedrog, 1911), p. 14, col. 1043, ll. 23–4; translation from Barber, *The Figure of Arthur*, p. 98.

22. B. G. Charles, 'An early charter from the Abbey of Cwmhir', *Transactions of the Radnorshire Society,* Vol. XL (1970), pp. 68–74, p. 68.

23. In the poetry of Llywarch Hen, which can be found in Jenny Rowland, *Early Welsh Saga Poetry* (D. S. Brewer, 1990).

24. E. K. Chambers, *Arthur of Britain* (Sidgwick & Jackson, 1927), p. 202.

25. A. W. Wade-Evans, *Nennius's History of the Britons* (SPCK, 1938), p. 75, n. 4.

26. Bartrum, *A Welsh Classical Dictionary*, p. 129.

27. The Welsh text can be found in *Bulletin of the Board of Celtic Studies*, Vol. V (1930), pp. 115–129, and was translated by Tom Peete Cross in *Studies in Philology*, Vol. 17 (1920), pp. 93–110.

28. John Rhys, *Celtic Folklore, Welsh and Manx* (Clarendon Press, 2 vols., 1901), p. 480. 'Carnedd' = 'cairn' or a burial mound of stones.

29. Bartrum, *A Welsh Classical Dictionary*, p. 134.

30. RCAHM [Royal Commission on Ancient and Historic Monuments], *An Inventory of the Ancient Monuments in Wales and Monmouthshire, Volume IV – County of Denbigh* (Royal Stationery Office, 1914), pp. 135–6. Grid reference SJ 051642. An example of 'Guinnion' becoming 'Gwynion' can be found in The Chester Apprentice Rolls for Ironmongers, 1557–1646, '22 Feb 1613 (1613–14) – William son of John Dalbin late of Kayegunnion Co. Denbigh'. From *The Cheshire Sheaf*, March 1910, p. 22.

31. Grid reference SJ 151341.

32. A. O. H. Jarman, *Llyfr Du Caerfyrddin* (University of Wales Press, 1982), p. 66, ll. 21–2.

33. Ibid., p. 67, l. 48.

34. Rachel Bromwich, A. O. H. Jarman & Brynley F. Roberts (eds.), *The Arthur of the Welsh: The Arthurian Legend in Medieval Welsh Literature* (University of Wales Press, 1991), p. 41.

35. John J. Parry, *Brut y Brenhinedd, Cotton Cleopatra Version* (Medieval Academy of America, 1937), p. 28.

36. Roger Sherman Loomis (ed.), *Arthurian Literature in the Middle Ages* (Clarendon Press, 1959), p. 4.

37. Bartrum, *A Welsh Classical Dictionary*, p. 56.

38. Ibid.

39. T. Gwynn Jones, *Welsh Folklore and Folk Custom* (Methuen, 1930), p. 52.

40. Michael Winterbottom, *Gildas, The Ruin of Britain* (Phillimore, 1978), p. 28, §26.

41. Ibid.

42. Bartrum, *A Welsh Classical Dictionary*, p. 87.

43. Gwyn Jones & Thomas Jones, *The Mabinogion* (Everyman, rev. edn, 1993), p. 117.

44. Thomas Jones, *Brut Y Tywysogyon or The Chronicle of the Princes, Peniarth MS. 20 Version* (University of Wales Press, 1952), p. 13.

45. G. Jones & T. Jones, *The Mabinogion*, pp. 118–19.

46. Ibid., p. 119.

47. Melville Richards, *Breudwyt Rhonabwy* (University of Wales Press, 1948), p. 47 and references therein.

48. G. Jones & T. Jones, *The Mabinogion*, p. 119.

49. Steve Blake & Scott Lloyd, *The Keys To Avalon* (Element, 2000), p. 104.

50. T. P. Ellis & J. E. Lloyd, *The Mabinogion* (Clarendon Press, 2 vols., 1929), Vol. II, p. 2.

51. 'In Praise of Owain Gwynedd' by Cynddelw Brydydd Mawr (*fl.* 1155–1200): 'Fal gwaith Fadon fawr wriawr oriain' – 'As at Badon fawr, valiant war-cry.' R. Geraint Gruffydd (ed.), *Cyfres Beirdd y Tywysogion* (University of Wales Press, 7 vols., 1991–6), Vol. IV, p. 8, l. 40; translation from Gwyn Jones (ed.), *The Oxford Book of Welsh Verse in English* (Oxford University Press, 1977), p. 26.

52. G. Jones & T. Jones, *The Mabinogion*, p. 83.

53. Rachel Bromwich & D. Simon Evans, *Culhwch and Olwen: An Edition and Study of the Oldest Arthurian Tale* (University of Wales Press, 1992), p. 60.

54. G. Jones & T. Jones, *The Mabinogion*, p. 87.

55. Ibid., p. 106.

56. Rachel Bromwich, *Trioedd Ynys Prydein* (University of Wales Press, 2nd edn, 1978), p. 140.

57. Jarman, *Llyfr Du Caerfyrddin*, p. 39, ll. 90–2; translation from Thomas Jones, 'Stanzas of the Graves', The Sir John Rhys Memorial Lecture, *Proceedings of the British Academy*, Vol. LIII (1967), pp. 97–137, p. 123, §30.

58. Bromwich et al., *The Arthur of the Welsh*, p. 47.

59. Bartrum, *A Welsh Classical Dictionary*, p. 274 and notes therein.

60. Several places which bear the name 'Dyfnaint' and other variants are often ignored in favour of the modern understanding for Devon. For example, the Dyfnant Forest near Lake Vyrnwy, Dyfnant near the village of Trefilan in Ceredigion, and a river called Dyfnant near Cwm Penmachno – to name but three. The name actually translates as 'deep river valley', and is usually used for a small river in a steep-sided valley.

61. Bromwich, *Trioedd Ynys Prydein*, p. 25.

62. Bartrum, *A Welsh Classical Dictionary*, p. 415.

63. Lewis Thorpe, *The History of the Kings of Britain by Geoffrey of Monmouth* (Penguin, 1966), pp. 214–15.

64. D. Simon Evans, *A Mediaeval Welsh Prince of Wales – The Life of Grufydd ap Cynan* (Llanerch, 1996), p. 64; original Welsh text in the same author's *Historia Grufudd ab Kynan* (University of Wales Press, 1977), pp. 11–12.

65. Grid reference SH 833767.

66. Hywel Wyn Owen, *The Place-Names of East Flintshire* (University of Wales Press, 1994), p. 276. Caer Estyn perhaps?

67. R. G. Gruffydd, *Cyfres Beirdd y Tywysogion*, Vol. VII, p. 619, l. 30.

Chapter 7

1. Dafydd Jenkins, *The Law of Hywel Dda* (Gomer Press, 1986), pp. 8–11.
2. See T. M. Charles-Edwards, Morfydd E. Owen & Paul Russell (eds.), *The Welsh King and his Court* (University of Wales Press, 2000), 'Teulu and Penteulu', pp. 63–81, for a detailed discussion of the Welsh term '*teulu*'.
3. The poem states that this war-band was an amalgamation of young men from several districts – such as Rhos, Arfon, Rhufoniog, Aeron, Dunoding, Eidyn, Gododdin etc. – who were brought together and feasted for a year before doing battle at Catraeth. The apparently large size of this *teulu* can therefore be explained by this war-band's being brought together for a particular and difficult objective.
4. Sir John E. Lloyd, *A History of Wales* (Longmans, Green & Co., 3rd edn, 2 vols., 1939), Vol. I, p. 316.
5. Rachel Bromwich, *Trioedd Ynys Prydein* (University of Wales Press, 2nd edn, 1978) p. 57.
6. Ibid., p. 61.
7. A. O. H. Jarman, *Aneirin: Y Gododdin* (Gomer Press, 1988), p. 64, l. 972.
8. Bromwich, *Trioedd Ynys Prydein*, p. 57.
9. A. W. Wade-Evans, *Vitae Sanctorum Britanniae et Genealogiae* (University of Wales Press, 1944), p. 69.
10. Hugh Williams, *Gildae De Excidio Britanniae*, Cymmrodorion Record Series No. 3 (Hugh Williams, 2 vols., 1899–1901), Vol. II, pp. 415–20.
11. Michael Winterbottom, *Gildas, The Ruin of Britain* (Phillimore, 1978), p. 29, §27.
12. Ibid.
13. Ibid.
14. Ibid., p. 28.
15. Ibid., p. 32. The reference to Maelgwn being of great stature is also preserved in Welsh material where he is often nicknamed Hir (Tall).
16. Ibid.
17. These are discussed in P. C. Bartrum, *A Welsh Classical Dictionary: People in History and Legend up to about A.D. 1000* (National Library of Wales, 1993), pp. 438–42.
18. John Morris, *Nennius: British History and the Welsh Annals* (Phillimore, 1980), p. 45.
19. Winterbottom, *Gildas, The Ruin of Britain*, p. 32, §33.

Chapter 8

1. Sir Thomas Malory, *Le Morte d'Arthur* (J. M. Dent (Everyman's Library), 2 vols., 1906), Vol. III, pp. 386–7.
2. Ibid., pp. 389–90.
3. Lewis Thorpe, *The History of the Kings of Britain by Geoffrey of Monmouth* (Penguin, 1966), pp. 260–1.
4. Ibid., p. 261.

5. Ibid., pp. 257–8.
6. Rachel Bromwich, A. O. H. Jarman & Brynley F. Roberts (eds.), *The Arthur of the Welsh: The Arthurian Legend in Medieval Welsh Literature* (University of Wales Press, 1991), p. 81.
7. John Morris, *Nennius: British History and the Welsh Annals* (Phillimore, 1980), p. 45.
8. Gwyn Jones & Thomas Jones, *The Mabinogion* (Everyman, rev. edn, 1993), p. 89.
9. Rachel Bromwich, *Trioedd Ynys Prydein* (University of Wales Press, 2nd edn, 1978), p. 144.
10. Ibid., p. 206.
11. Ibid., p. 147.
12. A. W. Wade-Evans, *Welsh Christian Origins* (Alden Press, 1934), p. 190.
13. T. Gwynn Jones, 'Some Arthurian Material in Celtic', *Aberystwyth Studies*, Vol. VIII (1926), pp. 37–93, pp. 43–4.
14. G. Jones & T. Jones, *The Mabinogion*, p. 104.
15. T. Gwynn Jones, *Gwaith Tudur Aled* (University of Wales Press, 2 vols., 1926), Vol. I, p. 266, ll. 43–50.
16. R. Geraint Gruffydd (ed.), *Cyfres Beirdd y Tywysogion* (University of Wales Press, 7 vols., 1991–6), Vol. IV, p. 130, ll. 266–7; translation from O. Padel, *Arthur in Medieval Welsh Literature* (University of Wales Press, 2000), p. 59.
17. Bromwich, *Trioedd Ynys Prydein*, p. 162.
18. Neil Wright (ed.), *The Historia Regum Britannie of Geoffrey of Monmouth I: A Single-Manuscript Edition from Bern, Burgerbibliothek, MS. 568* (D. S. Brewer, 1985), p. 131, §178.
19. Geoffrey Ashe, *The Traveller's Guide to Arthurian Britain* (Gothic Image, 1997), pp. 198–200.
20. O. G. S. Crawford, 'Arthur and his Battles', *Antiquity*, Vol. IX (1935), pp. 277–91, p. 289.
21. *Archaeologia Cambrensis*, 1872, pp. 71–3.
22. A. O. H. Jarman, *Llyfr Du Caerfyrddin* (University of Wales Press, 1982), p. 37, ll. 36–8; translation from Thomas Jones, 'Stanzas of the Graves', The Sir John Rhys Memorial Lecture, *Proceedings of the British Academy*, Vol. LIII (1967), pp. 97–137, pp. 120–1.
23. Bromwich et al., *The Arthur of the Welsh*, p. 51.
24. G. Jones & T. Jones, *The Mabinogion*, p. 102.
25. P. C. Bartrum, *A Welsh Classical Dictionary: People in History and Legend up to about A.D. 1000* (National Library of Wales, 1993), p. 98 and references therein.
26. Ibid.
27. Ibid., p. 192.
28. Bromwich, *Trioedd Ynys Prydein*, p. 42.
29. Patrick K. Ford, *Ystoria Taliesin* (University of Wales Press, 1992).
30. Bromwich et al., *The Arthur of the Welsh*, p. 51.

31. Bromwich, *Trioedd Ynys Prydein*, p. 493.

32. Ibid., p. 494.

33. Bartrum, *A Welsh Classical Dictionary*, pp. 548–9.

34. Michael Lapidge, 'Vera Historia De Morte Arthuri: A New Edition', in James P. Carley (ed.), *Glastonbury Abbey and the Arthurian Tradition* (Boydell, 2001), pp. 115–41, pp. 116–17.

35. Ibid., pp. 124–8.

36. Ibid., p. 135.

37. Ibid.

38. Lewis Thorpe, *Gerald of Wales: The Journey Through Wales/The Description of Wales* (Penguin, 1978), p. 182.

39. Lapidge, 'Vera Historia De Morte Arthuri: A New Edition', p. 137.

40. A rather free English translation was printed in Richard Barber, *The Arthurian Legends: An Illustrated Anthology* (Boydell, 1979), pp. 30–2. The first Latin text with a facing English translation appeared in 1981, and the latest edition, based upon all the manuscripts now found, is in Lapidge, 'Vera Historia De Morte Arthuri: A New Edition'.

41. Steve Blake & Scott Lloyd, *The Keys To Avalon* (Element, 2000), pp. 121–217.

42. Lapidge, 'Vera Historia De Morte Arthuri: A New Edition', p. 141.

43. T. Jones, 'Stanzas of the Graves', pp. 126–7.

44. R. G. Gruffydd, *Cyfres Beirdd y Tywysogion*, Vol. V, p. 122, ll. 7–8.

45. John Rhys, *Celtic Folklore, Welsh and Manx* (Clarendon Press, 2 vols., 1901), Vol. II, pp. 473–6.

46. David H. Williams, *Atlas of Cistercian Lands in Wales* (University of Wales Press, 1990), 1990, pp. 37–8.

47. Grid reference SH 828524.

48. V. E. Nash-Williams, *The Early Christian Monuments of Wales* (University of Wales Press, 1950), p. 125.

49. Ibid.

Appendix 1

1. Gwyn Jones & Thomas Jones, *The Mabinogion* (Everyman, rev. edn, 1993), p. 89.

2. A. W. Wade-Evans, *Vitae Sanctorum Britanniae et Genealogiae* (University of Wales Press, 1944), pp. 25–9.

3. G. Jones & T. Jones, *The Mabinogion*, pp. 90–1.

4. A. O. H. Jarman, *Llyfr Du Caerfyrddin* (University of Wales Press, 1982), p. 37, l. 38.

5. G. Jones & T. Jones, *The Mabinogion*, p. 126.

6. Rachel Bromwich, *Trioedd Ynys Prydein* (University of Wales Press, 2nd edn, 1978), p. 16.

7. Ibid.

8. Ibid.

9. Ibid., p. 25.

10. Ibid., p. 154.

11. G. Jones & T. Jones, *The Mabinogion*, p. 112.

12. Jarman, *Llyfr Du Caerfyrddin*, p. 40, l. 119.

13. Rachel Bromwich & D. Simon Evans, *Culhwch and Olwen: An Edition and Study of the Oldest Arthurian Tale* (University of Wales Press, 1992), p. 89.

14. Ibid., p. 97.

15. Rachel Bromwich, A. O. H. Jarman & Brynley F. Roberts (eds.), *The Arthur of the Welsh: The Arthurian Legend in Medieval Welsh Literature* (University of Wales Press, 1991), p. 40.

16. Thomas Jones, 'Stanzas of the Graves', The Sir John Rhys Memorial Lecture, *Proceedings of the British Academy*, Vol. LIII (1967), pp. 97–137, p. 137.

17. John Morris, *Nennius: British History and the Welsh Annals* (Phillimore, 1980), p. 45.

18. P. C. Bartrum, *A Welsh Classical Dictionary: People in History and Legend up to about A.D. 1000* (National Library of Wales, 1993), p. 442.

19. G. Jones & T. Jones, *The Mabinogion*, pp. 35–46.

20. Bromwich, *Trioedd Ynys Prydein*, p. 56.

21. Bartrum, *A Welsh Classical Dictionary*, p. 561 and references therein.

22. Bromwich, *Trioedd Ynys Prydein*, p. 193.

Appendix 2

1. Antonia Gransden, 'Glastonbury traditions and Legends', in James P. Carley (ed.), *Glastonbury Abbey and the Arthurian Tradition* (Boydell, 2001), pp. 29–53, p. 33.

2. Hugh Williams, *Gildae De Excidio Britanniae*, Cymmrodorion Record Series No. 3 (Hugh Williams, 2 vols., 1899–1901), Vol. II, pp. 323–5.

3. For the full version of this episode see A. W. Wade-Evans, *Vitae Sanctorum Britanniae et Genealogiae* (University of Wales Press, 1944), pp. 80–5.

4. The confident identification of the unnamed Scottish site of Cadog's monastery with Cambuslang seems to rest solely on the very late and dubious evidence of a will from 1533. For details see Molly Miller, *The Saints of Gwynedd* (Boydell, 1979), p. 128, n. 34.

5. Wade-Evans, *Vitae Sanctorum Britanniae et Genealogiae*, p. 85.

6. Ellis Davies, *Flintshire Place-Names* (University of Wales Press, 1959), 1959, p. 36.

7. F. T. Wainwright, 'Cledemutha', *English Historical Review*, Vol. LXV (1950), pp. 203–12.

8. The oldest reference to this phrase is found in *Y Gododdin*: for the Welsh text see Ifor Williams, *Canu Aneirin* (University of Wales Press, 1938), p. 10, l. 255. Bannog is also mentioned on several occasions by the later bards: see Rachel Bromwich, *Trioedd Ynys Prydein* (University of Wales Press, 2nd edn, 1978), pp. 278–9 and references therein.

9. Jenny Rowland, *Early Welsh Saga Poetry* (D. S. Brewer, 1990), p. 415.

10. Also associated with this area are folktales concerning the Ychain Bannog, a pair of large oxen known throughout Wales. These tales also preserve other names containing the element 'Bannog': see Rev. Elias Owen, *Welsh Folklore* (Woodall, Minshall & Co., 1896), pp. 129–33.

11. Gwyn Jones & Thomas Jones, *The Mabinogion* (Everyman, rev. edn, 1993), p. 85.

12. For a detailed look at the available information for each son of Caw see P. C. Bartrum, *A Welsh Classical Dictionary: People in History and Legend up to about A.D. 1000* (National Library of Wales, 1993), pp. 112–14 and references therein.

13. H. Williams, *Gildae De Excidio Britanniae*, Vol. II, p. 327.

14. Bartrum, *A Welsh Classical Dictionary*, p. 290.

15. Ibid., p. 330.

16. Ibid., p. 335.

17. Ibid., p. 357.

18. J. Gwenogvryn Evans & John Rhys, *The Text of the Book of Llan Dav Reproduced from the Gwysaney Manuscript* (Oxford University Press, 1893), p. 255.

19. Bartrum, *A Welsh Classical Dictionary*, p. 464.

20. P. C. Bartrum, *Early Welsh Genealogical Tracts* (University of Wales Press, 1966), p. 85: 'Kaw of Dwrcelyn'.

21. Ibid, p. 63. §59: 'Kaw, arglwydd Kwm cawlwyd'.

22. Bromwich, *Trioedd Ynys Prydein*, p. 409: 'Kaw of Prydein was the name of a chieftain who ruled over Edeirnion, in North Wales', translating from the chronicle of Elis Gruffudd in the manuscript NLW 5276D, p. 334, kept in the National Library of Wales in Aberystwyth.

23. G. Jones & T. Jones, *The Mabinogion*, p. 101.

24. Ibid., p. 103.

25. H. Williams, *Gildae De Excidio Britanniae*, Vol. II, pp. 401–3.

26. Lewis Thorpe, *Gerald of Wales: The Journey Through Wales/The Description of Wales* (Penguin, 1978), p. 259.

27. H. Williams, *Gildae De Excidio Britanniae*, Vol. II, pp. 325–7.

28. For a full translation of the original text see, Steve Blake & Scott Lloyd, *The Keys To Avalon* (Element, 2000), pp. 225–7.

29. Thomas Jones, 'Chwedl Huail ap Caw ac Arthur', in Thomas Parry-William (ed.), *Astudiaethau Amrywiol* (University of Wales Press, 1968), p. 49.

30. Ibid., p. 58.

31. Ibid., p. 59.

32. Ibid.

33. Ibid.

34. Bromwich, *Trioedd Ynys Prydein*, p. 37.

35. Ibid.

36. For more details on this relic see Blake & Lloyd, *The Keys To Avalon*, pp. 161–4.

37. T. Jones, 'Chwedl Huail ap Caw ac Arthur', p. 64.
38. H. Williams, *Gildae De Excidio Britanniae*, Vol. II, p. 403.
39. *The Life of Gildas* states that Huail was killed by Arthur in 'the island of Minau' (ibid., p. 403). This has been identified as the Isle of Man, known to the Welsh as Manaw, but it is interesting to note that Mon (Anglesey) is also referred to as Manaw or Manua, with which Caw and some of his children are associated. See Blake & Lloyd, *The Keys To Avalon*, pp. 241–2 and references therein.
40. His notes on the history of Merionethshire were printed in the journal *Archaeologia Cambrensis*, 1850, p. 204.
41. V. E. Nash-Williams, *The Early Christian Monuments of Wales* (University of Wales Press, 1950), p. 170.
42. Ibid.
43. H. Williams, *Gildae De Excidio Britanniae*, Vol. II, p. 322. Also of interest is the website http://www.ucl.ac.uk/archaeology/cisp/database/ and click on Llanfor. This site is called 'The Celtic Inscribed Stones Project', and is a fantastic resource covering the whole of the UK and Ireland.
44. J. H. Davies, 'A Welsh Version of the Birth of Arthur', *Y Cymmrodor*, Vol. XXIV (1913), pp. 247–64, p. 248.
45. Ibid., p. 248.
46. Sir John E. Lloyd, *A History of Wales* (Longmans, Green & Co., 3rd edn, 2 vols., 1939), Vol. I, p. 247.
47. Thomas Roberts, 'Y Traddodiad am y Brenin Arthur yng Nghaergai', *Bulletin of the Board of Celtic Studies*, Vol. XI (1944), pp. 12–14, p. 13.
48. John Rhys, *Celtic Folklore, Welsh and Manx* (Clarendon Press, 2 vols., 1901), Vol. II, p. 693.
49. T. Roberts, 'Y Traddodiad am y Brenin Arthur yng Nghaergai', p. 13.
50. R. Morris (ed.), *The Works of Edmund Spenser* (Macmillan, 1912), Book 1, Canto IX, p. 4.
51. A. O. H. Jarman, *Llyfr Du Caerfyrddin* (University of Wales Press, 1982), p. 67, l. 64; translation from Rachel Bromwich, A. O. H. Jarman & Brynley F. Roberts (eds.), *The Arthur of the Welsh: The Arthurian Legend in Medieval Welsh Literature* (University of Wales Press, 1991), p. 43. 'Emrys' was used to denote Gwynedd in bardic poetry: see Chapter 5.
52. Jarman, *Llyfr Du Caerfyrddin*, p. 67, ll. 56–7; translation from Bromwich, et al., *The Arthur of the Welsh*, p. 43.
53. G. Jones & T. Jones, *The Mabinogion*, p. 87.
54. Stephen S. Evans, *Lords of Battle* (Boydell, 1997), pp. 118–20.
55. J. H. Davies, 'A Welsh Version of the Birth of Arthur', pp. 247–8.
56. Ibid., p. 247.
57. Some words have evidently been omitted at this place in the Welsh text.
58. This sentence is left unfinished in the MS – probably the scribe could not read the original.
59. Literally 'to play staff and shield, and to break spears'.

BIBLIOGRAPHY

Andrews, Rhian, 'Rhai Agweddau ar Sofraniaeth yng Ngherddi'r Gogynfeirdd', *Bulletin of the Board of Celtic Studies*, Vol. XXVII (1976), pp. 23–30

Arthurian Bibliography, The: Volume I, *Author Listing*, ed. C. E. Pickford & R. W. Last (D. S. Brewer, 1981)

—— Volume II, *Subject Index*, ed. C. E. Pickford, R. W. Last & C. R. Barker (D. S. Brewer, 1983)

—— Volume III, *1978–1992*, ed. Caroline Palmer (D. S. Brewer, 1998)

—— Volume IV, *1993–1998*, ed. Elaine Barber (D. S. Brewer, 2002)

Arthurian Literature (D. S. Brewer, 1981–)

Ashe, Geoffrey, *The Traveller's Guide to Arthurian Britain* (Gothic Image, 1997)

Bachellery, E. (ed.), *L'Œuvre poetique de Gutun Owain* (Librairie Ancienne Honoré Champion, 2 vols., 1950–1)

Barber, Richard, *The Figure of Arthur* (Longman, 1972)

——, *The Arthurian Legends: An Illustrated Anthology* (Boydell, 1979)

——, *King Arthur: Hero and Legend* (Boydell, 1986)

Bartrum, P. C., 'Arthuriana from the Genealogical Manuscripts', *National Library of Wales Journal*, Vol. XIV (1965), pp. 242–5

——, *Early Welsh Genealogical Tracts* (University of Wales Press, 1966)

——, *A Welsh Classical Dictionary: People in History and Legend up to about A.D. 1000* (National Library of Wales, 1993)

Bell, Alexander (ed.), *L'Estoire des Engleis By Geffrei Gaimar* (Anglo-Norman Text Society, 1960)

Bibliographical Bulletin of the International Arthurian Society, 1949–present

Biddle, Martin, *King Arthur's Round Table* (Boydell, 2000)

Blake, Steve, and Lloyd, Scott, *The Keys To Avalon* (Element, 2000)

Bromwich, Rachel, *The Poems of Taliesin* (Dublin Institute for Advanced Studies, 1968)

——, 'Concepts of Arthur', *Studia Celtica*, Vol. X–XI (1975–6), pp. 163–81

——, *Trioedd Ynys Prydein* (University of Wales Press, 2nd edn, 1978)

Bromwich, Rachel, Jarman, A. O. H., & Roberts, Brynley F. (eds.), *The Arthur of the Welsh: The Arthurian Legend in Medieval Welsh Literature* (University of Wales Press, 1991)

Bromwich, Rachel, & Evans, D. Simon, *Culhwch and Olwen: An Edition and Study of the Oldest Arthurian Tale* (University of Wales Press, 1992)

Chadwick, H. M., & Chadwick, N. K., *The Growth of Literature* (Cambridge University Press, 2 vols., 1932)

Chambers, E. K., *Arthur of Britain* (Sidgwick & Jackson, 1927)

Charles, B. G., 'An early charter from the Abbey of Cwmhir', *Transactions of the Radnorshire Society,* Vol. XL (1970), pp. 68–74

Charles-Edwards, T. M., Owen, Morfydd E., & Russell, Paul (eds.), *The Welsh King and his Court* (University of Wales Press, 2000)

Crawford, O. G. S., 'Arthur and his Battles', *Antiquity*, Vol. IX (1935), pp. 277–91

Crick, Julia *The Historia Regum Britanniae of Geoffrey of Monmouth III: A Summary Catalogue of the Manuscripts* (D. S. Brewer, 1989)***

Davies, Ellis, *Flintshire Place-Names* (University of Wales Press, 1959)

Davies, J. H., 'A Welsh Version of the Birth of Arthur', *Y Cymmrodor*, Vol. XXIV (1913), pp. 247–64

Dumville, David, 'Nennius and the Historia Brittonum', *Studia Celtica*, Vol. X–XI (1975–6), pp. 78–95

——, 'Sub-Roman Britain: History and Legend', *History*, Vol. LXII, (1977), pp. 173–92

Ellis, T. P., & Lloyd, J. E., *The Mabinogion* (Clarendon Press, 2 vols., 1929)

Evans, D. Simon, *Historia Grufudd ab Kynan* (University of Wales Press, 1977)

——, *A Mediaeval Welsh Prince of Wales – The Life of Grufydd ap Cynan* (Llanerch, 1996)

Evans, J. Gwenogvryn, *Report on Manuscripts in the Welsh Language* (Historical Manuscripts Commission, 2 vols., 1898–1910)

——, *The Book of Taliesin* (Llanbedrog, 1910)

——, *The Poetry in the Red Book of Hergest* (Llanbedrog, 1911)

——, *Poetry by Medieval Welsh Bards* (Llanbedrog, 1926)

Evans, J. Gwenogvryn, & Rhys, John, *The Text of the Book of Llan Dav Reproduced from the Gwysaney Manuscript* (Oxford University Press, 1893)

Evans, Stephen S., *Lords of Battle* (Boydell, 1997)

Ford, Patrick, K., *Ystoria Taliesin* (University of Wales Press, 1992)

Gransden, Antonia, 'Glastonbury Traditions and Legends', in James P. Carley (ed.), *Glastonbury Abbey and the Arthurian Tradition* (Boydell, 2001), pp. 29–53

Gresham, Colin A., 'The Cymer Abbey Charter', *Bulletin of the Board of Celtic Studies*, Vol. XXXI (1984), pp. 141–57

Grooms, Chris, *The Giants of Wales* (Edwin Mellen, 1993)

Gruffydd, R. Geraint (ed.), *Cyfres Beirdd y Tywysogion* (University of Wales Press, 7 vols., 1991–6)

Gruffydd, W. J., *Math vab Mathonwy* (University of Wales Press, 1928)

Haycock, Marged, '"Preiddeu Annwn" and the Figure of Taliesin', *Studia Celtica*, Vol. XVIII–XIX (1983–4), pp. 52–78

——, *Blodeugerdd Barddos o Ganu Crefyddol Cynnar* (University of Wales Press, 1994)

Hughes, Kathleen, 'British MS. Cotton Vespasian A. XIV ("Vitae Sanctorum Wallensium"): its purpose and provenance', *Studies in the Early British Church* (Cambridge University Press, 1958), pp. 183–200

Huws, David, *Medieval Welsh Manuscripts* (University of Wales Press, 2000)

Jackson, Kenneth, *The Gododdin: The Oldest Scottish Poem* (University of Edinburgh Press, 1969)

Jarman, A. O. H., *Llyfr Du Caerfyrddin* (University of Wales Press, 1982)

——, *Aneirin: Y Gododdin* (Gomer Press, 1988)

Jarman, A. O. H., & Hughes, Gwilym Rees, *A Guide to Welsh Literature Volume 1* (Christopher Davies, 1976)

Jenkins, Dafydd, *The Law of Hywel Dda* (Gomer Press, 1986)

Johnston, Dafydd (ed.), *Iolo Goch Poems* (Gomer Press, 1993)

Jones, Gwyn, & Jones, Thomas, *The Mabinogion* (Everyman, rev. edn, 1993)

Jones, T. Gwynn, 'Some Arthurian Material in Celtic', *Aberystwyth Studies*, Vol. VIII (1926), pp. 37–93

——, *Gwaith Tudur Aled* (University of Wales Press, 2 vols., 1926)

——, *Welsh Folklore and Folk Custom* (Methuen, 1930)

Jones, Thomas, *Brut Y Tywysogyon or The Chronicle of the Princes, Peniarth MS. 20 Version* (University of Wales Press, 1952)

——, 'Datblygiadau Cynnar Chwedl Arthur', *Bulletin of the Board of Celtic Studies*, Vol. XVII (1958), pp. 237–52

——, 'The Early Evolution of the Legend of Arthur' (1958), trans. Gerald Morgan, *Nottingham Medieval Studies*, Vol. VIII (1964), pp. 3–21

——, 'Teir Ynys Prydein a'e Their Rac Ynys', *Bulletin of the Board of Celtic Studies,* Vol. XVII (1958), pp. 268–9

——, 'A Sixteenth-Century Version of the Arthurian Cave Legend', in Mieczyslaw Brahmer (ed.), *Studies in Language and Literature in Honour of Margaret Schlauch* (Polish Scientific Publishers, 1966)

——, 'Stanzas of the Graves', The Sir John Rhys Memorial Lecture, *Proceedings of the British Academy,* Vol. LIII (1967), pp. 97–137

——, 'Chwedl Huail ap Caw ac Arthur', in Thomas Parry-William (ed.), *Astudiaethau Amrywiol* (University of Wales Press, 1968), pp. 48–66

Kendrick, T. D., *British Antiquity* (Methuen, 1950)

Keynes, Simon, & Lapidge, Michael, *Alfred the Great: Asser's Life of King Alfred and Other Contemporary Sources* (Penguin, 1983)

Lapidge, Michael, '*Vera Historia De Morte Arthuri*: A New Edition', in James P. Carley (ed.), *Glastonbury Abbey and the Arthurian Tradition* (Boydell, 2001), pp. 115–41

Lapidge, Michael, and Dumville, David (eds.), *Gildas: New Approaches* (Boydell, 1984)

Lewis, Henry, *Brut Dingestow* (University of Wales Press, 1942)

Lloyd, Sir John E., *A History of Wales* (Longmans, Green & Co., 3rd edn, 2 vols., 1939)

Lloyd-Jones, J., *Geirfa Barddoniaeth Gynnar Gymraeg* (University of Wales Press, 8 vols., 1931–63)

Loomis, Roger Sherman (ed.), *Arthurian Literature in the Middle Ages* (Clarendon Press, 1959)

Lynch, Frances, *A Guide to Ancient and Historic Wales: Gwynedd* (Cadw, 1995)

Malory, Sir Thomas, *Le Morte d'Arthur* (J. M. Dent (Everyman's Library), 2 vols.,1906)

Mommsen, Theodore (ed.), *Monumenta Germaniae Historica, Chronica Minora,* Vol. III (Berlin, 1894)

Morris, John, *Nennius: British History and the Welsh Annals* (Phillimore, 1980)

Morris, Rupert H. (ed.), *Parochialia: being a summary of answers to 'Parochial queries in order to a geographical dictionary, etc., of Wales' / issued by Edward Lhwyd* (1698) (Cambrian Archæological Association, 4 vols., 1909–1911)

Nash-Williams, V. E., *The Early Christian Monuments of Wales* (University of Wales Press, 1950)

Owen, Rev. Elias, *Welsh Folklore* (Woodall, Minshall & Co., 1896)

Owen, Hywel Wyn, *The Place-Names of East Flintshire* (University of Wales Press, 1994)

Padel, O., *Arthur in Medieval Welsh Literature* (University of Wales Press, 2000)

Parry, John J., *Brut y Brenhinedd, Cotton Cleopatra Version* (Medieval Academy of America, 1937)

RCAHM [Royal Commission on Ancient and Historic Monuments], *An Inventory of the Ancient Monuments in Wales and Monmouthshire, Volume IV – County of Denbigh* (Royal Stationery Office, 1914)

Rhys, John, *Celtic Folklore, Welsh and Manx* (Clarendon Press, 2 vols., 1901)

Richards, Melville, *Breudwyt Rhonabwy* (University of Wales Press, 1948)

Rider, Jeff, 'Arthur and the Saints', in Valerie M. Lagorio and Mildred Leake Day (eds.), *King Arthur Through the Ages Volume I* (Garland, 1990)

Roberts, Peter, *The Chronicle of the Kings of Britain* (E. Williams, 1811)

Roberts, Thomas, 'Y Traddodiad am y Brenin Arthur yng Nghaergai', *Bulletin of the Board of Celtic Studies*, Vol. XI (1944), pp. 12–14

Rowlands, E. I., 'Bardic Lore and Education', *Bulletin of the Board of Celtic Studies*, Vol. XXXII (1985), pp. 143–55

Rowland, Jenny, *Early Welsh Saga Poetry* (D. S. Brewer, 1990)

Sims-Williams, Patrick, 'The Irish Geography of *Culhwch and Olwen*', in Donnchadh Ó Corráin, Liam Breatnach, Kim McCone (eds.), *Sages, Saints and Storytellers: Celtic Studies in Honour of Professor James Carney*, Maynooth Monographs No. 2 (An Sagart, 1989), pp. 412–26

——, 'Clas Beuno and the Four Branches of the Mabinogi', in *150 Jahre Mabinogion Deutsch-Walisische Kulturbeziehungen* (Max Niemeyer Verlag, 2001), pp.111–27

Southern, R. W., 'Aspects of the European Tradition of Historical Writing 1. The Classical Tradition from Einhard to Geoffrey of Monmouth', *Transactions of the Royal Historical Society*, Fifth Series, No. 20 (1970), pp. 173–96

Spanuth, Jurgen, *Atlantis of the North* (Sidgwick & Jackson, 1979)

Stevenson, William Henry, *Asser's Life of King Alfred* (Clarendon Press, 2nd edn, 1959)

Tacitus, *De Vita Agricolae*, ed. R. M. Ogilvie & Sir Ian Richmond (Clarendon Press, 1967)

Tatlock, J. S. P., *The Legendary History of Britain* (University of California Press, 1950)

Thorpe, Lewis, *The History of the Kings of Britain by Geoffrey of Monmouth* (Penguin, 1966)

——, *Gerald of Wales: The Journey Through Wales/The Description of Wales* (Penguin, 1978)

Vinaver, Eugene (ed.), *The Works of Sir Thomas Malory* (Clarendon Press, 3 vols., 1947)

Wade-Evans, A. W., *Welsh Christian Origins* (Alden Press, 1934)

——, *Nennius's History of the Britons* (SPCK, 1938)

——, *Vitae Sanctorum Britanniae et Genealogiae* (University of Wales Press, 1944)

——, *The Emergence of England and Wales* (Heffer, 2nd edn, 1959)

Ward, Charlotte, 'Arthur in the Welsh Bruts', in Cyril J. Burne, Margaret Harry & Padraig O'Siadhail (eds.), *Celtic Languages and Celtic Peoples: Proceedings of the Second North American Congress of Celtic Studies* (St Mary's University, 1992), pp. 383–90

Weiss, Judith, *Wace's Roman De Brut: A History of The British* (University of Exeter Press, 1999)

Williams, David H., *Atlas of Cistercian Lands in Wales* (University of Wales Press, 1990)

Williams, Hugh, *Gildae De Excidio Britanniae* (Cymmrodorion Record Series No. 3, 2 vols., 1899)

Williams, Ifor, *Pedeir Keinc y Mabinogi* (University of Wales Press, 1930)

——, *Canu Aneirin* (University of Wales Press, 1938)

Williams, J. E. Caerwyn, *The Poets of the Welsh Princes* (University of Wales Press, 1994)

Winterbottom, Michael, *Gildas, The Ruin of Britain* (Phillimore, 1978)

Wright, Neil, 'Geoffrey of Monmouth and Gildas', *Arthurian Literature*, Vol. II (1982), pp. 1–40

——, 'Gildas's geographical perspective: some problems', in Michael Lapidge and David Dumville (eds.), *Gildas: New Approaches* (Boydell, 1984), pp. 85–106

—— (ed.), *The Historia Regum Britanniae of Geoffrey of Monmouth I: A Single-Manuscript Edition from Bern, Burgerbibliothek, MS. 568* (D. S. Brewer, 1985)

——, 'Geoffrey of Monmouth and Bede', *Arthurian Literature*, Vol. VI (1986), pp. 27–59

—— (ed.), *The Historia Regum Britanniae of Geoffrey of Monmouth II: The First Variant Version: A Critical Edition* (D. S. Brewer, 1988)

USEFUL ADDRESSES

The Authors

If you would like to contact the authors, please either write care of the publishers or contact us through our web site: www.blakeandlloyd.com This site will also contain short articles on points raised in this book and other material of interest.

Source Publishers

Boydell & Brewer
PO Box 9
Woodbridge
Suffolk
IP12 3DF
England
UK
Tel: 01394 411320
Fax: 01394 411477
www.boydell.co.uk

Dublin Institute of Advanced Studies
School of Celtic Studies
10 Burlington Road
Dublin 2
Ireland
www.cp.dias.ie/celtic.html

The National Library of Wales
Aberystwyth
Cardiganshire SY23 3BU
Wales
UK
www.llgc.org.uk

University of Wales Press
10 Columbus Walk
Brigantine Place
Cardiff
CF10 4UP
Wales
UK
Tel: 02920 496899
www.uwp.co.uk

Other Resources

Flintshire Library Headquarters
Mold
Flintshire
CH7 6NW
North Wales
Over 3000 volumes concerning all aspects of the Arthurian Legend, dating from the sixteenth century and updated continually.

The Welsh Academic Press
www.ashleydrake.com/dragon_books/Welsh_Academic_Press.html
A book containing all of the Welsh sources is currently in preparation by the authors.

A reprint of A.W. Wade-Evans' *Vitae Sanctorum Britanniae et Genealogiae*, containing the Lives of the Welsh Saints is also in preparation and due for publication in 2003.

Early Manuscripts at Oxford University
http://image.ox.ac.uk
This excellent site contains digital facsimiles of dozens of important manuscripts. Those most relevant to the study of Arthurian materials are:
Jesus College MS.20 which contains the earliest copy of *A Conversation Between Arthur and the Eagle* and some of the earliest Welsh genealogies
Jesus College MS.28 which includes a version of *Brut y Brenhinedd*
Jesus College MS.111 which gives the complete text of *The Red Book of Hergest*, including *The Mabinogion*, *Brut y Brenhinedd*, a large percentage of the poetry of the *Gogynfeirdd* and various other poems of interest

INDEX

Aaron, martyr 42
Aber Deu Cleddyf 130–1
Aberconwy Abbey 61, 195, 201, 237
Aberdaron 99
Abererch 99
Aberffraw 116, 120
Abergele 107, 148, 192
Aberhafesb 233
Aberporth 192
Afarnach's hall 136
Afon Gamlan 190
Afon Medrad 187
Afon Meirchion 154
Afon Trystan 154
Agned Mountain 156
Alcock, Leslie 23
    Arthur's Britain 24
Aled, River 153
Alexander, Bishop of Lincoln 33, 34, 164–5
Alliterative Morte Arthur, The 17–18, 30
Ambrosius Aurelianus 6, 11–12, 85, 108,
    109
Amhar ap/son of Arthur 103
Amlawdd Wledig (Arthur's grandfather) 71,
    86–8, 89, 90, 92, 93, 94, 96, 100,
    107, 108
Andrews, Rhian 115
Anglesey (Mon) 89, 95, 96, 97, 116, 120,
    123, 136, 138, 151, 224, 231, 233,
    243
Anglo-Saxon Chronicle 175, 176
Anna ferch/daughter of Uthyr (Arthur's sister)
    12, 82
Annales Cambriae (Welsh Annals) 39–40, 44,
    45, 46, 58–9, 75, 102, 120–1, 144,
    148, 157, 160, 173, 180, 185, 222,
    260–1
Annwas Adeiniog 213, 214
'anoeth bid' 199–200
Antor (Arthur's foster father) 83, 241 *see also*
    Cynyr Ceinfarfog of Penllyn
Aran mountains 124
Archaeologica Cambrensis 190

Archfedd ferch/daughter of Arthur 103
Arecluta 228–9
Arthur, alternative historical figures 144–5
Arthur, son of Henry VII 20
Arthurian studies 23–5, 142–5, 271–2
Ashe, Geoffrey 23
Asser, monk 117
Aurelius Caninus 176
Avalon, Isle of 8, 12, 15, 18, 75, 183
    location 197

Badon (Baddon, Caer Faddon, Mons
        Badonis) 41, 59, 76, 77, 141, 179
    location 157–60
Bala Lake (Llyn Tegid) 124, 193, 241
Baldwin, Archbishop of Canterbury 80
bards *see* Welsh bards and bardic poetry
Bardsey Island 40
Bartrum, P. C. 153, 154
Baschurch 151, 152
Basingwerk Abbey (Dinas Basing) 61, 100,
    151–2
Bassaleg 151
Bassas, River 151
Beardsley, Aubrey 22–3
Bedd Geraint 164
Bede *Historia Ecclesiastica Gentis Anglorum*
        (Ecclesiastical History of the English
        People) 13, 36, 43, 108, 175, 176,
        257–8
Bedivere 182, 191
Bedwini the Bishop 213, 214, 219
Bedwr 42, 55, 72, 213, 214–16, 237
Berwyn Mountains 154, 156
Betws Geraint 164
Bicanus (Arthur's uncle) 88, 96
Black Book of Carmarthen, 40, 42, 63–7,
        84–5, 91, 104, 108, 163, 174, 212, 267
    see also Pa Gur?; Stanzas of the Graves
Bleddyn Fardd 104, 115, 166
Bodfari 90
Bodferin 161
Boece 189

Bonedd Gwyr y Gogledd (Lineage of the Men of the North) 94, 96, 125, 127
Bonedd y Saint (Lineage of the Saints) 81, 89, 90, 91, 93, 94, 95, 96, 97, 99, 103, 186–7, 192
Bonedd yr Arwyr (Lineage of the Heroes) 89–90, 94
Boniface VIII, Pope 17
Book of Aneirin 60–1, 96–7, 125, 153, 266–7
Book of Llandaf 35, 39, 43, 44, 93, 117, 233
Book of St Germanus 57
Book of St Patrick 57
Book of Taliesen 40, 61–3, 73, 135–6, 149, 156, 194–5, 212, 221, 266
Branwen ferch Llyr 115–16
Bray Head, Ireland 122
Brecon 68
Breidden hill 158
Britannia 10, 36, 37, 113, 117–18
denoting Wales 38–9, 55, 117–18, 174
Britons 6, 10, 11, 13, 32, 48, 52, 57, 68, 127, 141, 142, 143, 146, 147, 155, 157, 168, 179, 196
denoting inhabitants of Wales 7
Brittany 41, 226
association with Llydaw 88
denoted by Britannia 38
Bromwich, Dr Rachel 51, 52, 65–6, 66–7, 77, 143, 189, 237
Bron Bannog 230
Brut y Brenhinedd (Chronicle of the Kings) 45, 80, 82, 90, 100, 112, 169, 187, 262–3
Brut y Tywysogion (Chronicle of the Welsh Princes) 46, 158
Brutus 10, 32
Bryn Euryn *see* Dinarth hill fort

Cadbury Castle 9, 18–19, 21, 23, 47
Cadfarch, St 99
Cadwaladr 28, 33
Cadwallon Lawhir 43, 149
Cadwy ap/son of Geraint (Arthur's cousin) 88, 213
Cadyrieth ap/son of Saidi 213, 216
Caeaugwynion Mawr 154
Caer Cybi (Holyhead) 148
Caer Dathal 94–5
Caer Faddon *see* Badon
Caer Gai 240, 241–2
Caer Llwydcoed (Kaerluideoit) 40, 164–6
Caer Oeth ac Anoeth 162–3, 199, 206
Caergwrle 166
Caerleon 39–40
Caerleon on Usk 34, 43, 120, 168, 233
Caerlleon (City of Legions) 42–3, 120–1 *see also* Urbes Legiones
Caerloyw 222

Caernarfon 95, 116, 123
Caerwyn Williams, J. E. 69–70
Caerwys 235, 236
Caeugwynion farm 154–5
Caesar 117
Cai (Cei) ap/son of Cynyr (Kay) 42, 55, 72, 80, 83, 161–2, 206, 211, 213, 222, 237, 241–4
Caledfwlch *see* Excalibur
Caliburn/Caliburnus *see* Excalibur 40
Camel, River 21
Camelot 14, 18–19, 30, 118–19
location 18–19
Cameron, Julia 22
Camlan 8, 12, 36, 44, 181–95, 206
location 1, 21, 189–91, 198
survivors 191–5
Welsh sources 59, 160, 184–9
Canterbury records (1152) 34
Capel Gwynog 233
Capel Marchell 96
Caradog Freichfras ap/son of Llyr Marini (Karadeues Briebaz) (Arthur's cousin) 99, 187, 213
Caradog of Llancarvan 56, 226–7
Life of St Gildas 54, 226–30, 234, 238–9
Cardigan Castle 164
Carmarthen priory 63
Carmarthenshire 135
Carnedd Arthur 201
Carnedd Llywelyn 154
Carnwennan (Arthur's dagger) 73, 75, 133
Carreg Gwynion hill fort 154
Castell Meirchion 154
Castell y Gawr hill fort 192
Castelldwyran 176
Castellmarch 100
Castello Guinnion (Gwynion) 154–5
Catraeth 60, 171–2
Catterick 60
Caw of Prydein 133, 134, 228–30
children of 206, 230–3
Llanfor Stone 239–40
Cawdraf, St 99
Caxton, William 18, 30
Cedwyn, St 192
Celidon Wood *see* Coedd Celyddon
Celtic culture and tradition 27, 73, 49–50
Celyddon Wledig 152
Ceredigion (Cardiganshire) 89, 91, 99, 164, 192
Cernyw 96, 99, 121
location 124–6
Chadwick, H. M. and N. K. 144
Chambers, E. K. 23, 38, 152
Charles, Prince 20
Chester 43, 120, 145, 146, 152, 155
Chrétien de Troyes 14, 30, 69
Erec et Enide 14, 104

Lancelot 14, 30, 119
Perceval (Le Conte de Graal) 14, 75
Christianity 15, 16, 49, 175
Chronicle of John of Glastonbury 217
Church of England 16
Chwilog 123
Cilydd ap/son of Celyddon Wledig (Arthur's uncle) 88, 152–3
Cistercian monks 16–17
Cleddau rivers 131
Clwyd, River 229–30 *see also* Vale of Clwyd
Coed Celyddon (Celidon) 40, 141, 152–4
Constantine, Duke of Cornwall 183
Constantinus, King 11, 176
Continental campaigns 8, 12, 42, 47, 162, 168
Conwy (Conway), River 88, 153
Corn Gaffalt 57
Cornwall 41, 68, 133, 193–4
  association with Cernyw 96, 121, 124
  claimed as site of Camlan 21, 183, 189
Cornwy 224
Cotton Ms. Vespasian A. xiv 54
Crawford, O. G. S. 189
Cregiau Gwineu hill fort 126
Creuddyn (Great Ormes Head) 137
Criccieth 97
Croes Feilig 233
Crown of Arthur 237–8
Culhwch and Olwen 39, 42, 44, 51–2, 70–6, 106, 121, 124, 125, 152–3, 161–2, 174, 214, 230, 234, 243, 264
  Arthur's possessions 40, 73–6
  Arthur's relatives 89, 90, 91–2, 93, 94, 95–6, 97, 99, 104, 186
  battle of Camlan 185–6, 188
  places visited by Arthur 120, 130–5, 136
  survivors of Camlan 191, 192, 195
  warrior list 64, 66, 72, 88, 93, 103, 122, 135, 212, 214, 216, 217, 218, 219, 220, 221, 222, 223, 224
Culhwch ap/son of Cilydd (Arthur's cousin) 71–3, 89
Cuneglasus (Cynlas Goch) 129, 176
Custennin ap/son of Mynwyedig (Arthur's uncle) 89
Cwm Cawlwyd 233
Cwm Cerwyn 217, 219
Cwmllan valley 200
Cydfan ap/son of 103
Cymhir Abbey 151
Cymmer Abbey 124
'Cymry' 115, 117
Cynan Garwyn of Powys 28, 149
Cynddelw, bard 26, 69, 115, 122, 188
Cynddelw Brydydd Mawr 160
Cynfeirdd (Early Poets) 52
Cyngar ap/son of Geraint (Arthur's cousin) 89, 93

Cynwal Garnhwch (Arthur's uncle) 89–90, 92
Cynwyl, St 192
Cynyr Ceinfarfog of Penllyn (Arthur's foster-father) 241 *see also* Antor
Cysceint ap/son of Banon 213, 216–17
cywydd poets 53

Dafydd Nantmor 193, 194
Dark Ages 7, 23–5, 26–7, 50, 52, 146–7
  warrior societies 168–73
Darowen 97
David, St 44
Davies, J. H. 240–1, 245
Dee, John 21
Dee, River (Peryddon) 100, 106, 151–2, 154, 187, 241
Deganwy 107, 222
Deheubarth 68, 114
Denbighshire 90, 100, 134, 137, 153–4
Derfel Gadarn 193, 206
Devon 88, 91, 163, 164
Dialogue of Arthur and the Eagle 85, 267
Diheufyr ap/son of Hawystyl Gloff (Arthur's cousin) 90, 94, 96, 97
Dillus Farfog 162, 243
Dinarth (now Bryn Euryn) hill fort 123, 129–30, 176
Dinas Emrys 138, 200
Dindraethwy 88
Dinhengroen 192
Dinorben hill fort 107
Disethach 136–7
Disserth, Powys 137
Diwrnach 42, 131, 221
Doged, King 88, 153
Dolgellau 1, 190, 198, 200
Doré, Gustave 22
Dream of Macsen Wledig, The (Breuddwyd Macsen) 44, 70
Dream of Rhonabwy, The (Breuddwyd Rhonabwy) 70, 74, 76–7, 97, 157–60, 188, 264
  Arthur's forty-two counsellors 77, 88, 92, 100, 103, 212, 214, 216, 217, 218–19, 220, 221, 222, 223, 224
  location of Badon 77, 157–60
druids 49
Dubglas *see* Dulas
Dubricius (Dyfrig) 39–40, 41, 44
Dulas (Douglas, Dubglas), River 40, 141, 151
Dumville, David 24
Dunstan, St, relics 226–7
Dyce, William 22
Dyfed 41, 104, 131, 132, 135, 217, 219, 223
Dyfi, River 190, 198
Dyfnaint/Dyfneint 163
Dyfnog, St 186, 187

Dyfyr ap/son of Alun Dyfed 213, 217
Dyserth, Denbighshire 137

Eadmer, monk 227
Edeirnion 116, 233, 234, 239
Edern ap/son of Nudd 213, 217
Edward I 17, 20, 237–8
Edward III 19
Efadier ap/son of Llawfrodedd (Arthur's grandchild) 103
Efrog, King 155
Eglwys Dudur 97
Ehangwen (Arthur's hall) 135
Eidyn 137, 207, 221
Eifionydd 97, 125
Eigr ferch/daughter of Amlawdd Wledig (Arthur's mother) 12, 81–2, 90, 92, 99, 102, 107
Einion ap/son of Gwalchmai 148
Eleanor of Aquitaine 13, 14
Elei 136
Elen 44
Elerich ferch/daughter of Iaen 94, 103
Elis Gruffydd 69, 138, 235–6
Eliwlod ap/son of Madoc ap Uthyr (Arthur's nephew) 85, 267
Elizabeth I 21
Ellis, T. P. 158
Elvodugus, Bishop of Gwynedd 148
'Emrys' (Gwynedd) 137–8, 243
Erging 88, 93
Esgeir Oerfel, Ireland 122, 132
Eugrad ap/son of Caw 231
Evans, Theophilus 164
Excalibur (Caledfwlch/Caliburn) 18, 40, 73, 74–5, 131, 182, 191, 221
Excalibur (film) 23

Fergus mac Roig 74
Ffleudur Fflam 213, 218
Ffynon Dudur 97
Flintshire 89, 90, 100, 137, 153–4
Foel Fenlli hill fort 166
folklore 271
fosterage 244

Galahad, Sir 167
Gallgo ap/son of Caw 231
Gamber Head, Llanwarne 103
Garwen ferch/daughter of Henin Hen (Arthur's mistress) 106–7, 213
Garwy Hir 106
Gawain see Gwalchmai ap/son of Gwyar
Geiriadur Prifysgol Cymru 113
Gelliwig 121–6, 206
Geneid Hir 193
Geoffrey of Gaimar L'Estoire des Englies (History of the English) 38
Geoffrey of Monmouth 9, 31–2, 48, 53, 207

Historia Regum Britanniae History of the Kings of Britain) 5–8, 10–13, 17, 20, 30, 32–46, 54, 56, 58, 66, 67, 69, 73, 84–6, 75, 76, 79, 81–2, 90, 108–9, 120, 124, 126, 160, 162, 164, 165, 168–9, 183–4, 188, 234, 262
Prophetiae Merlini (Prophecies of Merlin) 5–6, 25, 33
sources 35–46, 183–4
Variant versions 37
Vita Merlini (Life of Merlin) 33, 69
George I 21
Geraint ap/son of Erbin 64, 89, 91, 93, 163–4, 219
Geraint ab/filius/mab Erbin 103, 161, 163, 174
Geruntius of Dumnonia 163
Gildas 59, 134, 230
De Excidio Britanniae (The Ruin of Britain) 27, 35, 41, 42, 55, 108, 118, 129, 157, 160, 175–80, 206, 225, 256–7
see also Life of Gildas
Gillamuri, King 42
Giraldus Cambrensis
De Princips Instructione 15, 30, 198
Description of Wales 80, 131, 196–7, 234–5
Glastennin 54
Glastonbury 9, 15–16, 21, 30, 47, 54, 69, 197–8, 208, 217, 226–7, 234
Glein, River 150
Gleiniant 150
Gleis ap/son of Merin 206
Glewlwyd Great Gasp 162, 213, 218
Glyn Dyfrdwy, North Wales 106
Gobrwy ap/son of Echel Big Hip 213, 218
Gododdin, Y 60–1, 63, 133, 137, 153, 171–2, 173, 194, 204
Gofan ap/son of Caw 231
Gogledd (the north) 127–9, 133–4, 135
Gogynfeirdd (Bards of the Welsh Princes) 52, 53, 67–70, 85, 88, 90, 112, 114, 115, 116, 137–8, 149, 160, 187, 198, 206, 268–9
Goleuddydd ferch/daughter of Amlawdd Wledig (Arthur's aunt) 71, 88, 91, 153
Gorchanau 60
Goreu ap/son of Custennin (Arthur's cousin) 72, 89, 91–2, 162, 213
Gorlois 8, 12, 81–2, 84
Gormant ap/son of Ricca (Arthur's half-brother) 92
Gorthyn ap/son of Urfai 153
Grays Inn Library 195
Greidiol Gallddofydd 213, 218–19
Groes Gwenhwyfar 93
Gruffudd ap/son of Cynan 67, 115, 132, 135

Gruffudd ap/son of Maredudd 106
Gueltas, St 226
Guinevere *see* Gwenhwyfar ferch/daughter of Ogrfan Gawr
Gungrog fach 158
Gungrog fawr 158
Guto'r Glyn 114, 269
Gutun Owain 114, 123, 269
Gwair ap/son of Gwystyl (Arthur's cousin) 92, 93, 213
Gwalchmai (place) 100
Gwalchmai ap/son of Gwyar/Gawain (Arthur's nephew and cousin) 42, 80, 82, 99–100, 213
Gwalchmai ap/son of Meilyr 8, 48–9
Gwallawg 149
Gwanos 162
Gwarddur 60, 63
Gwarthegydd ap/son of Caw 213, 219
Gwen (Arthur's mantle) 74
Gwen Alarch 90
Gwen ferch/daughter of Cunedda Wledig (Arthur's grandmother) 92, 102
Gwenhwyfach, sister of Gwenhwyfar 185–6
Gwenhwyfar ferch/daughter of Ogrfan Gawr (Guinevere) 12, 14, 17, 30, 42, 73, 82, 92–3, 102–3, 183, 185–6, 213, 220
Gwenwynwyn ap/son of Naf 213, 219
Gwilym Ddu 224
Gwrddelw ap/son of Caw 231
Gwrfoddw Hen (Arthur's uncle) 88, 93, 96
Gwrhai ap/son of Caw 232
Gwrial ap/son of Llawfrodedd (Arthur's granchild) 103
Gwryd Cai 243
Gwyar ferch/daughter of Amlawdd Wledig (Arthur's aunt) 93
Gwyddog ap/son of Menestyr 162, 206, 243
Gwydre ap/son of Arthur 104
Gwyn ap/son of Nudd 217
Gwyn Godyfrion 213, 219
Gwyn Hyfar 188
Gwynedd 8, 40, 60, 61, 68, 95, 114, 124, 136, 137–8, 148, 153, 161, 176, 179–80, 195, 196–7, 198, 200, 207, 208, 224, 231, 243
Gwynion *see* Castello Guinnion
Gwynnog ap/son of Gildas 134, 233
Gwystyl (ap/son of Nwython) (Arthur's uncle) 93
Gwythur 63
Gwythyr ap/son of Greidiol 213, 220
Gyrthmwl Wledig 213, 220

Hanoverians 21–2
Harleian MS 3859 43, 46, 58, 102
Haverfordwest 131
Hawystyl Gloff (Arthur's uncle) 94

Hengroen (Arthur's horse) 192
Henin Henben 107
Henllan 90, 100
Henry of Huntington 10, 25, 69, 141, 175
Henry I 10, 33, 67
Henry II 13, 34
Henry VII 19–20
Henry VIII 16, 20
Herefordshire 39, 88, 93, 233
Historia Brittonum (History of the Britons) 36, 39, 41, 43, 56–8, 75, 102, 103, 108, 118, 133, 138, 173–4, 216, 258–60
  battle list 40, 57, 140, 141, 142, 147–60, 161, 178, 205
History of Gruffudd ap Cynan 40, 61, 165
Holy Grail 14–15, 16, 17, 30, 69, 119
Hopcyn Thomas 123
Hope 89, 166
Hopedale 165–6
Huail ap/son of Caw 207, 227, 233–9
Hualla ap/son of Tudfwlch Corneu (Arthur's cousin) 94, 97, 125
Huw Conwy 123
Hyffeidd One-Cloak 213, 220
Hywel ap/son of Owain Gwynedd 188

Iaen of Caer Dathal, sons of (Arthur's in-laws) 94–5, 206
Iddawg the Embroiler of Prydein 188
Iestyn ap/son of Geraint (Arthur's cousin) 93, 95, 96
Ieuan ab/son of Einion 123
Illtud, St (Arthur's cousin) 95
Indeg ferch/daughter of Garwy Hir (Arthur's mistress) 106, 213
International Arthurian Society 23
Iolo Goch 123, 269
Ireland 11, 41, 42, 49, 50, 77, 116, 122, 131, 132, 221
Irish, the 79, 146
Isle of Avalon *see* Avalon

Jesus College MS 20 85
Jones, T Gwynn 69, 156
Jones, Thomas 47, 142, 143, 236, 237, 238
Joseph of Arimathea 15–16, 17
Julian, martyr 42
Julius Caesar 49

Kaerluideoit *see* Caer Llydcoed
Kay *see* Cai (Cei) ap/son of Cynyr
Kentigern, St (Cynderyn Garthwys) 129
Keys to Avalon, The (Blake and Lloyd) 37, 80, 100, 112, 217, 222, 237
Knights of the Round Table 14, 119, 167, 168
Knucklas Castle 93

Lady of the Lake 18, 75
Lake Lumonoy, sixty islands 41
Lancelot of the Lake 14, 17, 30, 92, 109, 167
Layamon 15
Leland, John 19, 20–1, 100
   Assertio Inclytissimi Arturii Regis Britanniae (A Worthy Assertion of Arthur King of Britain) 21
   Itinerary 21
Lewis Glyn Gothi 193, 236–7, 269
Lewis Jones, W. 23
Lhuyd, Edward 90, 93
   Parochialia 134
Life of Gildas (Caradog of Llancarfan) 54, 226–30, 234, 238–9
Life of Gildas (monk of Rhuys, Brittany) 226, 228, 231, 234, 239
Life of St Alfred 117
Life of St Cadog 42, 70, 174, 214, 228
Life of St Carranog 88
Life of St Gwynllyw 39
Life of St Illtud 39, 42, 86, 88, 95, 96
Life of St Padarn 42
Life of St Pedrog 193
Life of St Samson 39, 41
Life of St Teilio 42, 44
Life of St Winefred 90
Lin Ligua 41
Lincolnshire 150, 151
Linnius, region 150, 151
Lives of the Welsh saints 42, 54–6, 70–1, 117, 135, 179, 180, 212, 261–2
Livre de Carados 99
Loch Garman, Ireland 221
Loughor 220
Lucan (Arthur's butler) 182, 191

Llacheu (Loholt) ap/son of Arthur 64, 104, 207, 213
Llanbedrog 193
Llancarvan 42, 54, 56
Llandaf 35, 40, 42, 56
Llanddoged 88, 153
Llanddyfnog 186
Llanderfel 193
Llandyfrydog 97
Llandyrnog 97
Llanfaelog 233
Llanfaethlu 99
Llanfor Stone 239–40
Llangedwy, Llanrhaeadr y Mochant 192
Llangedwy, Ystrad Yw 192
Llangefni 89
Llangernyw 125
Llangoed 99
Llangorwda 99
Llangwyllog 231
Llangwm 134, 187, 233

Llaniestyn, Anglesey 95
Llaniestyn, Lleyn Peninsula 95
Llanilltud Fawr (Llantwit Major) 41, 95
Llanuwchllyn 241
Llanwnog 233
Llanwynnog 233
Llary ap/son of Casnar Wledig 20, 213
Llawfrodedd Farchog 103
Llawfrodedd Farfog 103, 213, 221
Llech Eidy 137
Llenlleog Wyddel 213, 221
Lleyn Peninsula 40, 95, 99, 100, 122, 123, 124, 125, 153, 192, 193
Llifris of Llancarvan 174, 228
Lliwedd 200–1
Llongborth 64, 91, 163–4, 207
Lloyd, J. E. 241
   A History of Wales 67–8, 158
Llwch Llaw-Wynniog 213, 221
Llwyd, Humphrey 20
Llydaw 88, 221
Llygad Amr 103
Llygadrudd Emys (Arthur's uncle) 95–6
Llys Meirchion 154
Llywarch ap/son of Llywelyn 69
Llywarch Hen 204, 230
Llywelyn ap/son of Iorwerth, Prince of Gwynedd 195
Llywelyn ap/son of Gruffudd 67

Mabinogion (Four Branches) 51, 64, 66, 70, 74, 95, 115, 158, 223, 263–4
   see also *Culhwch and Olwen*; *Dream of Rhonabwy*
Mabon ap/son of Mellt 213, 221
Mabon ap/son of Modron 213, 222
Macsen 44
Madog ap/son of Maredudd 48–9, 76
Madog ap/ son of Uthyr 85
Maelgwn Gwynedd (Maglocunus) 8, 55, 59, 107, 117, 120, 129, 176, 179–80, 213, 222
Maen Huail 236
Maes-y-Camlan 190, 198
Maesglas 164
Maethlu, St 99
Mallwyd 1, 190, 198
Malory, Thomas *Le Morte d'Arthur* 18, 19, 22–3, 30, 181–3, 241
Manawydan ap/son of Llyr 214, 222–3
March ap/son of Meirchion (King Mark of Cornwall) (Arthur's cousin) 100, 153–4, 206, 214, 219
Marchell ferch/daughter of Hawystyl Gloff (Arthur's cousin) 94, 96, 97
Marie de Champagne 14
Math fab Mathonwy 95
Matilda 10, 33, 67
'Matter of Britain, The', 10–11, 20, 21

Medrod (Mordred) 12, 44, 59, 82, 181, 183, 184–5, 186–8, 200, 206
  possible identification with Medrod ap/son of Cawdraf 187
Medyr ap/son of Medredydd 122
Meilig ap/son of Caw 233
Meilyr Bryddydd 26, 67, 115
Melwas, King 54
Menai Straits 138
Menw ap/son of Teirgwaedd 214, 223
Mercia 116, 117
Merionithshire 137
Merlin (Myrddin) 3, 5–6, 7, 12, 16, 17, 18, 47, 63, 81, 83
Meurig ap/son of Iorweth 123
Middle Ages 49, 79–80, 109
Mil Du ap/son of Dugum 206
Mirabilia 57–8, 103
Moel y Don (Bon y Don) 138
Monmouth 54
Mons Aravius 44, 124
Mons Badonis see Badon
mons Bannauc 228, 229–30
Mons Breguion 156–7
Montgomery castle 119
Montgomeryshire 233
Morfa Rhianedd 107, 129
Morfran ap/son of Tegid 193, 206, 214, 223
Morien Mynog 214, 223
Morris, John The Age of Arthur 24
Mynydd Carn 132
Mynydd Mynnyddog 60
Mynydd Rhiw 126
Mynyddog Mwynfawr 171
Mynyw see St David's
Myrddin see Merlin
Myths and Legends of King Arthur and the Knights of the Round Table (musical homage) 23
Myvyrian Archaiology 22

Nant y Gleiniant 150
Nantlle 222
Nash-Williams, V. E. 239
Neath 92
Nennius 56–7, 147–8
Nerth ap/son of Cadarn 214, 223
Noethon ap/son of Gildas, St 233
Normans 10–11, 25, 28, 32, 46, 48, 53, 79, 204, 206–7, 227
north British kingdoms ('Old North') 127–9, 137
North Wales
  Arthur's battle sites 145–6, 151–7, 159, 162–3, 165–6, 190, 192, 195
  association with Arthur's family 98, 100–102, 109

  association with Arthur's mistresses 105, 106, 107
  association with Caw and his family 230, 236
  association with Cernyw 124–6
  possible denotation by 'y Gogledd' 127–9, 133–4, 135
  setting of Branwen ferch Llyr 115–16
Northumbria 116

Offa's Dyke 117, 154–5
Ogof Llanciau Eryi 201
Ogrfan Gawr 93
Old Oswestry 93
Olwen ferch/daughter of Ysbadden Pencawr 71–2
'once and future king' 9, 17, 30, 68–9, 200
oral tradition 28, 51, 79
Orddu hill 134
Oseny Abbey 32
Osfran 190–1
Owain ap/son of Urien Rheged 149
Owain Gwynedd 34, 115, 122
Oxford 32, 38, 165

Pa Gur? (Who is the Porter?) 63–4, 84, 108, 136, 138, 155, 161, 180, 214, 216–17, 218, 219, 221, 222, 242–3
Padel, Dr Oliver 121
Parry, John J. 39
Pedrog, St 193–4
Peithien ferch/daughter of Caw 231
Pembrokeshire 44, 131, 135, 231
Penbryn 164
'Pendragon'
  Geoffrey of Monmouth's interpretation 7
  meaning in Welsh literature 8
  possible origin connected with Maelgwyn Gwynedd 180
Penllyn 193, 241
Penmon 96
Pennant Gouut yg gwrthir Uffern 133–4
Penrhos 192
Penrhyn Bay 129–30, 140
Penrhyn Rhianedd 126–30, 206, 220
Penymymydd 123
Penystrywaid 233
Perceval 109
Peredur Paladr Hir 214, 223–4
Perlesvaus 104
Perth Geriant 164
Peters, Ellis 90
Picts 11, 12, 57, 142, 143, 146, 165, 168, 175
place-name lore and studies 51, 166, 270–1
Port Cerddin 131–2
Porth Cleis 132, 135
Porth Mawr 131

Powys 48, 68, 76, 104, 114, 123, 137, 176, 198
Preiddeu Annwn (The Spoils of Annwn) 61–2, 73, 135–6, 194–5, 221
Preseli mountains 104, 131
Price, Sir John of Brecon 63
Privilege of St Teilio, The 117
Pryddyd y Moch 115, 200
Prydwen/Pridwen (Arthur's ship) 61, 73, 130, 131
    name used by Geoffrey of Monmouth for Arthur's shield 40, 74
Puffin Island (Ynys Seiriol) 222
Pwll Crochan 131
Pwllheli 136
Pyle, Howard 22

Red Book of Hergest, The 66, 76, 163, 264
Retho 44 *see also* Rhita Gawr
Rhahawd ail Morgan 214, 224
Rhienwylydd ferch/daughter of Amlawdd Wledig (Arthur's aunt) 96
Rhita Gawr 44, 90, 124–5
    identified with Ricca 92
Rhodri ap/son of Owain 8, 115
Rhongomyniad/Ron (Arthur's spear) 40, 73, 75
Rhufon Befr 214, 224
Rhufoniog 153
Rhun ap/son of Maelgwyn Gwynedd 107
Rhyd Llanfair 201–2
Rhyd-y-Groes 157, 158–60
Rhys, Sir John 23, 240
Rhys ap/son of Maredudd 115
Ricca *see* Rhita Gawr
Rider, Jeff 55, 56
Robert de Boron *Merlin* 16, 30
Robert de Chesney 31
Robert of Gloucester 10, 33–4, 38
Robert of Shrewsbury 90
Roberts, Thomas 242
Roman histories 27
Romans 11, 27, 49, 57, 118, 146, 175
Rome and Roman Empire 10, 12, 16, 44, 207
Rossetti, Dante Gabriel 22
Round Table 13, 15, 30, 69, 118, 167–8, 206
    at Winchester 19, 30, 168
Ruabon mountain (Rhiwabon) 222
Ruthin 235–6, 239

Samson, Archbishop of York 41–2
Sandde Angel-face 194
Sandde ap/son of Llywach Hen 194
Saxons 6, 10, 11–12, 22, 25, 40, 57, 82, 116, 118, 120, 142, 146–7, 155, 157, 165, 168, 170, 175

not Arthur's main opponents 143, 161, 178–9, 205–6, 225
Scotland 25, 46, 152
    association with Caw questioned 228–30, 239–40
    invasion by Edward I 17, 20
    north British kingdom theory 127–8, 137
    Ynys Prydein confusion 116, 126
Scots 11, 57, 127, 142, 143, 146, 168
secondary localisation 128
seers/poets 49
Seisgeann Uairbheoil 122
Selfan/Selyf ap/son of Geraint (Arthur's cousin) 93, 96
Shrewsbury Abbey 90
Sims-Williams, Patrick 51, 122
Snowdon 125, 200
Snowdonia 138, 154, 191, 200–1, 216, 222, 233, 243
Somerset 3, 29, 91, 163 *see also* Cadbury Castle; Glastonbury
South Wales
    Anglo-Norman quest for domination 53
    early Arthurain tradition 57
    denoted by 'dextralis britannia'117
    nineteenth century historians 145
    provenance of *Culhwch and Olwen* 135
    see of Llandaf's claims to land 34–5
    twelfth century hagiographical school 42, 54–6, 70–1, 109, 117, 135, 206–7
Southern, R. W. 38
Spanuth, Jurgen 111
Spenser, Edmund *The Faerie Queene* 21, 242
St Asaph 34, 129
St Cadfan church, Tywyn 190–1
St David's 44, 70, 120, 131, 132, 135, 222
St Govan 231
St Mary's chapel (Arthur's burial place) 199
    possible location 3, 201–4
'Stanzas of the Graves' (*Englynion y Beddau*) 50–1, 65, 99, 106–7, 162–3, 190–1, 199, 216, 220, 222
Stephen, King 10, 13, 33, 34, 67
Stirling Castle 168
Strabo 49
Survey of Denbigh, The 165
Sutcliff, Rosemary *Sword at Sunset* 23
'sword in the stone' 16, 18, 30, 83
Sword in the Stone (film) 23

Tacitus 117
    Agricola 27
'taleith' 237–8
Tangwn, St 99
Tebaus (Teilio), Bishop of Llandaf 44
Tegid Foel of Penllyn 193
Tennyson, Alfred Lord *The Idylls of the King* 22
teulu (war-band) 169, 170–3, 244

Theobald, Archbishop 34
Tintagel 8, 9, 47
Tre Beddau cemetery 202–4
Tre'r Ceiri hill fort 95
Treaty of Wallingford 34
Trefilan 89
Tremeirchion 100, 154
Tresaith 91, 164
Treuddyn 137
Triads see Welsh Triads
Tribuit, River *see* Tryfrwyd, River
Tryfan 191, 216
Tryfrwyd (Tribuit), River 155–6, 161, 206, 207, 216
Trystan ap/son of Tallwch 153, 154, 206, 214, 224, 237
Trwyth (great boar) 57, 93, 96, 104, 120, 132–3, 217, 219, 222
Tudfwlch Corneu (Arthur's uncle) 96–7, 125
possible identification with Tudfwlch Hir 96–7
Tudors 19–20
Tudur Aled 106, 188, 193, 269
Tudur ap/son of Hawystyl Gloff (Arthur's courin) 94, 97
Tudur Fychan 123
Twain, Mark *A Connecticut Yankee in King Arthur's Court* 22
Twrcelyn 231, 233
Tyfrydog ap/son of Hawystyl Gloff (Arthur's cousin) 94, 96, 97
Tyrnog ap/son of Hawystyl Gloff 94, 96, 97
Tyrrhenian Sea 221
Tywanedd ferch/daughter of Amlawdd Wledig 94, 96, 97, 99
Tywyn 191

Urbes Legiones 42–3, 145–6, 155
Urien Rheged 29, 43, 149, 156, 204
Uthyr (Uter) Pendragon 6–7, 11, 12, 81–2, 84–6, 90, 100, 107–9, 222, 223

Vale of Clwyd 97, 123, 186, 187, 229–30
Valle Crucis Abbey 123
Vaughan, Robert 241
Vera Historia De Morte Arthuri (The True History of the Death of Arthur) 195–9
Vergil, Polydore 20
Vortigern 11, 109
Vortiper 176
Vulgate Cycle 17, 30
Vulgate Merlin 83, 240–1

Wace *Roman de Brut* 13–14, 15, 30, 69, 167
Wade-Evans, A. W. 145, 152, 187

Wagner, Richard 22
Waleran of Worcester, Count 33
Wales
    Arthurian tradition 20, 22, 28, 47–8, 57, 77–8, 79, 145–6, 184, 204, 205–9, 211, 225
    denoted by Britannia 38–9, 117–18, 174
    denoted by Ynys Prydein 112–16, 118
    Norman interest in 46
    place-name studies 166, 270–1
    rebellion and renaissance 67–8
Walter, Archdeacon of Oxford 32, 33, 36, 37, 38
Ward, Charlotte 46
Welsh bards and bardic poetry 8, 25–6, 48–53, 59–63, 113–14, 122–3, 124–5, 149, 199, 236–7, 242, 265–7
    Arthur's battles 160–6
    place names attached to Arthur 135–8
Welsh genealogies 43, 46, 58, 79–81, 230–1, 270
Welsh Triads 65–7, 91, 99, 119, 105–6, 160, 162, 164, 172, 184, 185–6, 193, 212, 214, 216, 218, 219, 220, 222, 223, 224, 237, 265
'Welsh version of the Birth of Arthur, A' 240–4
    reprinted 245–55
Welshpool 158, 160
Whitchurch 96
White, T. H. *The Once and Future King* 23
White Book of Rhydderch, The 66, 163, 263–4
William, Prince 20
William Lleyn 241–2
William of Malmesbury 10, 25, 69, 139, 141, 175, 200
    De Antiquitate Glastoniensis 217
William the Conqueror 135
Winchester 6, 18
    Round Table 19, 30, 168
Winchester Cathedral 18
Wynebgwrthucher (Arthur's shield) 73, 75

Ynys Gyngar 89
Ynys Prydein 112–16
    denoting Wales 113–16, 118, 128
Yorkshire 60, 151
Ysbaddaden Pencawr 71–2, 91–2
Ystoria Taliesin (History of Taliesin) 107, 193
Ystoria Tristan (History of Tristan) 153–4
Ystrad Tywi 96
Ystrad Yw 93, 192